HUMAN FAITH

DALE SEGREST

WITHIN A CONSCIOUS BIOSPHERE

Human Faith Within a Conscious Biosphere

Print ISBN: 978-1-66783-896-0
eBook ISBN: 978-1-66783-897-7

TABLE OF CONTENTS

ACKNOWLEDGMENTS

I worked on the project that resulted in *Human Faith in a Conscious Biosphere* for over twenty-eight years. The work was more a study than a writing project. It evolved. It involved a writing effort from the beginning, but moved through countless stages and drafts. During the early stages, the late Dr. Frank Buckner, head of the department of religion and philosophy at Huntingdon College, read earlier versions of the manuscript and provided feedback. I will always regret that Frank did not live to see the finished project. Also in early stages, while the project was still focused primarily on faith, Don Bryant and Darryl Pendergrass led discussions in a small group study at First United Methodist Church, Tallassee. Afterward Darryl's wife, Kristina Pendergrass, read an early manuscript and offered her suggestions. Dr. Jamie Rhinehart also read an early draft of the manuscript and expressed his thoughts. As the project evolved, I bored my family and friends with these ideas that had become my obsession, and appreciate the patience and courtesy that they all exhibited! My wife Betty's niece, Kathy Drews, and her husband, Don, patiently listened to my thoughts and discussed the ideas presented here for hours and hours! After the project was moving into its final stages, Dr. Henry Findlay, retired director of continuing education at Tuskegee University began reading drafts of the essays, and became a great mentor and advisor. After COVID-19 arrived, he and I hit on the idea of a group discussion of the ideas, using the ZOOM app. So, we organized a group that discussed the drafts of the essays, one essay at a time. The discussions continued on a weekly basis for several months, and I am deeply appreciative for all who took part in those discussions. Participants in the discussions, in addition to Dr. Findlay and me, included Dr. Mark La Branche, Rev.

Mike Thurmond, Dr. Meigan Fields, Sarah Catherine Richardson, the late Mike Letcher, Allen Stanton, Jimmy McCain, Dr. Vivian Carter, and Tiffany Johnson Cole. Of course, not all the participants were able to participate in all the discussions, but the discussions were lively and helpful, and they resulted in considerable improvement in the essays. And most importantly, my wife, Betty Segrest, has listened to the ideas and patiently endured the uncountable hours of study, and thinking, and trying to reduce my thoughts to writing!

INTRODUCTION

IT FINALLY CAME TOGETHER IN my eightieth year on earth. The evolution of these ideas was slow, and involved a lot of reading as well as writing. The difficulty for someone traversing new territory is sometimes deciding when the journey has reached its destination. Many times along the way, I thought that I might be near the completion of the work. But I kept encountering new thoughts, and the theory kept expanding.

I am a lawyer and retired judge. I wrote a book, *Conscience and Command,* that was published in 1994. It dealt with legal philosophy. In the course of writing that book, I realized that law, and other important *social systems* are totally dependent on *faith*. When I say dependent on faith, I am not talking about *religion*; I am saying that law and other faith-based systems receive their motivational force from *what people really believe*, as I explain in these essays. So, after I completed that book, I intentionally undertook a study of *faith and its functions*.[1] Let me briefly summarize the concept of faith that I will be describing. Faith is what humans actually believe. It is what we know. It is the basis for our judgment. It is the data base on which we draw when we decide what to do.

The study of faith led inexorably to the role that **consciousness** plays in faith, and I expanded my interest to include a study of consciousness. Consciousness is the basis for how we think, and in a sense, **psychology** is the **study of consciousness**. I had already done a great deal of reading in psychology in an effort to improve my skills as a judge, and in researching legal philosophy, but I expanded the study of psychology, and also got into the philosophy of the mind. There are many questions about consciousness for which no one has answers. Its very existence is a mystery. But looking at **faith and consciousness** together, I realized that humanity is composed of individuals and groups that evolved in the **biosphere**, and the important **function** of consciousness for humans is that it enables humanity to cope in the biosphere. And the faith that consciousness empowers enables humanity to **collect knowledge** about the biosphere, and that is an important function of faith. So, in these essays, I am writing about faith, consciousness, and humanity in the biosphere. More specifically, in these essays I will be writing about humanity, and how *faith* and **consciousness** enables humanity to cope in the biosphere.

It is all fairly complicated, but let me briefly summarize how it all works. Humans are animals that evolved in the biosphere. Like other animals, they **participate in consciousness**. They are aware of their surroundings and consciousness empowers them to decide what they will do next. They developed **language** and can communicate. That enabled them to transfer information from person to person, collect and store information, and transfer information from generation to generation. Evolution of the **capacity** for language was the giant step for human **participation in consciousness**. Language is obviously a **group** thing; an individual would never develop it acting alone, although **individuals** had to evolve the **capacity** for it. So how did language develop? Consciousness utilizes **nonphysical essences** to connect human minds to the **physical objects** of the biosphere. Groups of humans create **words** that they substitute for the **nonphysical essences**. Words

2

enable group members to talk to each other about the objects. They enable the group to collect and store information in memory and to pass information from generation to generation. Words are **abstractions**. Children acquire them by learning to talk, and internalized language is the basis for abstract thinking. So, **concepts** actually originate in the **language** of the **group** and are **internalized by individuals**, who use them for abstract thinking. And all of that enables humanity to cope much more efficiently in the biosphere. Consciousness is a **system that runs the biosphere**. It came with creation. It **did not evolve** in humans and other sentient beings—they just **participate** in it. It probably induced evolution.

That's it in a nutshell. But this oversimplification is just a hint. A lot more explanation will be necessary to enable you to make to the paradigm shift, and embrace the conclusions that I finally reached in my eightieth year. So now I will begin to expand on it. I'll start with language.

"In the beginning was the word." This biblical statement, which is the first verse of the biblical gospel according to John, has a powerful literal meaning that may be quite different from the meaning intended by its writer. The development of **words**—**language**—was the beginning of humanity's most important expansion in human **participation in consciousness** and **faith**. For **words** to represent **objects** and **essences**, there had to be **faith**. If humans had not **believed** that words—the oral sounds humans invented—represented objects and essences, languages would not have served their purpose. But that is not all. Words **stored knowledge** and passed it from person to person and from generation to generation. And words provided a basis for individual **abstract thinking**. What did humans think about before language appeared? They certainly didn't "look out the **window** (or cave door) and see **green trees**" as such, because that entire sentence is composed of words, and words did not exist at the time. Those words and their meanings are now familiar to us, and have become a part of the way we think. But although the **essences** that have now been assigned words no doubt presented themselves to the senses of prelinguistic humans, those humans would have had no words—no internalized concepts—for dealing with the essences the way that modern humans deal with them.

After humans learned to talk, and had been talking for a long period of time, they learned to **write**. With writing, words that humans had invented and used came to be represented by written symbols. Knowledge and human *participation in consciousness* expanded even faster after the human ability to write developed, and so did religions, governments, and economics. Writing was a necessary precursor for the development of those *social systems* as we know them. And then came the *printing press* and the modern age. Abstract thinking and storage of knowledge with the use of symbols (*written words*) was even more powerful than the abstract thinking that had used only spoken words in oral communication.

Today, we have moved to a new and different level of *participation in consciousness*. We now use *electronic means of communication*. The literate public knows that we are into the "postmodern age," but it is not as aware of the fact that we are into what can be called a new *axial age*. The concept of the *Axial Age* was first suggested by Karl Jaspers soon after World War II. He identified it as the period from about 800 BC to 200 BC. He named it the *Axial Age* because it is the period during which the great world religions, governments, economics, and practically all modern *cultural systems* and *institutions* arose and began evolving. I suggest that Jaspers *Axial Age* is not a mysterious period in which unique cosmic forces were at work in the universe: it was the period in the biosphere during which human consciousness began to experience the effect of the newly developed ability to *write and read*. It brought into existence a new level of human *participation in consciousness*. I am suggesting that we have now moved into a new *axial age* that is again transforming human *participation in consciousness*. Information is literally exploding. Its content is growing rapidly, even as the space required to store it shrinks. Human *participation in consciousness* and *human faith* are growing exponentially. In this series of essays that, as the title indicates, describe *human faith within a consciousness biosphere*, I plan to fully develop and expand upon these thoughts dealing with faith and consciousness.

Let me make my contentions about consciousness clear. Consciousness is a *system*. It is the system that operates the biosphere. Consciousness did not *evolve* in humans, rather humans and other sentient beings evolved the *capacity to participate in consciousness*. Consciousness is inherent in the biosphere and is an obvious prerequisite for human faith. But it is interesting to find that *human faith* has also played an important role in the *evolution of human consciousness*.

For over twenty-eight years, I have worked to assemble these thoughts about *faith and consciousness*. My study of faith has focused on the importance of *things unseen*. By *faith*, I mean *what we think that we know for sure*. As stated previously, my effort started with an attempt to understand and describe what *faith* is, how it develops, and how it functions in society. That study led me inexorably into the *mysteries of consciousness*. The mysterious existence of consciousness and imperfect human participation in it make humans absolutely dependent on faith. Human *faith* and human *participation in consciousness* are totally inseparable, and that is not just because of the truism that we can believe something only if we are aware of it. Human *faith* and human *participation in consciousness* have dramatically interacted and affected each other in their evolution over the past one hundred thousand years. Human faith has grown enormously as a result of the expansion of human *participation in consciousness*. But human *participation in consciousness* has also grown dramatically, as a result of the growth of human faith.

So, what is faith? When I use the word *faith*, I am talking about *what humans really believe*, that is, *what they think that they know for sure*. By carefully studying faith as described in these essays, what it is and does, and how it operates, I gradually realized the even more important truth that *consciousness is the system that operates the biosphere.* Although the *cause* of consciousness may involve a single essence, or some subatomic particle, the *functions of consciousness* are not a single *phenomenon* that evolved in the human species and exists only in individual human brains. Consciousness is much more than any single concept; it is the basis for all concepts. In fact, as Russian psychologist Lev Vygotsky figured out almost a hundred years ago, *higher mental functions* exercised by individuals are dependent on the *internalization of language* of the *cultural group* into which the individual is born. So, the discussion of *faith* leads into the discussion of the *philosophy of consciousness* very naturally.

My study of faith and consciousness culminated in 2020, when I first became aware of the writings of Lev Vygotsky and his follower, Alexandr Luria, who had articulated some of the ideas in which I was interested. Unfortunately, although they did their work almost a hundred years ago, the importance of the work of these two Russian psychologists is still not understood and appreciated in western Europe and the United States as well as it needs to be. The school of thought that they founded is called the *Cultural-Historical School.* A key element of their theory is that *concepts* originate and are perpetuated in *language* that is maintained by social groups, and are *internalized* by individuals during the course of personal development. These ideas that had been developed by Vygotsky and Luria almost one hundred years ago fit perfectly with my own ideas about human faith and consciousness that I had been working on for twenty-six years!

Vygotsky died in 1934 at the early age of thirty-eight. Although he adequately described the idea that individuals develop conceptual thinking by internalizing the concepts reflected in language, he did not live to fully develop the philosophical implications of his ideas. I hope that these essays will articulate the philosophy of consciousness that appears to me to be implicit in Vygotsky's writings.

Vygotsky suffered from diabetes. He was a brilliant psychologist, and it is difficult to understand how a man with his poor health could have developed and articulated the penetrating thoughts that he was able to articulate during his short lifetime. Although Freud's theories about the child's *internalization* of the image and commands of parents as the basis for *moral formation* were brilliant, his explanation of the role of *internalization* pales in comparison to the far more complete explanation of the role played by *internalization* as described by Vygotsky. Émile Durkheim had provided a brilliant description of the formation of *collective representations*, a form of concepts or categories that resulted as a social consequence of elementary religious practices. However, Durkheim's description of the role that *society* plays in the development of important *concepts* does not equal the way that Vygotsky explains how individual members of cultural groups internalize the language of the group in the course of personal development, so that the concepts reflected in the language become a part of the individual's mental functioning.

Human *faith* and human *participation in the consciousness system* that operates the biosphere are inseparable. I deal with both *faith* and *consciousness* in this series of essays. I develop the concept of *faith* and its important *functions*, both for their own importance and in order to show how growth of human faith has brought dramatic growth in human *participation in consciousness*. I deal with both *individual* faith and *collective* faith. The first five essays anticipate the discussion of *consciousness* and *philosophy of the mind*. They demonstrate the importance of the *nonphysical*. They explain that consciousness is not a single essence, but is the *system the operates the biosphere*. The system includes the *physical*, and the work of *perception*, but for humans much of the most important work is with *conceptual consciousness*. The *abstractions*—the *concepts*—with which human consciousness deals are *nonphysical*, and they are derived from *nonphysical essences* in the biosphere. The *third* and *fourth essays*, that deal with the individual human's **differentiation** of **self** from the **biosphere** and **establishment** of **self-identity,** anticipate the **mind-body** and **dualism** issues dealt with in the **eighth** and **ninth essays** that develop the **consciousness theory** and dispose of **dualism.** And the **fifth essay** deals with the **institutionalization** of important **social systems** and **social entities,** and the **nonphysical values** and **principles** on which they rely: **law, morality, religion** and **economics.** In short, I describe the importance of the **nonphysical** part of reality on its own merits, rather than discussing it defensively with arguments purporting to deal with scientific theories that cannot actually deal with it.

The **first essay** recognizes the obvious fact that faith has developed in the biosphere. The biosphere itself contains **essences** that humans must internalize in order to cope within the biosphere. The **second essay** expands on the faith environment by describing **stages** of faith development and **sources** of faith. What individuals actually believe—their **faith**—is the basis for their motivation. As Abraham Maslow suggested, humans do what they do to get what they need from the biosphere, and that is the theme of the **third essay.** To get what they need from the biosphere, individuals differentiate themselves from the rest of the biosphere, and that differentiation lays the foundation for establishing individual identity. The **fourth essay** fully describes how individuals establish their personal identity. In their efforts to do what they do to get what they need from their physical and social environment, humans naturally cooperate, and in doing so, they create **social systems.** The **fifth essay** deals with **social systems** and the establishment of **social entities** by **institutionalization.** In it, I describe large, faith-dependent **social systems** that are essential for human existence, whose qualities are nonphysical and cannot be measured and evaluated by science and technology. It is essential that we understand the importance of these **social systems,** because the current intellectual focus on **physicalism** is a significant threat to their continued effectiveness. We must revalidate the reality of the nonphysical **consciousness** *system* from which these *social systems* derive their existence, and on which they depend.

After discussing faith in depth in the first five essays, I transition into a discussion of philosophy, consciousness, and the *philosophy of consciousness* in *essays six, seven* and *eight*. The *sixth essay* fully develops the important concept that I call *"consensus reality." Consensus reality* is the total collection of human knowledge that was made possible by the development of language and is maintained by faith. The discussion of *consensus reality* that develops from and is maintained by faith provides a natural transition to the philosophy of the mind and consciousness. The *seventh essay* examines Western philosophy itself, with a description of the work of Plato and Aristotle. It traces the influence of that work into the modern era, and shows how the work that I have done fits with traditional philosophy. These discussions culminate in the *eighth essay* that shows that consciousness was a prerequisite for *evolution in the biosphere* and is the *system that operates the biosphere*. After developing the theory of *consciousness* as the *system that operates the biosphere*, I explore important implications of that theory in two essays dealing with dualism, freewill, and related topics. I then conclude with a final essay, recognizing unfathomable mysteries.

The focus of my discussion of faith is not about *religion* as such, but it is important for religion, because it describes a worldview in which claims of religion can be credible. It shows the existence of important reality that is *not physical*, or at least not physical in terms of what humans have traditionally understood about physicality. The vistas that opened for me as I gained insight into the reality of consciousness, operating as a system and operating the biosphere, are magnificent. The possibilities that this new understanding of consciousness offers, both for *cultural groups* and *individuals*, are virtually *unlimited*. I invite you to travel with me, one essay at a time, into this vast mental terrain. But I have tried to write each of these essays with independent significance, and they don't have to be read in the order in which they are presented. So, if you can't wait to read the discussion about consciousness as the **system that operates the biosphere**, go directly to the **eighth essay**! Or start with the **focus on philosophy**, which begins with **essay six**. But all the essays contribute to an understanding about the operations of **human faith** and **consciousness** in the biosphere, so I hope you will read them all!

The effort to present nonsequential, nonlinear thoughts in a traditional book format, which loses every hint of intonation and inflection, can be difficult to follow. Therefore, I have liberally used **bold, italicized** print, to suggest **inflection** and **intonation** in an effort to promote better understanding. Bold, italicized print also helps hold together key concepts that involve more than one word. Because I have tried to present these ideas in free-standing essays, you will encounter repetition of key concepts in the separate essays.

I drew on many sources in assimilating these concepts, and I have used **endnotes** to identify and acknowledge some of the sources. I have also occasionally used endnotes to cite **reliable sources** in an effort to **authenticate** certain ideas or concepts. However, for ideas or concepts that are widely accepted and understood, and that come from well-known sources, I have not ploddingly noted every source. Today, such sources can usually be easily found on the internet, and the easily accessible information found there is much more objective and useful than anything I can put in a footnote or endnote. In the essays, I refer to Scripture. I am **not** using Scripture to **authenticate** the thoughts under consideration, but to illustrate how deeply and quite unconsciously Scripture is embedded in the faith of the Western world.

With these things explained, we are ready to delve into the role of human faith and consciousness in the biosphere.

1) THE FAITH AND CONSCIOUSNESS ENVIRONMENT

LET ME REITERATE WHAT *I* mean by *faith*. *Faith is what we really believe.* It is what we think that we *know*. Faith must not be dismissed as "mere belief." And I am not talking about religion as such. The faith I am describing includes what humans, including scholars and scientists, believe most strongly. Their strong beliefs about their chosen area of expertise *is* their faith! Professor James Fowler of Emory University described *faith* as our *image* of the *ultimate environment*.[2] By *ultimate environment*, he meant *the whole of reality*. Throughout these essays, I will use the term *ultimate reality* to mean the same thing as Fowler's *ultimate environment*. The *ultimate environment* is what faith seeks to embrace. Faith includes what we think about science as well as other disciplines. Unfathomable mysteries and imperfect human *participation in consciousness* prevent perfect connection to *ultimate reality*, so faith is humanity's imperfect attempt to use consciousness to try to connect to *ultimate reality*. An imperfect, but a very necessary endeavor!

The faith of cultural *groups*—not just what one individual believes, but what the larger group believes—provides an important approach to truth. *Objectivity* arises from the *group effort* to decide what is true. As I will show in these essays, individual perception is always completely *subjective*. But even though individual perception is always subjective, refinement of knowledge by the group in *consensus reality*, particularly the work of science, gives the faith system an increasingly accurate image of *ultimate reality*. The meaning of *consensus reality* will become clear as we proceed through these essays.

Individual faith includes all of the important beliefs on which individuals base their actions. *Faith* encompasses all of whatever humanity thinks is real. It even includes strongly held beliefs about mysteries that humans cannot resolve. Faith evolves. Accurate faith produces beneficial results and endures; inaccurate faith does not produce beneficial results and eventually disappears. Faith is the confidence we humans place in ideas that work. Of course, the faith of individuals is important. But the beliefs shared by society and humanity as a whole are even more important. A practical test for whether individual faith is real is *whether the "belief" affects the way the individual behaves.* If an individual believes something, that belief will likely affect his or her behavior, but only if he or she *really believes* it.

THE BIOSPHERE

The purpose of the current essay is to focus on the *environment* in which human faith developed and in which human *participation in consciousness* evolved. Of course, that environment is the biosphere. A Russian scientist, Vladimir Vernadsky, provided the first definitive description of the earth's *biosphere* in 1926.[3] He worked under the constraints of communism, but his book, *The Biosphere*, has been available in English since mid-twentieth century. The biosphere is the layer of soil, rock, oceans, and air at or near the earth's crust, which supports life. Human *participation in consciousness*, and the resulting human faith, developed within that *biosphere*. Darwin's theory of *evolution* led Vernadsky to the theory of the *biosphere*. Understanding those two theories—evolution and the biosphere—is the starting point for understanding the environment that produces human faith. The dynamics of human faith are intimately involved with the biosphere. Of course, the actual human faith that I am describing started to evolve long before these two theories were described in words, but what we now know as the *biosphere* is the environment in which human *faith* and human *participation in consciousness* developed. Vernadsky's theory is an extension and expansion of Darwin's theory of evolution.

The *biosphere* is the huge, complex, interdependent system of evolving life on earth. Vernadsky described the evolution of life in the biosphere. All of the matter composing the part of the earth that is included in the biosphere is either alive or can become part of a living organism. The sun—although located millions of miles from the earth's biosphere itself—is the constant source of energy for the biosphere, and is a critical part of the system. All plant and animal life—*all life* in the biosphere—is *interdependent*, and is *dependent on solar energy*. No life in the biosphere exists independently of other life. Human life is no exception. There are no *individual* human beings or other living organisms that exist separately and apart from the biosphere and other life that exists in it. All is interconnected. The entirety of the earth's surface is a *living system*. Within the biosphere, there are numerous differing ecosystems that support a variety of forms of life: oceans, deserts, mountains, rainforests, and many others. All life that exists in these ecosystems depends on other life and the nutrients of the ecosystem. And the ecosystems themselves are interdependent. The flora and fauna of the deserts depend on the rainforests, and the rainforests depend on the oceans.

LANGUAGE

Teilhard de Chardin, a French paleontologist—who was also a Catholic priest—called the ***thinking part*** of the biosphere the ***noosphere.*** [4] The noosphere is the part of the biosphere in which humans and other animals that think live. Human faith obviously developed in this ***thinking part*** of the biosphere. De Chardin's work built on Vernadsky's description of the biosphere. The important thing that I learned from de Chardin was about a major development that occurred in the biosphere with the emergence of the ***capacity for language***, which he dated 100,000 years ago. There is no actual consensus as to when the capacity for language evolved in humans. Some estimates go back as far as two or three hundred thousand or even a million years. The development of language is often linked with the appearance of ***homo sapiens***. A precise date for its appearance is not important to the development of the concepts that I am describing in these essays. But de Chardin was right: the ***emergence of language***, whenever it happened, had a huge impact on ***human participation in consciousness***, and enabled the development of the human ***faith*** that I am describing. The huge contribution that language has added to ***human participation in consciousness*** is confirmed by the work of Lev Vygotsky. His work was totally independent of the work of de Chardin.

The ***development of faith*** as I am describing it started whenever participation in language emerged, regardless of when that happened! As we will see, and as Vygotsky's work confirmed, when language developed, humans began to develop a more powerful ***participation in consciousness*** than any sentient beings on earth had previously experienced. De Chardin called the new level of participation[5] in consciousness ***reflective consciousness***. By that, he meant self-awareness —***awareness*** of consciousness—consciousness that is aware of itself.

The term ***reflective consciousness*** is a bit technical, and it does not describe or even suggest ***all*** the mental elements that were necessary for the revolutionary change in human *participation in consciousness*. The level of *participation in consciousness* that supports language involves much more than the *awareness* of consciousness suggested by the phrase *reflective consciousness*. So, in these essays, I will use the phrase *linguistic participation in consciousness,* in an effort to reflect *all* of the necessary mental prerequisites for language, rather than the phrase *reflective consciousness* used by de Chardin. The necessary mental elements obviously include the capacities for *memory* and *abstraction*. Another subtler but vital requirement for language is the capacity for *faith*. Language would not have served its purpose if humans had not *believed* that words represent *objects and essences*. And this belief—this faith—in turn, implies a power to discern *truth*[6] or reality. The *capacity* for *linguistic participation in consciousness* includes *all* of the mental abilities that were necessary for humans to develop and maintain language. The phrase *linguistic participation in consciousness* is intended to fully describe the *participation in consciousness* involved in the use of language.

It would be difficult, if not impossible, to reconstruct all of the prerequisites for the initial development of *language.* I will just say that the evolution of the *big brain* of humans, and all the *physical* prerequisites for speech, that various biologists, psychologists, and philosophers have hypothesized and described in detail had to occur. Regardless of what was required, it worked. Humans can talk. Whatever was necessary for speech and language obviously happened, and that is what is important for the ideas I am presenting. Beliefs of humans prior to the development of language might be described as *faith*, but they were only precursors of the concept of faith that I am describing. And humans *participated in consciousness* prior to the development of language, but that participation expanded dramatically with the development of language.

Henri Bergson suggested that within evolving *life*, there is an internal energy, a *vital impulse* that drives it forward[7]—a surging force in life itself, which continually strives for higher forms of expression. Bergson related this *vital impulse* to the evolution of life. Maybe it was Bergson's *vital impulse* that pushed humanity to evolve the structures needed for the higher level of *participation in consciousness* that empowered language. Humans *needed* language to support their efforts to survive and continue to evolve in the biosphere. So, the human brain and other parts of the anatomy evolved to the point that the human organism could *support* language. The actual use of *language* engaged the full capacity of humans for *linguistic participation in consciousness*.

Humans were obviously surviving in the biosphere and doing pretty well before they developed the capacity for *linguistic participation in consciousness*. They were possibly creating tools, and may have developed pre-linguistic forms of communication. Their social nature had enabled them to cooperatively solve many problems that they had encountered in the effort to survive. But language tremendously enhanced their survival capability. Compared to other primates, and other animals generally, humans have a very large brain. The large brain is often associated with the ability to talk. Evolution responds to needs. Something in the human environment induced the evolution of the large brain with all the abilities that were necessary for *participation in consciousness* at a new and higher level. Both parents were needed for rearing children during the lengthy childhood that was required for the development of that large brain. The role of family has always been important in many ways. Parents and family—the entire village—were and are involved in teaching children to talk, and, as we will see, language played and still plays a key role both in the development of faith, as well as the capacity to think.

Development of language involved *abstraction*. In the use of language, *words* represent *physical objects* and/or *nonphysical essences*. That representation *is abstraction*. *Representation in words* combines with *memory* to empower the mind to deal with *physical objects* and/or *nonphysical essences abstractly.* The abstractions enabled individuals to think and talk about the physical objects and nonphysical essences anywhere, anytime, without actual examples being present. *Faith* was inherent in that process: humans had to understand, remember, and *believe* the information stored and communicated by language for the abstractions used for language to be useful. For language to work, both the individual and the group had to *believe* that *words* accurately represented the *physical objects* or *nonphysical essences* that they purported to represent. Armed with language, memory, the power of abstraction, and the ability to discern what is useful for survival, humans developed not only *individual* faith but also *collective faith*. As language expanded, human *faith* and human *participation in consciousness* also expanded.

Language is a *group function*, not an *individual* function as such. More than one person is involved in the use of language. This makes it clear that *cultural groups* created and maintain languages. Development of language, abstraction, and knowledge by the cultural group also makes it clear that *cultural groups* are deeply involved in the development of *individual faith* and *participation in consciousness*. Faith at the group level became a key factor for human progress from the time that language developed and has continued to be a key factor ever after. Language empowered humans to not only *share knowledge* with each other but also to *collect and preserve knowledge*. The *group* could create a collective *body of knowledge* and *pass it from generation to generation*. Each generation added to the collection.

Describing the development of language as *linguistic participation in consciousness* accurately recognizes a very important point: *nonphysical essences* that are the biospheric basis for language play an important role in the operation of human *consciousness*. Words capture those nonphysical essences—the *phenomena*—that represent physical objects in the biosphere, and that enables human groups to share meaning in language. The *nonphysical essences* of objects—their *phenomena*—enable humans to represent both *physical objects* and things that are not physical in language. These essays will fully develop the meanings of *nonphysical essences* and *phenomena* as used here.

So how did humans develop the ability to use language? The answer to that question is not obvious, and we can only speculate. but I will share thoughts concerning how language possibly developed that occurred to me and that I found intriguing. It is generally believed that *musical participation in consciousness* preceded language. Before language emerged, *music* and human interaction probably elicited the ability to make the unique sounds that the human voice can make.

Participation in music may have also been a *social precursor* of language. Like music, language is a very social function. *Music* probably was a part of *religious rites* that attracted group participation, produced shared awe, and evoked group emotion in gatherings of humans. Religious activities, supported by music, likely brought groups of humans together. This would be consistent with Émile Durkheim's theory of the development of *collective representations* out of religious practices. *Musical participation in consciousness* requires a type of *mental participation* that is similar to language, although the two functions are now known to be supported by different parts of the brain. However, Vygotsky and his disciple Alexandr Luria have proven that the brain is a multifunctional organ. If one part of the brain is disabled, another may develop the function that the disabled part of the brain would have usually supported. So, as the speech function emerged, it could have mobilized a different part of the brain.

But regardless of *how* language developed, it *did* develop, and it brought all the advantages and progress in human thinking that I am describing. Human *participation in consciousness* has expanded dramatically since language first developed. That growth must be taken into account in any effort to understand *consciousness*. The evolution and expansion of *language* has significantly improved and expanded human *participation in consciousness*.

Humans began using language long ago. Human *participation in consciousness* today, filled with **abstractions** produced in ever expanding language, is far different from language when it first developed. Unlike Minerva, the goddess of **wisdom**, who according to Greek mythology sprang from the head of Jupiter fully developed, *linguistic participation in consciousness* evolved gradually, as the use of language evolved and expanded. It did not appear in the biosphere fully developed. Accordingly, human *participation in consciousness* has expanded gradually but dramatically from the point in time that humans first developed the use of language.

CONSENSUS REALITY

I mentioned **consensus reality** above in the current essay and also in the introductory essay. Let me provide a brief preliminary description of the concept. Language empowered humans to collect useful information and pass it from person to person and from generation to generation much more easily than could be done without language. That power to collect and transmit information enabled humans to build an ever-expanding body of knowledge. I use the term **consensus reality** to represent that collective body of information that language made possible. **Consensus reality** contains all collective human knowledge. The accumulated information, maintained by cultural groups, made the **cultural evolution** that I will describe in these essays possible. Continuing expansion of **consensus reality** steadily increased the ability of humans to *participate in consciousness*. Of course, there are multiple **consensus realities**, because there are multiple cultures.

Language is mainly a **group** function, rather than an *individual* function. (Why would an individual need language, if there were no other humans?) Languages, consisting of **abstractions,** exist and are maintained in the **collective minds** of cultural groups. The **abstractions** that language developed play a special role in human *participation in consciousness*. Although abstractions exist in and are maintained by the group, they are *internalized* by individuals, so that they also exist in the minds of individuals, where they empower *conceptual*, or *abstract, thinking*. Vygotsky used the term *higher mental processes* to describe this internal use of linguistic concepts by individuals. Without cultural groups, abstractions, as we know and use them, would not exist to the extent that they do. But *members* of cultural groups use the abstractions *individually* in their *abstract thinking*.

This means that a very important part of the human ability to think is transmitted from generation to generation *socially*, not *genetically*. *Genes* that enable humans to participate in language are located in *individuals biologically*, but maintenance of the power of abstraction that is involved in thinking is quite dependent on the cultural group to collect and maintain the abstractions. But after all, the genes of the cultural group are the genes of the individuals composing the group. And biological evolution itself is a function of species, not individuals. The group—the species—is the key to human operations in the biosphere. The group does not possess genes independently of individuals, but it participates in language, and maintains concepts represented by words that are used by individuals in their mental operations. Individuals develop the capacity for *speech* in order to utilize the *language* of the cultural group of which they are a part. And as they learn to talk, they internalize the abstractions, and use them as concepts for individual thinking.

TRUTH

The emergence of *language* depended on the existence of what we now call *truth*. As mentioned previously, *words* had to *accurately* represent *physical objects* and *nonphysical essences* in order for language to work. So, language requires *faith*, and faith *requires* something that we call *truth—an accurate portrayal of facts by words*. There could be no *faith* unless information could be accurately represented by words. *Truth* has at least two powerful meanings. The first meaning is that *truth* requires that words *accurately represent* the *physical objects* or *nonphysical essences* that they purport to represent. This is what we usually think about when we talk about *telling* the truth. If words do not accurately represent the *physical objects* or *nonphysical essences* that are involved in a statement then the statement they purport to make is not true. But please note that to use the word *truth* in this sense, there must be *consensus* about what the words are *intended* to represent, which ties *this* meaning of the word *truth* back to *consensus reality*.

Second, the word *truth* sometimes refers to an accurate understanding of *reality itself*. The word *reality* is a synonym of the word *truth*. *Truth*, in the sense of *reality*, simply reflects what is *real*. In the sense we are now discussing, *truth* is the *essence* of whatever is real. This second use of the word *truth* does not relate directly to *spoken or written words*. So, the word *truth* signifies more than just the accuracy of *things that are said*. It also represents *reality*. *Consensus* is not a direct prerequisite for this second meaning of the word *truth*: the *search* for *this* truth extends beyond existing *consensus reality*. But before truth that relates to *ultimate reality* that has not previously been captured in *consensus reality* can be *discussed*, there must be a *consensus* that gives meaning to the representational words. In short, for a newfound truth to be recognized by a cultural group, there must be *language* that can express the *truth* that describes the previously undescribed *reality*. But that again takes us back to *consensus*.

This discussion about truth and reality is not hypothetical; it is very practical. Scientists search for facts and theories that are not yet established. How does the search for unknown truths work? There is not yet a consensus about those facts and theories. The scientific search is for truth in the second sense described earlier. It is a search for an understanding of *reality* that is not yet known. Scientists hope to arrive at an understanding of the part of reality they are researching and create a consensus about it. They want to make it a part of *consensus reality*. After it is understood, and finds its way into *consensus reality* and language, everyone can use it! But at that point, the first meaning of truth described previously that requires **accurate representation** by words again asserts itself.

The **power of words** is the power of **truth** and the power of truth is the power of words. The power of words is immense. **Religion** and **mythology** recognize and are built on the **power of words**. The power exists because words capture the **essence** of something real. After a word captures the meaning of an object or nonphysical essence, that truth becomes part of **consensus reality**. Everyone can then share the meaning. Cultural groups maintain the meaning, and individuals use the information. Consciousness can function at the group level, using and maintaining the abstractions, and engaging the abstract thinking and communication that enables groups and individuals to do things made possible by the discovered truth. **Words** have power because **truth** has **consistency** and **duration**. Cultural groups can use it and rely on it. Falsity does not have consistency and duration, and the groups cannot rely on it.

To have a name for something is to have some degree of power or control over it. In an article that can be found on the internet, that was first published in 2009, Loren Graham, MIT and Harvard University wrote, "A common concept in history is that knowing the name of something or someone gives one power over that thing or person. This concept occurs in many different forms, in numerous cultures—in ancient and primitive tribes, as well as in Islamic, Jewish, Egyptian, Vedic, Hindu, and Christian traditions." http://www.philoctetes.org/news/the_power_of_names_religion_mathematics God did not want humans to take His **name** in vain. A folk story teaches children that **Rumpelstiltskin**'s name was important, a truth that the children's fictional story reveals and instills. In our daily affairs, remembering the names of people is important. Both **personal** knowledge and power, and **societal** knowledge and power, increase with growth of **vocabulary** and the ability to remember words and **names**. Growth of vocabulary represents expanding horizons of knowledge. Knowledge is power. None of that power was available in the biosphere before the human capacity for speech—*linguistic participation in consciousness*—evolved and language undertook to express reality, thereby creating *consensus reality*. In large measure, the accomplishments of humanity have resulted from the power of words and language.

If humans lose consensus, they lose the power of communication. That is the lesson of the biblical story of the *Tower of Babel*. In the story, God caused a *confusion of tongues* to prevent the people of Babel from building a tower to heaven. This mythical story carries powerful symbolic meaning. In these essays, I will show that the world's cultures have produced multiple, pluralistic *consensus realities*. The story of the *Tower of Babel* powerfully epitomizes the problems that are presented by pluralistic faith systems and *pluralistic consensus realities* that confront humanity today.

Language is not useful unless the words that are used represent, *as accurately as possible*, the *physical objects* and *nonphysical essences* they purport to represent. This is the function of truth. We use words in our effort to convey to others the meanings assigned to the words by the consensus that collective faith produces. Usually, multiple configurations of words are required to capture and convey meaning. Before humans can represent reality accurately with words, they must *understand* reality with some degree of accuracy. That *understanding* is also truth. *Faith* is the connecting link between humanity and reality. Faith depends on truth. Human understanding of reality will never be perfect, and the *power* that truth can add to human efforts depends on the degree of accuracy of words in representing the objects they purport to represent.

CULTURAL EVOLUTION

The emergence of *language, consensus reality*, and the power of *abstraction* marked a major turning point in human *evolution*. These developments greatly enhanced the role of *cultural evolution.* These developments allowed *intentional* change to affect the ways that humans dealt with their environment. With language, humans preserved *knowledge* about improved ways of doing things, and had access to the knowledge that predecessors had stored in *consensus reality.* They could make *intentional* decisions based on the knowledge that their cultural group had collected. The collected information was *faith*; it was what they *believed,* and that *faith* guided their actions. Evolving humanity used the preserved information *intentionally* to improve old practices and introduce new practices.

With the advent of language, new forms of *creative imagination* became possible. If I am familiar with the color *pink* (which is represented by a word) and also *elephant* (represented by another word), I *can* imagine a *pink elephant.* Creative thinking has the ability to produce new concepts that assist with intentional changes. *Creative, intentional change* became the key to *cultural evolution.* Before humans developed the use of *language,* *biological* evolution acting alone, without intentionality, produced changes in the human *species* on a much slower, more random basis. But language and the enhanced group *participation in consciousness* that language made possible allowed humans to participate collectively in consciousness and to make intentional decisions for change based on the knowledge that the group had accumulated. Of course, those developments started very slowly, but gradually gained speed.

The environment in which faith develops is a product of evolution. It includes the human social environment in which *cultural evolution* became a major factor after the development of language. *Evolution* of *human* life in the biosphere occurred in at least three different stages that culminated in *cultural evolution*. First there were the purely random *physical and chemical* actions and interactions that led to the **evolution of life,** that Darwin theorized and Vernadsky described in *The Biosphere*. Next, as Henri Bergson explained, *evolution* differentiated *animal life* from *plant life*. I will use the term *primary consciousness* for the consciousness in which humans partic-ipated before the development of language. Long before humans developed *linguistic participation in consciousness*, the animal kingdom developed the ability to participate in *primary consciousness*. *Participation in primary consciousness* was a very useful tool for mobile animal life, and might be the capacity that differentiates animals from plants. Evolution of life in the biosphere to that level took eons of time, in the random processes of *biological evolution*. The basic mental capability of *primary consciousness* was *awareness*. For humans it included other capabilities, such as memory. Different animal species *participate in consciousness* in varying degrees and use a variety of organs of perception. But *awareness* seems to be the ubiqui-tous element for all of consciousness. The biological evolution that created physical structures in animals that allowed them to *participate* in *primary consciousness* depended on *random* occurrences, enhanced only by natural selection and survival of the fittest. *Primary consciousness* likely promoted *natural selection* that led to further evolution. It helped select partners for reproduction and selected weak prey that either failed to survive and returned to soil or was removed from the gene pool when it became food. *Primary consciousness* was a major evolutionary accomplishment for the animal kingdom, but for humans, *primary consciousness* lacked the ability to store and transmit *conceptual* information to the next generation the same way *linguistic participation in consciousness* does.

But, as described earlier, humans eventually developed the capacity for *linguistic participation in consciousness*. Language empowered humans to participate in *communal faith* and empowered *cultural evolution*. *Cultural evolution* differs in kind from biological evolution and occurs at a *different level of organization*. It occurs at the social level rather than the biological level. The evolutionary changes brought by *biological evolution* occurred in the *genes* of individuals, but the changes brought by cultural evolution occurred at the *group level* and did not require *genetic* change. That is *not* to say that the new form of evolution did not produce *any* evolutionary biological change in the human *species* itself. After language developed, individual participation in the *process of abstraction* increased commensurately with the growth of language and the use of abstractions by the group. The individuals who *functioned well* in the evolving *social environment* had a better chance to survive and reproduce. New ways of meeting human needs produced by *linguistic participation in consciousness* altered the meaning of "*fittest.*" As Darwin had suggested, the *fittest* tend to survive and reproduce. With language, the best *speakers* and *thinkers* became the *fittest* and had a better chance to *survive* and *reproduce*. Those processes likely produced beneficial biological evolution—based on the natural eugenics that Darwin described! Although it occurred slowly, over a period of a hundred thousand years after the development of language, the natural processes of selection and survival of the fittest have probably produced appreciable biological evolution. But the evolutionary *biological* change in *individuals* composing the human *species* has been much less significant after the development of language than were the cultural skills derived from improved *group participation in consciousness* that language supported.

With the benefit of language, groups developed new skills and ways to work together. Cultural evolution brought dramatic change for humanity. Humans developed *social systems*, as described in the *fifth essay* in this series. Although individuals changed along with their groups, the cultural changes did not depend on, or necessarily involve, *genetic changes* in the individuals. Group *participation in consciousness* allowed by language was something new and different. It utilized *consciousness* at an entirely new level, and, allowed both individuals and groups of individuals to *participate in consciousness* at increasingly higher levels.

The development of language, with its ability to pass information to the succeeding generations, also lifted *faith* to a totally different level. No doubt faith existed, in the sense of emotional and intellectual *belief*, and enabled

26

rudimentary social cooperation before language developed, but most of what we now recognize as *faith* could not exist without language maintained by an ongoing group. What individuals are capable of believing, with the benefit of *language and abstractions* maintained by a group, is on an entirely different plane from the elementary psychological elements involved in any form of *faith* that preceded language.

Language not only enabled human groups to *participate in consciousness*, but the development of language also expanded *individual participation in consciousness*. Words are *abstractions* of the *objects* and *nonphysical essences* that they represent. This is the point at which the theory that I developed and am explaining coincides with work of Vygotsky and Luria. But the analysis of the issue by Vygotsky and Luria did not approach the issue from the standpoint of *collective faith* as my analysis did. Humans *believed* that the abstractions represented something real. *Faith* is an important element in the process. Vygotsky and Luria approached the issue of *internalization* of higher mental functions from language from the standpoint of individual psychology.

The word *faith* is so often associated with *religion* that many people think that *faith* is always just a matter of personal opinion and preference. However, faith is not just *personal* but extremely *social* in nature. Little individual faith of any significance exists independently of faith shared by a cultural group. The belief that faith is purely a personal matter combines with a strong Western dogma of *individualism* so as to almost sacralize the thought that every person has a right to believe whatever he or she pleases, regardless of consequences. Of course, it is true that every person has a right to believe whatever he or she pleases, but that fact creates significant dangers. Beliefs that are *not* true won't promote progress. Inaccurate opinions are dangerous. Truth is a very powerful force. It is important that what individuals and groups believe *be* true. My *third essay* in this series, "Faith in Action" points out that faith is the driving force of human *behavior.* And the *fifth essay*, "Faith, Social Systems and Institutions," argues that society harnesses that driving motivational force to create *social systems* that serve human needs. Inaccurate beliefs are a threat to those important social processes that are quite necessary for modern human existence. Continuing progress in cultural evolution is contingent on the continuing ability of cultural groups to make wise decisions.

Cultural evolution is obviously a *group* process. In biological evolution, *species evolve*, but individuals do *not* evolve. Individuals receive their genetic heritage at birth, and it changes very little over a lifetime. However, *cultural evolution* can occur during the lifetime of an individual, and individuals can experience the benefits of *cultural evolution*. There has been significant *cultural evolution* during my lifetime. My father was using a mule in his farming operations when I was born. He bought a tractor to replace the mule when I was about four years old. He never owned a cell phone. I remember the time *before* electricity, telephone, television, or even running water was available in my home. *Cultural evolution* and ever-increasing *participation in consciousness* have brought great changes. They have created the modern world.[8]

STAGES OF PARTICIPATION IN CONSCIOUSNESS

Collective faith creates *consensus reality* and *consensus reality* creates *collective faith*. The two have evolved together in recognizable stages. The first stage of collective faith was the *oral stage*. It began when humans developed the capacity for *linguistic participation in consciousness*. Humans developed language capable of preserving and exchanging knowledge 100,000 years ago according to de Chardin's guess about the point in time at which language developed. Most scientific students of evolution of language agree with that guess. Based on that guess, the purely oral stage of *consensus reality* lasted at least 90,000 years, but it may have gone back much further than that. Humanity's collection of words, stories and *abstractions* steadily expanded after language developed. With language, humans were able to tell stories. The stories they developed helped expand and preserve knowledge. The use of language and abstractions enabled humans to create stories now collectively called *mythos*, which we will discuss in more detail later in this essay. The oral tools of *mythos* include myths, legends, stories, and religious rituals and practices. Humans collected, remembered, and exchanged their beliefs orally. The ability to memorize stories was a key skill during this oral stage. Some individuals reportedly had the uncanny ability to recall, word for word, very long narratives,

The expansion of *faith* was an expansion of the understanding of what we now call the *biosphere*. Directly, it was part of the effort to survive in the biosphere. Indirectly, it represented a growing effort to comprehend *reality*. The abstractions included in language represent something *real*. They represent the *physical objects* and *nonphysical essences* that present themselves to the human mind in the biosphere as *phenomena*, and although the objects may be physical, the *abstractions* are *invisible* and *nonphysical!* The real trick here is the way consciousness transforms whatever it is that makes its way to the human brain from the biosphere, including the *social environment*, into knowledge in the human mind. The *phenomena* somehow match with *nonphysical essences* that exist in undeveloped consciousness before they become words in human languages. But after the group *develops* the abstractions as words, *individuals* internalize the abstractions that are included in their language and use them in their *individual thinking*.

About 6,000 years ago, a *second stage* of collective faith began to emerge as humans developed the ability to *write* and *read*. I call this the *manual writing stage* and have coined the phrase *symbol recognition participation in consciousness* to represent the increased human *participation in consciousness* that it involved. Writing carried the *process of abstraction* to a new level: the *written or printed word* stands not only for the *object* or *essence* that exists in the biosphere but also for the spoken *word* that humanity had already created using *linguistic participation in consciousness.* To create language, humans substituted a *word* for the *phenomenon* presented by the *physical object* or *nonphysical essence.* Words acquired an existence in the biosphere in their own right. *Words* existed in *language* and were used orally before they could be represented in writing. The fact that dictionaries give a "correct pronunciation" for written words makes it clear that *written* words represent *spoken* words. And now, in this electronic age, the internet will actually pronounce them for you! So, *symbol recognition participation in consciousness* evolved from *linguistic participation in consciousness.*

Symbol recognition participation in consciousness is not limited to written *words. Musical notation* that represents tones, and mathematical *numerals* that represent numbers are also *written symbols.* Written words used in speech, symbols used to write music, and numerals used to represent numbers are all maintained by *groups* of people. The involvement of multiple people is what makes them so useful. Composers write music that musicians can play without ever meeting the composer, and different musicians can play the same piece to produce very similar sounds. Whole orchestras can create beautiful sounds! Mathematical notation is almost universal, transcending languages and cultures. Art also engages *symbol recognition participation in consciousness.*

But the use of written *words* was extremely significant. *Symbol recognition* was a major development for human *participation in consciousness,* ending the requirement that human beings either be at the same place at the same time or send oral messengers to communicate with each other. With writing, humans were able to send messages by any transportation available. They were also able to use *writing* to collect, record, preserve, and exchange knowledge. Human memory was no longer the only way to preserve information.

Symbol recognition participation in consciousness required new *skills and technology.* The creator of the written message, or an assistant, had to be able to *write.* The recipient or an assistant had to be able to *read.* The skills of reading and writing required a new application of *consciousness* and invoked a new type of *intelligence.* The requirement for new skills gave an advantage to the individuals who had the ability to learn those skills. These new skills reduced the crucial role of the remarkable ability of certain individuals to memorize and recite very large volumes of information. At the same time, it put a premium on the key skills required for *symbol recognition participation in consciousness*: reading and writing. The new skills required for *writing, in turn, required new technologies.* The writer or his scribe had to have suitable writing *equipment* and *material.*

Writing significantly advanced the capabilities of *collective faith* and profoundly affected the development of religion, economics, and government. It enabled both religions and governments to expand their influence to include larger groups. It tremendously enhanced human ability to *institutionalize social structures* and *practices. Institutionalization* results from *faith.* It enables humans to believe that things like *religion, morality, government, law,* and other *social structures* are *real.* And they are very real, with essences their own, although not physical. The *manual writing stage* ushered in the *historical era.* With writing, *faith* took on a new dimension.

Karl Jaspers identified the period from about 800 BC to 200 BC as the *Axial Age* in history. It was the period that gave rise to all the great religions.[9] It was the age of Plato and Aristotle, Gautama Buddha, Confucius, Lao-tse, and many other great names in the development of religions and philosophy. It saw the rise of Judaism, Zoroastrianism, Buddhism, and other great religions in Europe, the Middle East, India, China, and Egypt. The writings of Homer were assembled early in this period. Jaspers thought it to be interesting, and almost mysterious, that parallel changes occurred at about the same time in all these widely dispersed cultures. The *Axial Age* affected many human activities in addition to *religion*. It was pivotal for the development of the entire institutional structure that is used by the modern world.

I contend that the *Axial Age* was brought about by an expansion of *participation in consciousness*. It was the period when *oral traditions* were being converted into *writing*. *Symbolism* was taking on increased importance in consciousness. The period was pivotal for every facet of history. The transition from the oral stage to the writing stage was almost certainly a principal causative factor giving rise to this period. And if so, the 800 BC to 200 BC time period needs to be expanded, and the dynamics of transition from oral to writing needs to be taken into account in discussing the time frame. Muhammad could not read or write, and the Arabian area was apparently rich in oral tradition right down to Muhammad's time, as reflected in the Koran. The Mayans learned to write, and the time frame for their development of writing needs to be taken into account when assigning a time frame to the *Axial Age*, if my suggestion that the *Axial Age* was caused by the appearance of writing is correct. Among some peoples, the transition from oral communication to writing is occurring even today, and is greatly complicated and accelerated by the simultaneous availability of the electronic means of communication, with sound and images.

The next significant stage in the development of collective faith evolved in the fifteenth century. The invention of the *printing press* revolutionized *written* communication. This *third stage* of collective faith was the *print stage*. The print stage enabled *mass dissemination* of knowledge. It coincided with the rise of science and ushered in the modern era. The *print stage* brought major progress in the evolution of *consensus reality*. Although it did not seem to involve a completely new *level of human participation in consciousness,* it greatly expanded *symbol recognition participation in consciousness*. It was the culmination of *symbol recognition participation in consciousness*, and a strong precursor of *electronic participation in consciousness*. It empowered science and technology. As more and more people learned to read and write, group *participation in consciousness* expanded, and *faith* moved to a higher *functional* level in society.

Ironically, as the *Age of Print* unfolded, the church tried to control the dissemination of knowledge, including religious material. It tried to control publication of scientific material that challenged its dogmas. The Church was instinctively trying to protect its power by controlling *consensus reality* and the creative power of *mythos*. However, evolving *consensus reality* and *mythos* possess revolutionary motivational force. They find and act on truth. It is never easy to suppress the power of *faith* acting on *truth*. *Truth* and *consensus reality* are likely to overcome opposition from any quarter, including the Church.

The *printed word*, and *reading*, introduced an unprecedented expansion of faith and participation in the *consciousness system. Symbol recognition participation in consciousness*—the ability to read and write—became the epitome of *intelligence*. Those talents actually affected the human *conceptualization* of intelligence. Skillful readers and writers have a large advantage over their contemporaries who lack those skills, and tend to do better on intelligence tests. But the skill set is strange. The ability to read is the ability of the human eye to follow a sequential line of print that presents words, using letters, from the beginning to the end of the written material. Although most common objects can be recognized from almost any angle, and reading is a highly prized skill, most people can't recognize printed words if the book is upside down! Readers must *consciously* absorb *information* represented in the intended *meaning* of the words, sentences, and paragraphs displayed in the long, sequential lines of a book.

The unique role that the ability to read has played during the past 500 years is impressive. It became more important to individuals than physical strength, mechanical ability, physical agility, and any other human ability. It was the precursor of the *electronic age*, just as writing itself led to Jasper's *Axial Age*. The new *axial age* to which it has led is likely to have even more profound effect on every facet of human endeavor and existence than the *Axial Age* that Jaspers described.

The invention of the printing press and expansion of its use enabled full development of *symbol recognition participation in consciousness.* In the realm of *consensus reality, print* reigned in the West for over 500 years. Faith evolved dramatically. In those 500 years, writers, scholars, and publishers collected a large portion of the basic beliefs of the human race. The writings included sacred, scientific, mathematical, musical, classical, Greek and Shakespearian tragedies and comedies, novels, poetry, and every imaginable form of literature. *Mythos* took a giant step, and so did *science* and every other aspect of human faith and knowledge. Humanity *printed* a large percentage of its basic beliefs during the 500-year *Age of Print.* Many cultures printed and stored their basic beliefs during that period. The *printed beliefs* of that period provided humanity's understanding of today's world.

And it brought us to the current stage of collective faith, the *electronic stage,* which differs in kind from all previous *participation in consciousness.* The electronic stage has gradually expanded. It started with telegraph, but rapidly expanded to telephone, movies, radio, and television. Then came the computer chip and computers in all their varieties. Telegraph sent written communications with a set of signs and symbols. Dots and dashes represented written words. Written words represented spoken words. Spoken words represented *physical objects* or *nonphysical essences.* That is a lot of representation and needed simplification! So, telephones were invented to transmit spoken words. Radio carried the spoken word to wide audiences. Its networks brought Franklin Roosevelt and World War II to the fireside and inner sanctum of families. Movies made images available, and eventually added sound. Television takes both *images* and *sound* into the heart of the home as the events occur, largely bypassing *written* symbolism. Computers and the internet expand human *participation in consciousness* to extremely high levels of performance. The capability for mass transmission of *images and sounds* is completely revamping the way the human mind processes *information*.

The expansion of *human participation in consciousness* brought by *electronic participation in consciousness* is obvious. Opportunities for communication and expansion of collective faith are almost unlimited. They now include an unprecedented ability to send and receive *emotional* and *spiritual* elements along with information. The information that is shared electronically often includes *inflection and tone* as well as facial expressions and other body language. The *affective* parts of communication are no longer missing in communication, as happened with the transition from the oral stage to writing and print. Electronics has virtually eliminated the time lag in the transmission of information. Electronic transmission can be almost instantaneous, a major step forward for consciousness itself! Cell phones expand human use of consciousness. That is why people cannot put their cell phones down. The attraction of human consciousness is very powerful. It is the essence of existence.

A prime example of the significant new capabilities created by electronics is illustrated by televised presidential election debates. The audience sees all the body language and hears the tones and inflection. The physical appearance of Kennedy and Nixon in their televised presidential debates is believed to have affected the outcome of the election. The current environment for the development of faith differs greatly from any that has ever existed in the past. The robust Teddy Roosevelt portrayed in early movie media could be elected today, but what about the three-hundred-thirty-pound William Howard Taft and the somber looking politicians of the Victorian Age? It is difficult to predict the ultimate outcome of the markedly different faith *environment* that exists today in comparison to the faith environment of the past. There is hardly any question that *electronic participation in consciousness*, with communication that connects the entire world, has brought a *second axial age* that will impact all human *participation in consciousness*, and every facet of human activity on the entire planet earth.

But the beginning of a new stage in the development of *consensus reality* has never completely displaced the methods of earlier stages. Written history did not eliminate oral mythos. The mythological method of thinking is still very much in use! Manual writing did not eliminate speech; it added a new dimension for the use of words and language in the art of communication. But people still talk. *Symbol recognition participation in consciousness* was built on and added to *linguistic participation in consciousness*. Print did not eliminate oral and manually written communication. It supplemented both.

But that is not to say that addition of a new stage does not impact the faith and the *consensus reality* that it produces. Channeling knowledge into print may have had a significant effect on the faith of human beings. When information moves from oral communication into writing and print, it loses the *emotion* inherent in *imagery*, *inflection*, and *tone*! Perhaps it gains some glow of its own by engaging imaginative powers. There may never have been princesses as beautiful or romantic as those found in fairy tales! Of course, the benefits of the broad, rapid expansion of *consensus reality* brought by the advent of writing overshadowed the loss of some of the *affective* parts of human communication. But now *electronic communication*, in this new *axial age*, has integrated many aspects of all previous stages of *participation in consciousness*, and it is having a profound effect on collective human faith. It will impact all human *social systems*, and is truly a new pivotal point in the history of humanity. Of course, there is a downside. Virtual reality is not completely "real." I can make a virtual visit to a restaurant, but virtual food will not satisfy the need for food that Maslow described! And the possibilities for false, deceitful representations increase along with the possibilities of truthful, positive communications. I get as many spam calls and messages as meaningful ones.

MATHEMATICAL PARTICIPATION IN CONSCIOUSNESS

Let me digress from the description of sequential development of *participation in consciousness* by *oral* and *written language* and talk briefly about *mathematical participation in consciousness*. Mathematical *participation in consciousness* is a critical element for all modern technology, including electronic means of communication. *Mathematical participation in consciousness* arrived at a level of development capable of supporting the forthcoming science and technology just two or three hundred years before the printing press was invented. Numbers are sometimes described as the *universal language* because they seemingly transcend cultures. Of course, the concept of *numbers* has been around for a very long time. But the development of the *base 10*, and inclusion of *zero as an integer*, occurred in *India*, where so-called *"Arabic"* numbers actually originated. Participation in mathematics at that level occurred in India several hundred years before these critical developments entered into the mathematics of the West. The system was transmitted to the West via the Arabic world and the symbols for *numbers* in *base 10* were mistakenly named *"Arabic" numerals* in the West. As noted previously, the use of numerals in *mathematical participation in consciousness* engages *symbol recognition participation in consciousness*. *Numerals* are *symbols* that represent *numbers* that are *nonphysical essences*, or *abstractions*. *Numerals* stand for *numbers* the same way *words* stand for *physical objects* and *nonphysical essences*. *Nonphysical essences*, including *numbers*, are important parts of reality. *Mathematical participation in consciousness* was very present in ancient Greece and the Middle East, and were integrated into the philosophy of the West early on, and has continued to evolve. It has played an essential role in the development of Western science and technology. Computer technology could not have developed without the recognition of *zero* as an integer. Of course, numbers and numerals are a part of *consensus reality. Mathematical participation in consciousness* will continue to develop its important role as the electronic era unfolds. A full treatment of **mathematical participation in consciousness** is beyond the scope of this series of essays, and my competence, but its importance cannot be overestimated.

FAITH AND RELIGION

The word *faith* is often used as a synonym for *religion*. As I have indicated earlier, I am not using the word *faith* in these essays to mean religion, but it is important to understand the strong relationship between religion and the concept of faith that I am describing. Every religion is centered on what its adherents **believe**, so it is not surprising that the word *faith* is often used interchangeably with the word *religion*. Even leading scholars use the word *faith* in this sense, more often than they use the word to simply mean what we **believe** or **think we know**. So, faith, as I am describing it, plays a central role in all religions. I am not attempting to distance my analysis of faith and consciousness from religion. Religion is an important function of faith, but I am describing a concept of *faith* that includes the entirety of what an individual or culture believes. Religious faith has been a cutting edge in the work of the noosphere in the past, and still has a key role to play. But I am describing *faith* as **what we really believe**, and I am focusing on **that** approach to **truth**, and dealing with what is **currently recognized** as religion only incidentally.

But I must point out that if an individual compartmentalizes or separates **religious beliefs** from other beliefs, the **compartmentalized** "religious" beliefs are probably not faith at all. Faith produces important functions that we will explore in other essays in this series that deal with **human motivation**, **self-identification**, and **social systems**. Those functions of faith are of critical importance. But they **only** occur as a result of faith that individuals and groups **actually believe**. What people actually believe, the actual faith of individuals and cultures, whatever it is, produces **social systems** and affects human behavior and affairs. Compartmentalized religion that is **not** what someone actually believes won't produce those results and will not have much effect on *social systems* and human behavior and affairs.

To be effective—to be real—*to affect conduct*—to *establish identity*— to *make social systems work*—religious faith must be what a religious person *really* believes. It must involve actual *spiritual participation in consciousness*. For religion to be effective, the belief in *nonphysical essences* associated with the religion must be as strong, or stronger, than belief in the physical world that surrounds us. If *"religious beliefs"* are not the faith on which a person acts, they really are not religious faith. They are not faith at all. But this discussion leads to a very haunting question: Is it possible that *faith,* as I am describing it, really *is* religion? I describe religion as a *social system* in the *fifth essay* in this series.

FAITH AND SCIENCE

Science is a specialized application of the more general principle that we confirm reality by having our perceptions and observations confirmed by other people. *Objectivity* is stronger within the power of a *group*—multiple observers—than with an individual. Confirming reality in the observations and experiences of other people is an integral part of the dynamics of *faith* as well as *science*. Science has carefully refined this process in its quest for greater *objectivity*. The formation of nonscientific *consensus reality* that I have described is humanity's broadest approach to truth, and it is less rigorous, and more informal, than the scientific method. The truths maintained by *consensus reality* generally arise from natural human social behavior and are confirmed by a much broader base of observers and maintained by a much larger group of believers.

Of course, *consensus reality* that the larger nonscientific culture produces makes mistakes. The rigor of science can cure many of those mistakes with regard to physical reality. However, *consensus reality* itself is the only cure for some problems that broad-based *consensus reality* created and has supported, such as *slavery, segregation*, and a *subordinate role for women*. But *consensus reality* now identifies those issues as *problems,* and identification is movement toward solution within *consensus reality* itself. *Consensus reality* itself *has* discovered and dealt, at least in part, with those problems. By its very nature, it will continue to search for and correct these kinds of problems, although the process may seem painfully slow to those impacted by the practices and beliefs that need to be changed.

Science requires *faith* and is a subset of faith. Science, like all faith, is *communal*. Individual scientists make great contributions to science. However, if science itself were not the property of a larger *group*, to what would the individual scientists be contributing? To be valid, the results of an experiment must be *confirmed*, and the results must be *maintained* by the *group*, like the rest of the *consensus reality*. Other scientists must be able to repeat a scientific experiment and get the same results.[10] The scientific method, with its requirements for confirmation, also provides an excellent example of group *participation in consciousness*. Its empiricism tends to confirm the concept of *direct realism*; that is, that the conscious mind deals directly with the objects detected by the senses. I will discuss *direct realism* further in the *ninth essay*.

Western culture *believes* in science. Science is part of the Western *faith* system. Unfortunately, many people believe that the scientific method is the *only way* to establish *truth*. But the fact is that many things are true and important, but the scientific method cannot examine them. Generally speaking, science, as it has evolved in Western culture, actually *disproves false* theories. The scientific method cannot test a theory unless it is *falsifiable*. Science deals with *matter and energy*, and things that can be measured and that mathematics can deal with—not *intangible values*. Many values that are absolutely necessary for human life to have any quality depend on truths that are not *falsifiable*, and science cannot deal with them. That makes the ideas described in these essays critically important. The German philosopher Karl Jaspers, writing after World War II, used the term *scientific superstition*. He had seen and experienced the horrors of the "scientific" Nazis. Concerning matters of morality, it is better to accept as *true* the facts strongly posited by *consensus reality*, until science proves that those facts are *not* true, or until the consensus changes. Of course, if there is good reason not to accept such facts as true, it is important to challenge them, and that is the way *consensus reality* changes. But my main point here is that rejection of good principles *just because* science cannot *substantiate* them is not the right approach. And equally important, there are many *social values* that science is not equipped to deal with. Science should not assert itself as the proper tribunal with regard to matters involving values reflected only as *nonphysical essences*. This argument is particularly important with regard to the wisdom of the ages reflected in *morals* and *values* that science can neither prove nor disprove. The argument that everything that exists is physical is dangerous.

Unfortunately, in Western ideology, the *scientific method* has somehow become a litmus for *individual faith*. The *scientific superstition* that Jaspers spoke of is quite strong. Westerners—not necessarily the scientists themselves—consider *questionable* any matter that science has not "*proven*." This belief combines with the belief suggested previously that every individual is entitled to his or her own opinion to cause some people to believe that one opinion is just as good as another, unless there is scientific proof to the contrary. Although freedom of opinion is important, some opinions *are* better than other opinions. Human faith can bring progress in the biosphere only by choosing the *best opinions*, regardless of whether those opinions can be validated by the scientific method. Humanity must seek truth concerning matters that science cannot address. Only *ideas that work* can move humanity forward. Human survival depends on our finding *right solutions* to problems—including both the right solutions that science establishes with regard to *physical matters* and those that science cannot address dealing with values and other *nonphysical* matters. Humanity must find other, nonscientific methods to seek truth with regard to those matters that science cannot address, and must resist any efforts of *pseudo-scientists* to assert control over those matters. *Religion*, *morality*, and *law* are all based on *nonphysical* principles, but those *social systems*, and the principles on which they are based are very important and depend on nonscientific truths. They operate as functions of *faith*. They are based in large measure on *nonphysical* aspects of reality, *essences* that cannot be physically measured.

Science cannot evaluate *normative force*. Normative force is the *moral force* that compels compliance with the norms or standards of behavior in society. *Faith* produces the *normative force* of *morality*, based on widely held convictions and beliefs. The *emotional components* that faith invests in *morality* cause humans to behave properly when the system works. Humans expect other humans to properly behave themselves, and human emotions are aroused when others do not behave themselves properly. But to produce normative force, the individuals involved must have the same or similar beliefs about right and wrong. The shared convictions evoke *emotional commitment* from the members of the group. That's where the *group* garners the *energy* that enforces its *norms*. Individuals supply it. Normative force is an important element of both *morality* and *law*.

The scientific method cannot even prove that it is *wrong* to *lie*. Science assumes the reality of truth. Of course, science would not work at all if scientists do not believe that it is wrong to lie. Science cannot prove that commission of murder, theft, assault, burglary, or any of the cardinal sins is *wrong*. Nazi Germany was proficient with science. The *values* reflected in *law and morality* are essential to humanity's continued existence, but science cannot prove them. An adequate faith system *must* address these important issues, without the benefit of scientific proof, while continuing to embrace the many important evolving truths offered by science. Reduced to its essentials, the scientific method is a refined approach to *consensus reality* that uses group objectivity to disprove *falsifiable* assertions about the *physical world.* But science cannot prove what is true or false concerning human values.

GEOGRAPHIC DIVISION AND PLURALISM

Humanity expanded and migrated all over the earth in the distant, irretrievable past. Distance and geographical barriers divided the dispersed humanity and prevented direct contact and direct communication between and among the widespread groups. Humanity continued to migrate around the globe even while language, abstraction, and faith systems were developing.[11] Different cultures, languages, and faith systems evolved. Many of the widely dispersed cultures were almost completely isolated from other cultures. Many cultural differences developed, and *differing faiths* shaped the mindsets of the people in the different regions of the earth. But the *faith* that arose in the different geographic areas produced complex *cultural systems* within their respective areas. Multiple *cultures* emerged with fundamentally different sets of beliefs. Despite the fact that the advent of writing caused the *Axial Age* to occur at approximately the same time in all the leading cultures of the day, continuing cultural development produced and retains significant differences among the geographically divided groups.

All humans are born into specific families, in specific communities or locations, in particular countries. They are born with specific racial and ethnic characteristics. They learn specific languages. They hear specific stories in those languages. Those stories influence their faith as it develops. Parents and peers who influence the developing faith of the individuals are deeply embedded in the immediately surrounding culture and its beliefs. All of these factors cause humans to believe certain things in certain ways. Other humans, in different cultures, with different languages and different religious faiths, hear different stories and believe differently. *Individual faith* always arises in a specific *cultural* environment. There are many different cultures, each with very different *faith systems.* But every individual participates in at least one of those faith systems. They have no choice. All individuals are born in the interdependent biosphere and are dependent on other life, including other humans, in the biosphere. They are born in the human race and are connected to and nurtured by one or more cultures. Cultural systems depend on individual behavior for their own continuation as institutions. It is quite difficult for individuals to change basic beliefs once those beliefs are instilled in their psyche by the surrounding culture. And culture depends on the stable, predictable behavior of its constituents.

Different cultural faith systems produce *social systems* that perform similar functions, but there are many significant differences in those *social systems*. Families, religions, morality, economic practices, legal systems, education, political, and governmental systems differ greatly from culture to culture. The faith system within each culture puts its imprimatur on the *social systems* of that culture. The *social systems* of each culture, in turn, put their imprimatur on each child born in the culture. The cultural systems are self-perpetuating. The culture and faith systems that exist in America, Russia, the Middle East, India, China, the South Pacific, and Africa are not the same. The *social systems* are not the same. The faith of individuals within those cultures are shaped by the culture and its *social systems*, and although there are significant parallels, there are also significant differences.

Regardless of what cultural system surrounds humans, the culture systematically instills *its* values into its constituents so that the individuals believe certain things. Beliefs are neither accidental nor unimportant. They are essential, both for the individuals and for the functioning of their cultural groups. Not *every* belief supported by a culture is essential for *every* individual in the culture, but the *systems* that faith produces are essential both for the individuals and their cultural groups. They are, and must be, supported by the collective faith of the group in order for the group to survive, and meet the needs of its individual members.

Pluralistic faith systems created pluralistic *consensus realities*. The *pluralistic cultures* remained divided by geography, language, and other factors until the recent past. But recently, the technologies of transportation and communication have connected all of humanity for the first time since its initial wide dispersion. Cultures that have very different faith systems are now in close communication with each other, even though significant differences between and among the cultures and their faith systems remain. The differences are as basic as *beliefs about what it means to be human*. The close contact among differing faiths that has occurred with modern communication is unprecedented. It produces conflict. The faith system of each culture firmly believes that it and only it is right. The intransigence of cultural beliefs presents a significant challenge in today's faith environment.

CONCLUDING SUMMARY

The earth's biosphere is the environment in which *life*, *language*, *faith*, and the ability to *participate in consciousness* evolved. That *participation* resulted in the evolution of the animal kingdom, and may run even deeper in the operation of the biosphere. But for humans, *participation in consciousness* took a giant step with evolution of the development of capacity for *linguistic participation in consciousness*. The prize possession of humanity is the ability to participate in reflective, communicable *consciousness*. *Participation in consciousness* is endowed with *memory*, *cognition*, *affection* and *imagination*, and the subtle *ability to separate truth from falsity*.

With the evolution of the human capability for *linguistic participation in consciousness*, human minds first developed the ability to deal with *nonphysical essences* as *phenomena* and gave them oral expression. That evolution empowered humans to create a very useful *consensus reality*. Although very useful, *consensus reality* is only a shadow of *ultimate reality*, but represents *ultimate reality* as accurately as is humanly possible at any given time. Human ability to capture reality was substantially augmented by the arrival of *symbol recognition participation in consciousness* that created writing and ushered in the *Axial Age* that enabled the evolution of the *social systems* that operate today's world. *Linguistic participation in consciousness, symbol recognition participation in consciousness*, and *consensus reality* set humanity apart from other animals. They involve unparalleled *group participation* in *consciousness*. As the *consensus reality* that was made possible by *linguistic participation in consciousness* continues to grow, the human faith environment expands. We have entered into a new *axial age* of *electronic participation in consciousness*, and the opportunities and dangers are unlimited.

Faith is what we *really believe*. It is both individual and social. Memory is essential to faith. Like language, faith is communal. It is a function of human *participation in consciousness*. Faith engages the entire person: emotions as well as intellect. Science engages faith and requires faith for its operations. It is a specialized form of *consensus reality*.

2) STAGES AND SOURCES OF FAITH

INDIVIDUAL FAITH AND THE ***INDIVIDUAL consciousness*** that maintains it develop over the lifetime of an individual. The ***development of faith*** involves expansion of ***individual consciousness***. Individual faith develops incrementally over a lifetime, but there are identifiable ***stages*** in the development of both ***faith*** and ***individual consciousness***. Different ***sources*** contribute to faith at different ***stages*** of an individual's physical, mental, and emotional growth and development. ***Sources*** of faith are ***external*** to the individual. They exist in the individual's environment. The individual ***internalizes*** them with the help of surrounding cultural groups, in a process that Lev Vygotsky called ***semiotic mediation***. This discussion of ***stages*** of faith focuses on ***development*** that occurs ***within individuals***. The discussion of ***sources*** later in this essay focuses on information and groups that surround the individual in the faith environment. The individual internalizes those sources. Vygotsky explained that the individual ***internalizes*** the information from the individual's cultural groups, and this forms the basis in the individual's ***higher mental functions***.

Cultures and societies perpetuate their ***faith***—their ***consensus reality***—by instilling beliefs into children born in the society. Needless to say, *education* is an extremely important part of the process. Vygotsky only differentiated *natural* and *"scientific"* lines of development of mental processes. This seems to identify only two *sources* for the knowledge that individuals develop. The *natural* development that he identified stems from heredity and the relationship with parents and other humans. Those relations are social, but they differ from the more formal social learning that occurs in school and vocational training. Vygotsky's use of the term *scientific* apparently includes *all educational activities*. Use of *language* is the key to both the *natural* and *scientific* categories posited by Vygotsky. The key to both "lines" of development (scientific and natural) is *internalization. Internalization* is not a complicated process. Internalization is simply learning to talk, then learning to read, and acquiring the knowledge that is stored in the language of the cultural group. But the thing that Western thinking (embedded, as it is in the ideology of individualism) seems to miss about Vygotsky's theory is that important parts of the *mental processes* that individuals internalize and use in abstract thinking are actually stored and maintained in *society*, and transmitted and maintained in systems *external* to the individual who *internalizes* them. Concepts—the elements of higher mental processes—are found in the language of the culture that surrounds the individual. The culture itself "found" these essences *in the biosphere* and incorporated them into its *language*. Important parts of consciousness and the faith it empowers are not merely the products of the individual's heredity, or brain, but are culture dependent.

Long before I discovered Vygotsky's writings in 2020, I had arrived at the conclusion that language plays a key role in the internalization of abstractions for conceptual thinking, extrapolating from Émile Durkheim's concept of *collective representations*, which he described in *The Elementary Forms of the Religious Life* (1912). But as I envisioned the role of internalization of concepts provided by the surrounding culture, it appeared to me that internalization included material that was more diverse and received from many more sources than Vygotsky described. Seemingly, he considered only the two sources mentioned above: (1) *natural* (heredity and family), on the one hand, and (2) *scientific*, which based on my reading of his translated works really seems to mean *formal schooling* or its equivalent. Perhaps all the sources of faith that I identify can be placed into one of those two categories, but I believe that it is helpful to more fully differentiate the cultural sources and identify them more specifically.

Vygotsky was born in Russia well before the 1917 Bolshevik Revolution, but did his scholarly work in the Soviet Union after the revolution. It may be significant to note that he was actually twenty-one years old by the time the revolution occurred, and his own early educational and mental development actually occurred in Czarist Russia, and not under the rule of communism. His most formative years were not necessarily dominated by the ideology of *dialectic materialism*. But he developed his psychological theories *after* the revolution. If he had articulated some of the sources that I mention in this essay in my discussion of sources, they might not have been well received in the environment in which he was working. But there is a lot more to culture than *family and schooling*, so I will identify many sources of faith that exist in the human cultural environment, and that individuals "internalize" so that they become a part of the individual's working faith. Development of faith and the expansion of *participation in consciousness* as a part of natural development are one and the same process. Before discussing the sources of faith in depth, I will describe the *stages* of faith—the "internal" development of faith.

STAGES OF FAITH

Emory University professor James Fowler developed the theory that *faith* develops in *definable stages* over the course of a lifetime.[12] He had worked at Harvard with Lawrence Kohlberg, who had described stages of *moral development*. Swiss psychologist Jean Piaget had previously introduced the concept of developmental *stages* in *moral development*,[13] describing *three* stages. Kohlberg drew on the work of Piaget and expanded the theory of stages of moral development that occur over a lifetime to include *six definable stages*. Following Kohlberg's lead, Fowler contended that *faith,* like moral formation, develops in *six definable stages*. Looking at their works, it becomes clear that *moral formation* is actually a subset of *faith formation*, and Fowler used the theories of Piaget and Kohlberg to develop his theory of *stages of faith*. *Faith formation* involves more components of personality and affects more human activity than does *moral formation*. Piaget's theories actually extended well beyond moral formation in individuals. Piaget dealt with psychological development generally, but Piaget did not recognize the role of language in concept formation in the same way Vygotsky did and he did not describe a role of *faith development* as such. However, as James Fowler realized, the same individual physical and mental developmental processes that are involved in moral formation are also involved in faith formation.

The theory of moral formation created by Piaget and Kohlberg is called the *cognitive developmental* theory. It holds that morality can be *taught*. Fowler also studied another theory called the *psychosocial theory*, developed by Sigmund Freud and Erik Erikson, that differs from the cognitive-developmental theory. Psychosocial theory places emphasis on *emotional* factors as well as *cognitive* factors in moral formation. Fowler drew on the works of Sigmund Freud and Erik Erikson, as well as Piaget and Kohlberg, to develop his description of the *stages* of *faith*. Both the *cognitive developmental theory* and the *psychosocial theory* play important roles in describing faith development. Needless to say, faith development involves participation in and the development of the individual's *participation in consciousness*. Unfortunately, Fowler did not consider the *Cultural-Historical School* of psychology propounded by Vygotsky and Luria. I believe that if he had been aware of it, it would have been prominently featured in his book.

But let's turn to the specifics of Fowler's theory of stages of faith. Fowler identified *infancy* as a *pre-stage* of faith development. In the *pre-stage*, the child establishes relationships of trust with parents or primary caretakers. *Trust* is the key component that develops (or fails to develop) during the infancy *pre-stage*. The *pre-stage* occurs during the period between birth and learning to talk.

Interestingly, what Fowler identified as the *first stage* of *faith* begins after the *pre-stage*, and starts with the development of *language*. Unfortunately, because he was apparently not aware of the work of Vygotsky and Luria, he did not mention the role that language plays in *participation in consciousness*, which obviously plays an important role in the development of faith. Fowler's *first stage* of faith development occurs during the *preschool years*. In the preschool *first stage*, the child is influenced by examples, moods, actions, and stories of the visible faith of the parents or other adults standing in the place of parents. The child imitates parents and internalizes and adopts both their *images* and their *language*. The failure of Fowler to consider Vygotsky's theory at this point is unfortunate. Vygotsky's ideas about *semiotic development* of concepts and consciousness through language would have tied well with Freud's concepts of *internalization*. Vygotsky's theory would have greatly enhanced the theories of Piaget and Kohlberg about the acquisition of concepts involved in morality and faith. Knowledge of Vygotsky might have caused Freud himself to realize that not only are *images* and *emotions* internalized; the very *concepts* that we use for thinking are internalized from the social environment. But in any event, Fowler recognized that parents, or people in their position, are the main *sources* of faith in both the *pre-stage* and the *first stage* of development that he described. I suspect that from and after the time Fowler wrote his book, TV and *electronic media* had begun to play a significant role in faith development, even in the *first stage*.

Fowler's *second stage* of faith development usually occurs during *elementary school* years. In this stage, the individual internalizes the stories, beliefs, and practices of his or her own *social group*. *Myth* plays an important role in this stage. Nursery rhymes and fairy tales play important roles. Children enjoy stories read by parents, teachers, and others at the *second stage* of faith. The individual internalizes the *values* or *lessons* embedded in the stories.[14] Teachers, schoolmates, and the peer group begin to exert influence on the child's developing faith, but parents also are still deeply involved. Educational experiences play an increasingly important part during Fowler's *second stage*.

The *third stage* comes with *puberty* and high school. This is the stage in which an individual comes to grips with the world *beyond the family*. The peer group plays an increasingly important role. Faith begins to synthesize *values* and *information*. The values and information begin to provide a basis for the individual's *identity* and outlook. At this *adolescence* stage, the individual *forms his or her personal myth*. The *personal myth* includes one's past and anticipated future. The image of what Fowler called the *ultimate environment* begins to evolve in the mind of the individual, and the individual begins to understand how his or her own personality fits into the big picture. Here is another point at which Vygotsky could have added much to Fowler's analysis. At this point, the developing individual develops a *concept of "humanity,"* which enables him or her to identify the *self* as *human*. This development enables *individual consciousness* to develop a concept of the *self* as an *object*. *Internalized language*, at this point, and memories that have developed, enable the individual to construct a *personal story*. At this stage, the individual develops *independent personality* and *identity*. We will develop the topic of *identification* of *self* in detail in the *fourth essay*, where we will see that *individual consciousness* is the seat *of self-identification* and is *totally subjective*, and the *self-concept* is a concept that it constructs and maintains. Most people never move beyond the *third stage* according to Fowler.

For those who move beyond stage three, Fowler contends that late adolescence or early adulthood may bring a *fourth stage* of faith development. In this stage, the individual begins to take seriously his or her responsibility for commitments, lifestyle, beliefs, and attitudes. The individual attains an identity independent of roles assigned by others. That identity is conscious of its own boundaries and inner connections. The individual develops a *worldview* that is aware of itself as such. For those who move beyond stage three, of course, *stage four* is usually the highest level that they will achieve.

However, according to Fowler, a few people move to a *fifth stage*. At this stage, "symbolic power is reunited with conceptual meanings," according to Fowler. At the *fifth stage*, one becomes aware of the effect of the myths, ideal images, and prejudices built deeply into the self because of membership within a particular cultural class, religious tradition, or ethnic group. This stage is *unusual before midlife.* Although one is well aware of the fact that he or she is a part of a group and shares in the meanings of that group, he or she also understands that those meanings are relative, incomplete, and only partial participation in total transcendent reality.

And then, according to Fowler, there is a rare, but possible *sixth stage* of faith. The *sixth stage* of faith—the highest level described by Fowler—one that is seldom attained—Fowler calls *universalizing faith.* At this stage, self-preservation is no longer a primary concern, nor is preservation of the *status quo*. One engages in absolute love of humanity, seeks justice, and constantly seeks to transform existing social structures to achieve universal justice and an ideal world. Because such persons seek to transform existing structures, they may be seen as a threat to the existing order, according to Fowler. For that reason, individuals who reach Fowler's *sixth stage* often suffer martyrdom.

A remarkable result of Fowler's *sixth stage* of faith is that it causes the individual to engage in activities that dramatically differ from expectations of conventional modern notions of motivation. Maslow's hierarchy of needs that we will discuss in the *third essay* in the series is seemingly turned upside down in Fowler's *sixth stage* of faith. Hobbes' adage that *self-preservation* is the first law of nature and Adam Smith's theory of economics based on the motivational force of *enlightened self-interest* are deeply embedded in the belief systems of Western cultures. But persons in the *sixth stage* of faith clearly see and demonstrate that this conventional wisdom, which often embraces an ideal of *rugged individualism*, is not universally desirable. Maslow, the guru of motivation, talked about *self-actualization*, and people who achieve Fowler's *sixth stage* of faith are certainly self-actualized. But self-actualization may idealize enlightened self-interest and self-preservation. In these essays, I argue that *self-actualization* can only be fully realized in *service to others*.

The welfare of the human race seems to take higher priority with each advance to a higher level in Fowler's stages of faith. This *faith evolution* in individuals involves an increasingly accurate assessment of *truth*, especially in the *nonphysical realm*. At the *sixth stage*, preservation of the human race is the central theme. The stages of faith development described by Fowler are very consistent with the kind of *faith* that supports the *evolution of beneficial social systems* in the *biosphere*. Fully developed faith supports *welfare of humans* in the biosphere and the opportunity for complete fulfillment of potential. It satisfies, so far as humanly possible, the human *quest for meaning* that we will examine in the essay about faith and human motivation. The *sixth stage* includes individuals like Jesus, Church martyrs, Dr. Martin Luther King, Jr., and Mahatma Gandhi as notable examples.

Fowler's description of stages of faith development probably holds generally true with regard to the development of faith for individuals in all cultures and faith systems. Its roots are tied to physical development, and development of *participation of consciousness*, so it is a *description* of *faith development* that could apply to everyone in the biosphere.[15] I am sure that is what Fowler intended. The stages of faith reflect stages of development of *individual consciousness* with regard to *participation* in the totality of *consciousness*.

Beginning in Fowler's *pre-stage*, faith development within individuals likely replicates the evolution of humanity's *participation in consciousness*. Throughout the process of development, in all stages, the individual is acquiring the conceptual framework for dealing with life with other individuals in the biosphere. *Participation in consciousness* plays a key role.

But let's do a little analysis of Fowler's work. Even though the most influential group during the *pre-stage* and *preschool* years may be *parents*, it is important to emphasize that *not all parents are alike*. And also, remember that activities of parents change with the passage of time. My children experienced parents quite different from my own parents. Likewise, the *peer groups* that my children encountered were not the same as mine. Understanding this dynamic, changing social environment is important in thinking through the application of Fowler's theory. The groups that are doing the influencing are composed of individuals who are *themselves* moving through *their own* stages of faith development. The whole process is a very fluid, dynamic process. Although we can see that there are stages of development that can be described generally, the fluidity of the factors just described should make it clear that the description of stages is not a template that is likely to produce the same *results* for all individuals in all times and places.

Parents *(or absence of parents)* have a significant impact on a child's development. Parents may do a good job of parenting or a poor job of parenting, and that affects the outcome of faith development, especially during the *pre-stage* and *first stage*. The influence of parents continues in the *second stage*, but the *peer group* then enters the picture. And not all peer groups are alike. The peer group that a child in the ghetto encounters is not the same that a child in the suburbs encounters. The peer group in China is not the same as in the United States. But whatever the peer group, and whoever the parents, parents and peer groups have a significant effect on the development of a child's faith.

Some of the stages that Fowler described have clearly defined biological benchmarks, such as the development of the capacity for meaningful use of language, puberty, and maturing into early adulthood. Others are not quite so clear. Vygotsky recognized the important changes in mental development that occur with puberty. But other than puberty, he might have argued for a continuum of development that is not so sharply defined by stages, and I tend to agree. Nevertheless, Fowler's analysis considered as a broad general description of stages of faith development is meaningful.

THE RELATIONSHIP BETWEEN STAGES AND SOURCES

As we have seen in the preceding discussion of stages, on some points, Fowler's description of stages seems to be *source* dependent. And a lot of what he describes has a close affinity with the education system that prevailed in the United States at the time Fowler wrote his book. To some extent, the stages that Fowler described seem to include what is *going on around a child* as much as what is going on within the child at particular times in the child's life. In large measure, the *sources* of faith and *stages* of faith are inseparable, but when thinking of *stages*, it would likely be helpful to focus on the *psychological stages* of development that are occurring *within* the individual—the development of *individual consciousness*—and to recognize that the *sources* are *external* to the individual. But Fowler was not trying to distinguish the two; he was focused on *stages* of faith. Although stages and sources are almost inseparable because of the important role played by internalization, the two need to be distinguished as much as possible. The sources that surround children, and are internalized, differ. They can be managed, to some extent. The stages are more internal, genetically controlled, and definitely psychological. The sources are external. The sources impact on the stages, and sometimes *need* to be managed.

The *sociological basis* for the stages that Fowler described are not limited to the fluid, changing social factors described above that are implicit in his description of the stages. Of course, internalization—the sociological impact on developing psychology—actually affects the ability of an individual to move from one stage to the next. *Educational opportunities* affect the *third* and *fourth stages.* There are good schools and schools that are not so good. Fowler says the *third stage* marks the final stage for many individuals. Is that because faith development, as he described it, ends for many with high school? Is high school dropout and failure to pursue education a factor? Is failure to fully develop, through educational opportunities, the highest levels of *linguistic, symbol recognition, mathematical,* and *electronic participation in consciousness* that I describe in other essays a limiting factor? Do *underlying factors* that *cause* dropout and failure to pursue education *also* adversely affect faith development itself? And taking this analysis to the next educational level, how much impact does *post-secondary education* have on the possibilities of moving into the *fourth* and/or *fifth stages*?

And there are still other sociological considerations. Although one would think that full faith development is possible for everyone, there is just so much room in society for certain roles. If everybody tried to do what Mahatma Gandhi, Dr. King, Nelson Mandela, Bishop Tutu, and others readily identifiable with Fowler's *stage six* did, hardly any would get to that stage or get the job done. The roles of these individuals were unique leadership roles that arose from special circumstances. For Gandhi, Mandela, and King, special cultural or political limitations imposed on certain races or cultures provided an opportunity for leadership and greatness. Do the struggles of class and race, and social and political differences find their way into Fowler's beliefs about the highest forms of faith development? These struggles certainly can and should have a place, but the question that I am raising is whether faith development to the highest stages can *only* occur in those limited circumstances. Society's capacity for creating the kinds of roles that Fowler identified with his highest stages is definitely limited. Did Fowler fail to adequately distinguish **faith development** from **social opportunity** for leadership? Is the capacity for faith development limited to such special circumstances? I do not think so. If not, it would be well to identify less well-known individuals who have achieved the highest levels of faith, and to describe them and **their** activities as examples of the top levels of faith development. Additional thoughtful work is needed with regard to the **stages** of **individual faith development**, especially the higher stages, taking into account the impact of social and political factors. The role of internalization that Vygotsky taught us needs to be carefully taken into account. Better understanding of the genetically controlled developmental processes that take place within individuals is also needed.

SOCIOLOGY, SOURCES AND STAGES

Sources of faith influence, but do not control **stages** of faith, although **stages** of faith are indeed closely related to **sources** of faith. Vygotsky has shown that the development of human **participation in consciousness** is inseparable from external sources. The sources tend to present themselves at different points in the life of the developing individual. To understand **stages**, we must focus on the **individual** whose faith is developing and underscore the significance of the expanding and changing role of **individual consciousness** over the course of a lifetime. The **stages** definitely are affected by the **individual's** processes of internalizing concepts and emotional aspects from the surrounding environment—particularly the social environment. Those changes and expansions reflect the development of the individual's **participation in consciousness**. The **sources** of faith are **external**—they are located outside the individual in the surrounding culture. Sources are found in the **environment of faith** described in **essay one** that identified the faith environment: the biosphere and noosphere. That environment is constantly changing and evolving. So, the sources of faith are constantly changing and evolving. In mainstream America, it is easy to identify basic sources of faith: *family*, *peer group*, *formal education*, *electronic media*, *church or religious institutions*, *literature in general*, and the *Bible and other religious literature*, but there are numerous other sources, and change is constant. Sources *are essential for* the optimal development of the stages of faith. The most influential sources for *every* individual are found in the culture that immediately surrounds that individual.

Individual developmental processes exist in a reciprocal relationship with the surrounding society. Each diverse group in that diverse society has a life of its own. Sources are the material that *society* uses to instill its faith into the individual. Sociologist Peter Berger has described the sociological development of social structures that the individual internalizes.[16] Berger strongly affirms the importance of *internalization*. And the reality that society constructs is immense. The entire community that surrounds the individual is involved in the internalization of that structure by individuals. Parents and peer groups do what they do naturally and it impacts individual development. But teachers *deliberately* use the process of *semiotic mediation* as described by Vygotsky to instill knowledge. Absence of appropriate sources at crucial times for development of a particular stage can retard or adversely affect faith development. *Development* of faith within the *recipient* and the way the *sources* supply the *content* of faith are inseparable, but they are very different functions. Psychology and sociology are inseparable, but they are legitimately separate disciplines.

Stages, which have to do with developments *within* individuals, tend to match categories of *sources* of faith; far example, *parents in the pre-stage*. But discussion of sources is not a repetition of the previous discussion of *stages*, even though different sources often match the different stages of faith development. For instance, parents deal with infancy and preschool and the peer group and teachers begin their influence as the processes of education begin. Vygotsky would say that as the individual develops, and moves to a new stage, his or her *zone of proximal development* expands. He or she becomes more capable of learning and of dealing with more complex sources. For instance, a preschooler is not ready for algebra, but may be ready to learn to read.

So, stages are internal, and sources external, but they are inseparable and affect each other, because *internalization* is a very significant factor in the development of mental processes, as Vygotsky indicated. Perhaps I could say that *stages* are rooted in *psychology*, while *sources* are rooted in *sociology*. Sociology is much more fluid and changing, and the changes affect psychology through the processes of internalization. I will now shift the discussion from the discussion of *stages* and focus on specific *sources* of faith.

FAMILY

The first and most influential *source* of faith for a child is *parents* and/or other adults with responsibility for the infant. Humans arrive in the world *helpless* and *dependent*. Parents and other family members begin *talking* to infants as soon as they are born! They surround the child with emotional care. *They instill their faith into the newcomer, beginning in infancy.* As the children develop, they begin to *understand* what the people around them are saying. They begin to develop their innate capacity for *linguistic participation in consciousness*, and their general *participation in consciousness* expands. They learn to communicate in the language of the surrounding culture. It is important to note that the language and vocabulary that is used in the environment that immediately surrounds the child is what the child internalizes. And it is not just the *images* and *commands* of parents, as described by Freud, that children internalize. As Vygotsky pointed out, they internalize *language*; they start acquiring the *abstractions*. They begin to acquire the concepts that will enable them to think abstractly. The first exposure to music and religion also often occurs during this period, which lays the foundations for *musical* and *spiritual participation in consciousness*.

Psychiatrist Sigmund Freud correctly identified **parents** as a source for development of **conscience**. Freud along with Erikson, Piaget, and Kohlberg were influential scholars in the background of Fowler's study of faith development as indicated in the preceding discussion of **stages of faith**. These psychologists focused on the role of parents in **moral** formation, but Fowler, like Piaget and Vygotsky, realized that parents instill a lot more than **conscience into their children. Faith development** includes, but is more comprehensive than, **moral development**. Children acquire many elements of their **faith** from parents. Children internalize the emotional examples that they see in their parents. Attitudes, values, views, opinions, and prejudices are often transmitted from parents to children, generation after generation. The family's transmission of these **nonphysical** elements of culture enables cultures to maintain their unique institutions and characteristics.

When children learn to speak, they acquire their parents' accent, inflections, tone, and all attributes of the art of linguistic communication. Southerners drawl. In the past, in the United States, Black parents instilled the Black dialect into their children. These peculiarities in the early environment affects the development of the individual's **participation in consciousness** itself. Social sharing of elements of consciousness through the medium of language is critically influential. If children hear profanity, they speak profanity. If they hear prayers, they pray. If parents scream at children to deal with misbehavior, the children will scream at others in their own emotional encounters. If they hear a dialect, they will speak a dialect. If the vocabulary of the parents is inadequate, the children will develop an inadequate vocabulary, and develop correspondingly inadequate **abstractions**, and inadequate **participation in consciousness** as the result. It is not clear whether educational efforts at a later stage of psychological development can correct such deficiencies. Individuals are genetically programmed to develop certain aspects of **participation in consciousness** at certain times.

For instance, a second language acquired after a certain age is likely to have a detectable accent.

Faith and mental functions of family that reflect the family's position in culture, and are largely *private*, move from generation to generation down the family line and out of public view. These attributes of culture and class that are embedded in the family maintain the attributes of the culture and class to which the family belongs. Attitudes about people of a different race, law enforcement personnel, the legal system, the value of education, marriage and sex, and practically everything else originate and perpetuate themselves in *family* or whatever alternative situation immediately surrounds a developing child. The family usually equips the child with the *personality* and *attitudes* that the child will use to deal with the world later in life. And the children pass them on to their own children. This is precisely how cultures, and cultural attitudes, are maintained and transmitted. Understanding this paragraph is a critical step in understanding, and eventually solving, the complex problems that arise from cultural differences and differences that involve subcultures, such as racial differences in the United States.

Sigmund Freud taught that *conscience* results from the internalization of the *image* and *commands* of parents. This occurs at a very early age—during the *preschool stage*—and even infancy. Children learn to talk before they learn to read. Much of the child's mental development occurs at a time when the child is still developing *linguistic participation in consciousness* and has not yet moved to *symbol recognition participation in consciousness*. Traditionally, as Sigmund Freud suggested, the *nurturing* mother and the *authoritative* father (regardless of whether the descriptive terms of *nurturing* and *authoritative* are accurate in every instance) played key roles in a child's development. The *superego* and *ego ideal* are terms that Freud used in describing the development of *conscience* that result from internalization of the image and commands of parents. Parents are involved not only in the *moral development* of children but also in the development of the entirety of the child's *faith.* The beliefs that children acquire from parents about what is right and wrong are a very important part of their *faith.* As Freud and Erikson suggested, *moral formation* has both *cognitive* and *emotional* components, and obviously, parents are involved in the development of both. Like moral development, *faith development* involves both cognitive and emotional components. Children can *learn* rules *cognitively*, but the development of *feelings* and *emotions* that *enforce* the rules internally through *conscience* is more complicated. Knowledge of good and evil arises and receives authenticity in the *faith* system. The parents, or the persons who take up the role of parents, introduce children to key components of the faith system and those components involve both *cognitive* and *emotional* elements. And moving beyond the matter of development of morality, Vygotsky has taught us that the very development of *intellect* is derived from the surrounding culture, starting with parents.

Knowledge of good and evil is knowledge that is produced and maintained in the *faith system.* The role that parents play in this process is very important. As I discuss in other essays, concepts of right and wrong are not subject to proof or disproof by the *scientific method.* They are valid because they work. *Knowledge of good and evil* is necessary for the functioning and continuation of society. Society adjusts its knowledge to meet changing circumstances. The traditional role of the *parents* has been a *central element* of the *faith system* that operates Western culture. The traditional family system is the *template* for *moral formation* in Western culture and will be difficult to replace if the traditional family system totally disintegrates. It affects every facet of faith development. A full discussion of the threat presented by the problems confronting family is beyond the scope of these essays.

ELECTRONIC MEDIA

In this *electronic axial age*, children precociously use *electronic devices.* They are exposed to TV from the time that they are born, and exposure to all kinds of electronic media continues throughout their lives. I believe this exposure to electronic media is very significant with regard to the development of their *participation in consciousness*. Media and *electronic participation in consciousness* in the earliest years probably play a more significant role in the development of their faith than does the peer group at that stage. The *electronic axial age* brought with it telephones, radios, movies, TV, computers, the internet, "smart phones," and a host of variations that are rapidly proliferating. *Images*, not just words, are now communicable. The shift from *words* to *images* is portentous. The impact that movies have had on people over the past one hundred years has been substantial. The impact that television has had on faith since the mid-1950s can hardly be overestimated. We spend an inordinate amount of time watching *television*. The exposure of children to *professional speakers* on TV during the *pre-stage* and *preschool* stage has likely done more than anything else to *standardize language* and eliminate drawls, dialects, and other linguistic peculiarities. And that exposure to TV with its images and standardized language changes the meaning and content of what the child internalizes and becomes the basis for the child's very thought processes. That is an important accomplishment for *electronic participation in consciousness*. It moved *linguistic participation in consciousness* to a new level, and in a sense, bypassed certain aspects of traditional *linguistic* and *symbol recognition participation in consciousness*. Children watch TV before they see books! They hear the professional voices on radio and TV almost as often as they hear the voices of parents. The continual exposure of developing individuals to trained speakers and performers via TV and other media is *changing language itself*. The exposure extends into the heart of every household. Television and electronic devices are an important source of faith and are also important media for education. When language changes, if Vygotsky is right, the very process of thinking changes.

Since the 1980s, the use of *personal computers* has rapidly expanded. A vast amount of information is available on the internet and is easily accessible.

Individuals now *participate* directly in the *exchange* of information via the internet, unlike the days of one-way communication when information—the news—was controlled by major TV networks. *Electronic participation in consciousness* is a remarkable expansion of *group participation in consciousness*.

Media is evolving. For hundreds of years, *reading* was the primary way for people to acquire information. It augmented and significantly expanded the earlier *oral* transmission of ideas and stories. *Writing and reading* were much more efficient means for disseminating and preserving information accurately than the ones that had existed previously. But now, newspapers are going out of business, and the primary means of communication are TV, the internet, and other forms of *electronic* communication. People use terms like the "*generation-x*" for those born from the mid-sixties to the mid-eighties, and "*generation-y*" for those born from the mid-eighties past the turn of the century. If we are going to use letters, I suggest that "*generation-TV* and *generation I-Phone*" would be more appropriate! I scanned one internet article that attempted to describe the *generation-x*, and saw no reference to TV, obviously a major influence on those born between the early '60s and the early '80s. *Mr. Rodgers* and *Captain Kangaroo* might have taught more than anyone else! But as time passed, computers and smart phones superseded TV as the attention-grabbers. As we consider the sources of faith, we must examine not just what people believe, but how they get their information and why they believe it. Electronics now play a major role.

When I left the practice of law in 1983 to become a judge, a *library* was a necessity for competent lawyers. When I returned to the practice in 2001, *law books were obsolete*. The primary storage places for information about law is now *electronic* and that information is moving more and more into the *public domain*. Research is much simpler.

But dangers to the faith system are inherent in electronic media. Economic interests that underwrite TV and electronic media are not necessarily the interests that promote religious, moral, legal, and economic *values* that are essential to civilization and continued cultural progress. Thirty-second vignettes on TV may not portray enough *reality* to sustain the *real picture*. Vignettes may not connect us to the essential truths of the *biosphere* that we must respect in order to maintain our existence. Our existence is still embedded in the biosphere. And in the biosphere, truth *survives* and reality has *duration*. The lack of duration and continuity in TV presentations and the internet and their *virtual reality* may be threats to the accurate *understanding of the reality that sustains us in the biosphere*. We *cannot turn reality off and on* the way that we turn a TV, computer, or cell phone off and on.

The world of electronics is expanding beyond TV, computers, and the internet, to even more complex permutations of electronic means of communication. Human *participation in consciousness* is *moving to a higher level*. It is expanding rapidly. Our *collective consciousness* is deeply embedded in electronically shared information. It is an important part of the way we think. The generations of individuals who remember when these devices did not exist is rapidly disappearing. It is difficult to predict the outcome of these important changes that can and will alter our basic beliefs about *what is real* and our participation in it. The functions and content of faith will continue to be impacted and changed by *electronic media* and *virtual reality*. *Electronic participation in consciousness* has carried *participation in consciousness* to a much higher level, and is still evolving. We are clearly into a new *axial age* that is impacting every facet of communication and knowledge. The new level of *participation in consciousness* will shape the continuing evolution of humanity, both collectively and individually. It starts at a very early age.

PEER GROUP

The *peer group* plays a powerful role in the development of what children—indeed all individuals—truly believe. The role played by *peers* underscores the connection between *moral formation* and *faith*. Jean Piaget emphasized the role that the *peer group* plays in moral development. He watched kids playing marbles, saw them devise their own rules, and realized that peers, like parents, are involved in *moral formation*. Unquestionably, peers also impact faith formation, as Fowler noted. As I mentioned above, *faith* and *moral development* are inseparable. Both result from the same processes. Piaget's theory about *stages* of *moral development* was a part of the basis for James Fowler's theory for his *stages of faith*. Moral values are embedded in what humans *believe*. Moral values are useful concepts, created and maintained by *faith*. The involvement of the *peer group* in moral formation and all mental development underscores the necessary role that *groups* play in individual faith development. I believe that Vygotsky would have agreed that individual members of a group internalize speech elements of other members. I believe that he would have considered the information internalized from the group a part of *natural* development, as opposed to *scientific* development. While Piaget believed that the socialization impact of peers only starts when meaningful communication *between peers* becomes possible, Vygotsky realized that the very development of speech, and internalization of language beginning at birth, began the process of socialization.

Moral values, like all other knowledge, are maintained by *groups*. Moral values, like other knowledge, exist within *consensus reality*. The power of *collective faith* enforces moral values. The influence of the *peer group* usually begins after parents have exercised considerable initial influence. However, the influence of both peer group and parents *continues throughout an individual's lifetime*. But it should be noted that parents have their *own* peer groups, and their own peer groups are still influencing them at the same time the parents are influencing their children. This is how culture maintains and instills its values, but also helps to explain how culture adjusts to changes. Families are the basic unit, but they do not exist independently of other families and societal structures. That is not the way human life in the biosphere works. Parents who do not do what they are supposed to do for their children incur the displeasure of their own peer groups. Those expectations gradually change and evolve with the passage of time.

Our groups—our peers—are important in many ways. In the *third essay* in this series that discusses the role of faith in *human motivation*, I will discuss how faith causes us to do the things we do. I will discuss Abraham Maslow's hierarchy of needs. One of the basic human needs that Maslow identified was the *need* for a group. We *need* the group for *friendship, self-esteem, respect*, and a host of other physical and emotional needs. We need our peer group! The group satisfies many of the needs of group members. And the individual must find ways to accommodate the group, because he or she is dependent on other people for meeting his or her own needs. Because individuals *depend* on groups, those groups—the peer groups—influence the beliefs of the individuals in the groups.

Most individuals are affected more by persons *within* their immediate circle of friends than by persons *outside* that circle. The immediate social environment exercises great influence, for obvious reasons. The people who instill core beliefs into individuals are the people whose opinion the developing individual cares about. *Emotional attachments* play an important role in the acquisition of faith. Cultural differences, such as the differences between *Black* culture and *White* culture in America, illustrate the importance of this point. Attempts to *mentor* persons who have violated criminal laws is likely to encounter difficulties if the effort crosses the lines of racial cultures. If an individual does not really care what another person thinks, the other person's beliefs and opinions are not likely to have much impact on the individual's moral development and behavior. The "honky" from the Methodist or Baptist Church on *Main Street* will experience difficulties mentoring in the *ghetto* (and vice versa). Social class and economic differences play an important role in the dynamics of internalization.

While serving as a circuit judge, I created a program that I called **Probation Sponsorship.** It enabled prospective probationers to recruit sponsors, including people from their **own cultural group,** to assist them with completing a successful period of probation. I encouraged **diversity** in the group of sponsors, but particularly emphasized the need for the probationer to recruit **friends**—persons from his or her own culture—as sponsors. The program had good success.

As a child matures, contacts with **peer groups** increase. Interaction with peers involve changes that correspond with the physical and mental developmental stages of the child. The **peer group** changes and is altered by circumstances as one goes through life. The first friends grow older and are themselves affected by the changes wrought by continuing development and cultural evolution itself. **Education** and **career development** of an individual brings new groups of **peers** and separates the individual from earlier groups. But ever-changing peer groups continue to exert influence throughout an individual's lifetime.

Everyone in a peer group must find ways to live comfortably with other group members. Friendship, rather than a sense of duty, often causes us to assist and accommodate other members of our groups. Cooperation is not really **optional.** We **must** adapt our behavior and accommodate the needs of others so that others will reciprocate and satisfy our own needs. Accommodations that we make to satisfy our group are **sometimes intentional**, but more often, we are **not even conscious** of the accommodations that we make in order to maintain good relationships with our groups. It is a natural, unconscious, and mutually beneficial cooperation. We **intuitively sense** that our **peer groups** expect certain behavior, and we comply and are happy to do so.

Peer groups change day by day, continually, over a lifetime. As my wife and I prepared for our fiftieth wedding anniversary, we reviewed cards that had accompanied wedding gifts fifty years before. Our "group" had changed dramatically between the wedding and the fiftieth anniversary! Nevertheless, the original group—most of them gone—continue to influence our lives. *Memories* of the commitment of people and groups that had been an important part of our past continue to play an important role in our commitment to values. That which is internalized with significant emotional attachment becomes a part of an individual's operating system. That is the way faith works. The influence of *peers* continues through all the stages of faith development, with lasting effect.

EDUCATION

Throughout these essays, I define *faith* as what we think we *know for sure.* The educational system is unquestionably the most important *source* of faith in the sense that I am using the word *faith*. Formal education provides much of the information that we think we *know*. Formal education is all about teaching and *learning*, which relates it directly to the concept of *faith* that I am describing. Education is the intentional use of what Vygotsky called *semiotic mediation* to produce what he called "scientific" development. Education begins in kindergarten, preschool, or even nursery. The entire *educational process* installs what I have defined as *faith*. The *education system* is a *social system* that I will discuss in the *fifth essay* in this series in the discussion of *social systems*. In the present essay, I am focusing on *education* as a *source of faith*.

We *believe* what we *learn*. Formal education teaches language, communication, and writing, so it develops both *linguistic* and *symbol recognition participation in consciousness*. It also teaches numbers and arithmetic. So, it develops *mathematical participation in consciousness*. It often promotes *musical participation in consciousness*. It teaches science, biology, chemistry, and physics, so it shapes what we think we know about the *physical* world. It also deals with *social sciences*. It teaches history, psychology, sociology, anthropology, geography, and economics—courses that describe

70

the ways people relate to each other in their *physical* and *social* environments. It installs into individuals a lot of what individuals *believe* about the world. In all these courses, students acquire their beliefs about the *ultimate environment*. The education system deliberately uses what Vygotsky called *semiotic mediation* to help students internalize knowledge about how to organize, categorize, classify, and retrieve information. Education is the primary bearer of *consensus reality* and expands *individual participation in consciousness.*

But while internalizing information, students in the education system also learn about behaving themselves and getting along with other people. Education requires an *orderly environment*, and maintaining an orderly environment requires *normative force*. Most people encounter their first *peer group* as schoolmates in *formal education*. Understanding the moral requirements of society, which begins in infancy with the parents, continues in the *peer group* and throughout the educational process. Teachers are authority figures and have a pronounced effect on both *moral development* and *faith development*. Social skills develop, often in ways that are not identified in the curriculum.

LITERATURE

Education introduces students to *literature*, but the effect of literature does not end with the completion of formal education. Truths that reflect the *core beliefs* of Western civilization are found in its literature. Meaning is found not just in the concepts represented by the words, but in the narratives presented in words.[17] *All of the literature* of a culture provides an important source of faith. Readership and leadership go hand in hand. The role that literature of all kinds has played in the operation and preservation of the faith of Western culture cannot be overestimated. Literature from other cultures is also important, because the *electronic axial age* has developed transportation and communication so that everyone in the biosphere can be in contact with everyone else. Humanity now needs a comprehensive, universal faith. Very comprehensive knowledge that extends to all cultures will be required for an adequate *universal system of faith*. Electronically shared information is now universally encompassing but not erasing specific culture-based knowledge.

For a period of 500 years after the invention of the printing press in the late 1400s, practically all knowledge was pressed into print. I am calling that the *Age of Print*. Reading and writing became the most important human skills during that time period. Those skills enabled readers and writers to participate in the expanding edge of the noosphere. The material printed during that 500-year period is a *transcript* of the growth and evolution of *consensus reality* during that period of unprecedented expansion in human *participation in consciousness*. So, the *faith* of that period is well documented. That period was the precursor of the *electronic axial age*.

During my tenure as a circuit judge, I participated in a number of *law and literature* courses. A central idea in the *law and literature movement* is that values, principles, and beliefs that support the legal system can be found in literature. The courses that I participated in included Greek tragedies, Shakespearian plays, modern novels, short stories, and other genres. Experts in literature led the discussions of the literature that the group had read in preparation for the course. We successfully identified *concepts of jurisprudential importance* in every genre of literature. Law is only one example of how our cultural foundations can be found in literature. The same would be true of every institutionalized discipline. Literature reflects the central ideas or beliefs that sustain *all aspects* of our culture.

While I served as a circuit judge, I was deeply involved in continuing judicial education. I used the *law and literature* concept to create a continuing judicial education event called *Foundations in Pluralism* that was co-sponsored by the Alabama Judicial College and Tuskegee University. In two three-day events on the campus of Tuskegee University, in 1995 and 1996, judges studied the writings of *significant Black authors*. The event provided a nonconfrontational opportunity to explore *cultural differences.*

After the invention of writing, literature became the *primary tool* for expansion of the noosphere. That process rapidly escalated after invention of the *printing press*. Until recent years, printed literature was the DNA of culture, carrying its sustaining values from generation to generation. It sustained society's *faith system*. But dramatic changes are occurring during this *new electronic axial age*. Printed literature no longer has center stage as it did during the *Age of Print*. There are more powerful ways to store and recall information. But despite the emergence of more powerful *media* for communication, literature still occupies a significant role as a *source of faith*, and the electronic means of communication simply expands and more fully presents the information in a rich variety of formats.

RELIGIOUS ORGANIZATIONS

Needless to say, religion plays an important role in *faith*. As I have repeatedly said, this series of essays is not about *religion* as such, and the recognized religions are certainly not the only sources of faith in the sense that I am using the word *faith*. But nevertheless, church and religious training are important sources of faith for those who participate in religion and the work of church, and religion has had many collateral effects. *Faith,* as I have defined and described it, develops whether or not the church or any religious organization is involved. Faith strongly influences the production of psychological and social functions as described in these essays, particularly the functions described in: (1) *essay three* dealing with the role of faith in *human motivation*, (2) *essay four* showing how faith establishes *personal identity*, and (3) *essay five* describing *social systems* and *institutions*. Most religions would like for the faith that they espouse to have impact in these important matters, but that won't happen unless its participants truly believe what they profess to be their faith

When Church does its job, it develops spiritual participation in consciousness among its adherents. A primary task of the Church is to preserve sacred teachings—sacred myths if you will—and use them to instill religious faith. Building the right kind of faith is an important part of personal development for every individual.[18] A myth may be a story too true to have actually happened, as one of my college professors said. Mythological stories create analogies that point to truths that lie beyond the stories themselves. The Church, as the bearer of sacred myths, is an important source of faith. It preserves and installs the stories of its faith into each succeeding generation of Christians. During its 2000-year history, the Church has embedded the tenets of Judeo-Christian belief into the core values of Western culture. The indirect effect of religious faith—the beliefs about what is right and wrong and preservation of the Platonic legacy, in a secular society that often thinks it is divorced from religion—is often as important in shaping secular cultural values as is the direct effect of Church activities. Church and Christianity have played pivotal roles in evolution of the faith of the Western world. Understanding the important functions of faith and the system that is consciousness as I am describing them can promote a better understanding of the role of the Church and Christianity.

Worship is central to the activity of churches. Humans have a capacity for *spiritual participation in consciousness* that is closely related to *emotional participation in consciousness*. *Musical participation in consciousness* is also an important factor in worship. Worship differs from other ways that humans *participate in consciousness*, in the ways that it engages the spiritual, emotional, affective part of the individual. In order for religious faith to work and produce its beneficial functions in society, the *entire person* must be engaged. Authentic worship is the actual *participation in spiritual consciousness*. It puts the individual in contact with the realm of unseen, *nonphysical essences*, and more fully in touch with total consciousness itself.

The *educational* work of churches is an important source of faith. Sunday school and study groups play vital roles in the very necessary educational process. The Church embodies the communal aspect of religious faith. Church can be deeply involved in an individual's *faith development*. As I have said repeatedly, faith *is* what we *really* believe. Otherwise, it is not faith at all, and will not produce the beneficial individual, social, and communal functions of faith. The principles of faith that I am describing in these essays fully apply to religious faith. For the work of the Church to be effective and relevant, church leaders must understand the *meaning and functions of faith,* which arise from what humans really believe.

The Church, as a *source of faith*, connects in a unique way with the *stages of faith* that develop within individuals. I question whether effective social *structures* for the intentional development of the *highest stages of faith* that James Fowler described are fully available to individuals who are in the process of development. I believe that the Church—all organized religions—should take the lead in creating very comprehensive, all-inclusive *structures* to accomplish that goal. I will discuss religion as a *social system* in the *fifth essay* in this series.

THE BIBLE

The Bible has probably had *more influence* in the development of the faith of Western culture than *any other book*. Over the past 500 years, it has been read by *more people* who have led in the formation of faith in Western culture than any other book. *Cultural literacy* still requires familiarity with the Bible. The Old Testament, which contains the primary Jewish religious literature, provides accounts of the creation of the earth and humanity, the gift of law, and the unique relationship between God and the descendants of *Jacob*, who was renamed *Israel.* Those beliefs are deeply embedded in the societal faith of Western culture. The New Testament tells the story of *the coming of Jesus Christ*. It contains the *teachings and story of Jesus Christ* and the *writings of St. Paul* and others. Jesus taught in *parables.* Parables were not told as factual stories, but as stories that illustrate larger truths. Searching for the larger truth rather than focusing on the literal stories is the best approach to reading *all Scripture* and religious writings. The role of narrative is not just to maintain existing knowledge, but to create metaphors that expand knowledge. Religious writings have done that.

The New Testament promotes the belief that Jesus was the *Son of God* and was put to death, that his death was an atonement for the sins of the world, and that he *arose from the dead.* It describes the important *role of faith.* The faith that Jesus described and exemplified may be something far more dynamic than anything captured in Church dogma. The New Testament describes the missionary work of *St. Paul* and the spread of Christianity to Gentiles. It describes the spread of Christianity throughout a Mediterranean region that was permeated by *Platonic philosophy.* More subtly, it describes the conflict between the early church and *Rome.* It includes philosophical underpinnings of *Neoplatonism.* The Old and New Testaments together show the *progressive revelation of God.* Many biblical principles have found their way into the *consensus reality* of Western culture.

MIXED, MULTIPLE SOURCES

Family and peer group play significant roles as sources of individual faith development. So do electronic media, education, literature, religion, and the Bible. I have chosen these examples as important and *illustrative* sources of faith. I am not asserting that they are *all* of the sources of faith. The description of all sources of faith would be a description of all the components of culture and the biosphere that individuals can internalize in the development of their capacity for *participation in consciousness.* That would be a lot! Internalization makes the internalized information a part of the very processes of thought that are available to individuals. So, there are a very large number of significant sources of faith. Not all sources affect every individual. Sources vary from culture to culture, but sources for most cultures are probably similar. The Bible is a source of faith in Christendom, the Koran in Islamic cultures, and the Vedas in Hindu culture. Family and peers are important in all cultures.

After infancy, sources and stages don't easily pair off. Individuals do not encounter sources one at a time, but all at the same time. The confluence of sources becomes very pronounced during and after puberty. The sources commingle and compete for attention. Parents, peer groups, TV, computers and the internet, church, school, movies, newspapers and magazines, sports events, cell phones, iPads, computer games, and other forms of "entertainment" and sources of information are in constant competition, vying with each other for attention. Every source of *information* is a potential source of *faith*. Every source can expand participation in an individual's *participation in consciousness*. All sources constantly and increasingly bombard the developing individual. They compete for attention and are in constant tension with each other. *Parents v. peer group* and *TV or iPhone v. education* are good examples of the *tension* between faith sources. After infancy, and particularly after puberty, all sources of faith compete with each other for the developing individual's attention.

MORE THAN KNOWLEDGE

Although I have emphasized that faith is what we think we *know*, I must also emphasize that development of faith is more than just *cognitive learning*. While cognitive learning—the internalization of *information* from the culture and the biosphere—is a part of the development of faith, the *internalization* of *images and values*, including moral qualities, is also an important part of faith development. The development of *faith* engages and develops the individual's *emotions* as well as the *cognitive* functions of the mind, as Freud and Erikson indicated. Howard Gardner introduced the concept of *multiple intelligences*.[19] He was on target. There are *many kinds* of valuable mental activities. Daniel Goleman suggested the concept of *emotional intelligence*, which recognizes the importance of *emotions* in human relations.[20] Emotions play an important role in many human activities. They play an important role in human *participation in consciousness*. The role and meaning of emotions cannot be readily translated into words, and the word *intelligence* standing alone does not capture the warm, *positive*, essential role that emotions play for successful human relations. *Multiple intelligences* suggest the existence of multiple ways that individuals *participate in consciousness*. The appropriate involvement of emotions plays an important part in *spiritual participation in consciousness* and is a necessary part of spiritual formation. German theologian/philosopher Friedrich Schleiermacher recognized the important role that *feeling*, as opposed to *intellection* plays in the spiritual life.[21] Emotions play a very positive role in human faith and human relations. Emotions can also play a strong *negative* role as well. They can be destructive. But "negative" *taboos* and *prohibitions* that individuals internalize help to support and enforce morality internally, and that is important.

The way emotions are acquired and developed is not what we usually think about when we use the word *learning*. The development of emotional content involves activation and development of latent hereditary structures and capacities through interaction with the cultural environment. Sigmund Freud used the term *internalization* in describing *moral formation*, and James Fowler echoed the word *internalization* in describing the development of stages of faith. And, of course, Vygotsky used the word *internalization* to describe how individuals acquire conceptual thinking from the language of the surrounding culture. Peter Berger shows that society creates and institutionalizes the myriad societal structures that individuals internalize. I am suggesting that *all* of these sources of faith provide material for internalization during the developmental processes.

INDIVIDUAL MIND AND INTUITION

Society, and the sources of faith that it controls, does not simply *"install"* faith into individuals. Societal forces do not produce **clones** that merely serve the needs of the group and perpetuate the group. Every child is born with the ability to **participate in consciousness**. Creative evolutionary processes are maintained and planted into new life by human genes. Humans are born with **senses** and a potential for developing a **mind—to participate in consciousness**. The individual, **participating in consciousness,** develops **affective, intuitive, emotional, spiritual,** and **cognitive** skills. He or she participates in the **consciousness system** and interacts with the biosphere that contains the **sources of faith**, including the social components that use language to reflect essences that exist in the biosphere. Thus, the subjective consciousness of each individual is connected to and participates in the **mysterious realm of essences**, which enable it, in concert with the minds of other individuals, to **interpret** the human environment.

Society does not automatically *"install"* faith. **Interaction** is involved. Each individual encounters the world and the sources of faith with **senses, mind, affections,** and **emotions**, with his or her own set of **needs**, and with **mysterious connection to the realm of essences** in **individual participation in consciousness**. Something about **individual participation in consciousness** connects the individual, albeit imperfectly, to the unseen realm of **nonphysical essences**—an important part of the **system that is consciousness**. Somehow, **nonphysical essences** that exist in the biosphere, including those that emanate from **physical objects**, as well as those that are not related to physical things, present themselves to human minds as **phenomena**, just as **time** and **space** and **numbers** somehow find their way into the mind. **Faith** arises from the interaction of all the sources that we have described with the **mind** and **soul** of the individual.

OTHER SOURCES

All of our observations of, and interactions with the world around us influence faith development. As I will point out in the next essay in this series, which deals with faith and human motivation, the inexplicably conscious individual, *participating in consciousness*, encounters the biosphere along with all other sentient organisms. He or she uses *individual consciousness* to participate in the *consciousness system*. Throughout this series of essays, I am developing a description of that *consciousness system* that operates the biosphere, and how it works. Individuals detect and identify with *other individuals* who also participate in the *consciousness system*. The collective consciousness of humanity creates *consensus reality* that is the shadow of *ultimate reality*. *Consensus reality* includes and permeates everything that human beings know, but reality extends beyond what human beings know. Everything that *exists* is a potential source of faith! Faith involves humanity's *participation* in the *consciousness that operates the biosphere*.

VYGOTSKY AND LURIA

Near the beginning of this essay, I pointed out that Vygotsky seemed to focus on *two categories of sources* of information in the articulation of his theory that conceptual thinking results from internalization of the language of the individual's surrounding cultural group. His categories were *nature* and *science*. And I pointed out that the word *science* he used as one of the two sources probably meant *formal education or its equivalent*. Vygotsky was a teacher and was deeply concerned with the role that teachers played in the learning process. In describing the *sources of faith*, I also indicated that *education* is the most significant source of faith. But I have identified numerous other sources of information. Most of them are *language intensive*, and they are internalized primarily from language. And I have pointed out that Sigmund Freud also used a theory of *internalization* to describe the process of *moral formation*. Children internalize the *image* and *commands* of parents. They internalize parental behavior. So, as I have mentioned above, *internalization* is not merely a matter of *formal learning*. Many aspects of society and socialization are *internalized* by individuals, and every internalizable part is important.

Language is a social function. In this essay, have shown that many sources of faith are dependent on *linguistic participation in consciousness.* The important point I am establishing here is that a *sociological approach*, in tandem with the *psychological approach*, is a necessary part of the study of the *internalization of language* as the source of conceptual thinking. Sociologist Peter Berger described the *social construction* of the *institutions* of culture. Those institutional social structures are captured in language and internalized by individuals as a part of reality.

The origin of *thought* in the human mind is a mystery. But the analysis provided in these essays may provide a clue to the solution of a part of that mystery. *Thought—meaning* itself—may actually result from *individual effort* to *understand what is being said*. This idea is subtle, and the meaning of the previous sentence can easily slide right by you! I will approach the idea in various ways in these essays. But Vygotsky proved that higher mental functions result from *internalization* of *language*. Language consists of sounds—oral symbols. So, *thought itself* may have evolved from the *mental effort* to *decipher those symbols. Thought* involves *meaning*, not just words, so humanity's struggle to apprehend meaning from the sounds other humans make may actually be the origin of *thought* itself. Words are in the language, and in dictionaries, but real meaning is in the mind. *Words* are used to try to convey *meaning* from one mind to another. But even if this paragraph describes what causes thought to happen, it doesn't explain *what consciousness is,* or how it enables the mind to create thought from oral symbols.

3) FAITH AND HUMAN MOTIVATION

In this essay, I will explain how individual faith guides individual motivation. Individuals are born into the biosphere, and the biosphere provides the things that they need for living. After individuals are born into the biosphere, *participation in consciousness* enables them to *differentiate* themselves from the rest of the biosphere. The purpose of human *participation in consciousness* is to allow the individual to cope in the biosphere. So, the current essay shows that the *individual* differentiates the *self* from the *environment*, and then engages the environment to satisfy his or her own needs. The next essay in this series moves beyond the *mere differentiation* of the *self* from the *environment*, and shows how individuals *form the concept of the self* that is *personal identity*.

So, what is the role of *faith* in *individual motivation*? *Activity* is necessary for survival. Humans *must* be *active* to cope in the biosphere. Faith is belief so strong that *we act on it*. We have seen that *linguistic participation in consciousness* results in *faith*. Faith is what we think we know. As we have seen, it develops in stages, over the course of a lifetime. As faith develops, individuals acquire the *knowledge* that enables them to cope in the biosphere.

Faith provides the basis for human decisions about what actions to take. Because *faith* guides the activity that is necessary for survival, what a person does is usually the strongest evidence of what that person believes. What we believe about our own *identity* and *character* and about the environment in which we live is reflected in our *actions*.

Life in the biosphere requires interaction with the biosphere. Some of the reasons for what humans do are *internal* to the individual, and some are *external*. *Interaction* of the internal and external factors is necessary for individual survival. In the previous essay, we saw that *internal* development of faith and *external sources* of faith are intimately related and interdependent. In the current essay, we will see that *internal* and *external* causes of *human activity* are also closely related, and we will explore that relationship.

In this essay, we will glean information from several important sources. Abraham Maslow will teach us that we do what we do to get what we need. Henri Bergson will suggest that we are compelled into action by the very force of life. Martin Buber shows us that the biosphere is composed of inanimate objects *(It(s))* and other people *(Thou(s))*. We differentiate ourselves from the *It(s)* and *Thou(s)* of the biosphere and establish our own identity, and then turn back to the *It(s)* and *Thou(s)* for the satisfaction of our needs. And in the course of the essay we develop a better understanding of *individual consciousness* and its role.

MASLOW AND MOTIVATION THEORY

Abraham Maslow is often identified as the twentieth-century mastermind of the psychology of motivation and we will begin the exploration of how faith guides individual motivation by examining his theory.[22] As indicated above, his theory was that human *motivation* arises from human *needs*. His thesis can be simply paraphrased: "***People do what they do to get what they need.***"

Maslow described a *hierarchy of needs* starting with basic needs such as the need for food and air, and moving to more complex needs.

His theory is often illustrated in the form of a triangle. Physiological needs are the most basic: food, air, water, protection from the elements. The hierarchy includes *safety* needs, *social* needs and *esteem* needs, in that order. Maslow identified *self-actualization* as the apex of the hierarchy. The theory is that individuals will give priority to the needs in the order listed, starting with the most basic, but tend to address the *most pressing need* at any given time. Scholars might differ about the identification and description of human *needs*, but few would disagree with Maslow's contention that people do what they do to get what they need. You will note that all of these needs can be satisfied by various elements of the biosphere. The *social* environment plays a prominent role in the satisfaction of needs.

An important part of the theory that I am developing involves the role of human *participation in consciousness*. In this regard, please note two important points. First, the satisfaction of needs involves *choice*. Individuals must decide what they are going to do to satisfy needs. Second, to satisfy needs, individuals must develop **knowledge** of the biosphere, that is, they must be able to identify the things that will satisfy their needs. This second requirement entails development of what I have described as *faith*. Understanding that people do what they do to get what they need enables us to easily understand how *faith* operates in the biosphere to govern an individual's activity, and human activity in general. (1) Humans must take action to get what they need from the biosphere. *To satisfy their needs, humans act on what they believe*. They make decisions. (2) Their needs are satisfied by things that are **provided by the biosphere**, which is the environment in which faith arises. Therefore, they must have **knowledge of the biosphere—faith**. For individual humans, the human *social environment*—the *noosphere*—is the most important part of the biosphere. Humans act on what they believe about themselves, other human beings, and the total environment to satisfy their own needs. It is a very natural process.

Scientists and philosophers sometimes differentiate things that **human culture has created** from things that exist *"naturally"* in the biosphere. But humans, like other animals, evolved in the biosphere, and the things that they do are just as "natural" as anything else that occurs in the biosphere. I believe that it is important to erase this popular differentiation between *"humanmade" and natural* when we are trying to discern the **reality** that humans deal with to satisfy needs. **Natural reality** includes **nonphysical essences** that play an important role in the **human construction of society** to satisfy needs. Human success in dealing with the biosphere arises from the fact that humans are very adept at recognizing and utilizing **nonphysical essences**. Using **nonphysical essences** that they encounter in the biosphere, humans are able to build language that enables them not only to identify the **physical things** that they need, but also to build the **social systems** and **social** *structures* that promote need satisfaction. *Cultural* and *social structures* and *activities* are quite *natural*.

BERGSON AND LIFE FORCE

For individuals to satisfy their needs, action is required. Humans are propelled into action by the very *force of life*. The force that I am suggesting is the force that Henri Bergson called *elan vital*—vital force. The Freudian branch of psychology possibly identifies that force as *libidinal energy*, but the word *libido* is often associated with the sex drive, especially as the term was used by Freud, although C. G. Jung may have used it in the same sense that I am suggesting here. For our purposes, the critical life force that pushes us into action involves a lot more than the desire for sex. As we have already seen, Bergson contended that this life force was instrumental in bringing about *evolution itself*, and that makes sense. Whatever it is, there is a force that propels humans and all other sentient beings—and even plants—into action. That force causes them to seek the things that they need for their own survival and the survival of their species, and sex is just one of those needs. The *life force* that Bergson described causes humans to take action to satisfy needs. The point that I am making is that *faith*—the *knowledge of the biosphere* that humans *internalize*—guides and shapes the choices that they make. And the causation involved is not a mechanical operation of *cause-and-effect*. It involves *purpose*. Consciousness enables individuals to make choices. *Bergson's vital force of life* pushes individuals into action. The needs that Maslow described set the goals and establish purpose for the activity. That is the beginning point for understanding how *needs* and *faith* shape the choices that individuals make to satisfy their needs.

BUBER AND I/THOU

To satisfy *needs*, one must deal with the *biosphere*. The biosphere includes other people and inanimate objects. Those people, and the *social systems* and *institutions* that they participate in, as well as those *inanimate things*, are required for the satisfaction of human needs. Individuals differentiate themselves—the person they identify as *I*— from other people and the other objects in the biosphere. Martin Buber described an *I/Thou* and/or *I/It* relationship that helps to explain how individuals differentiate themselves from world around them and interact with it.[23] Buber did not talk about the *biosphere*, but he talked about the world that surrounds individuals, that includes other human beings (the *Thou(s)*) as well as material stuff that can satisfy needs (the *It(s)*). Together, of course, the *Thou(s)* and *It(s)* comprise the entire biosphere. *Individual consciousness* enables individuals to develop an understanding of the world surrounding them. The individual (the person who identifies himself or herself as *I*) differentiates himself or herself from everything else, including other *people* (*Thou(s)*) and other *things* (*It(s)*). What each human identifies as *self*, or simply as *I*, must deal with the *Thou(s)* and *It(s)* of the biosphere to satisfy personal needs.

INDIVIDUAL CONSCIOUSNESS

Individual consciousness enables individuals to differentiate the *Thou(s)* and *It(s)* of the biosphere from the *self*. *Individual participation in consciousness* is something separate and apart from the *self-image*, or even the ego. It creates and examines the *self-image*. The *conscious component* of the individual is an unobserved, internal observer. This mysterious *unobserved observer* is the "camera operator" in the psyche. *Introspection* does not reveal this unobserved observer; the unobserved observer is the thing that does the introspection. So, the unobserved observer is not the "movie star" in the psyche; it is the *camera man*! The unobserved observer is *individual consciousness*—the *individual's participation in consciousness*. It controls and retrieves memories, including the thoughts one has developed concerning his or her own identity (the *self*), and the internal personality components. Those activities enable an individual to become conscious of what he or she identifies as *"I."* In the course of individual development, it eventually identifies the organism that it hosts (or should I say, that hosts it?) as an *object*—a *human being*— and that *object* is identified as the *self*. In *essay four* that deals with the *establishment of identity*, and other essays, I will further develop the concept and functions of *individual consciousness*. But my use of that term is special and needs further explanation now.

For years, I searched for words to capture the essence of the *inward awareness* that conducts introspection. Along the way, I realized that I was not alone in the quest. Philosophers of the Western Enlightenment, including but not limited to Descartes, Kant, Fichte, Hegel and Schleiermacher and others struggled with this issue, with no great success, possibly because of the way they conceptualized consciousness as an individual, brain thing. The problem they were trying to solve grew out of Descartes' famous statement, *"I think, and therefore I am."* His legacy suggested that an individual is a *mind*, that *has a body* and the "self" is a bit ambiguous. In this theory, the body was somewhat external to the individual, like the rest of the world. The mind had its own *construction* or *image* or *representation* of the *world* and the things in it, but all the things of the world were *outside* the individual. *"Things in themselves"* was what Kant called them. So, these philosophers accepted all of that at face value, and were trying to figure out how the *world image* contained in the individual *mind* was connected with the *apparent external world*. And the first task was to figure out what the *self* was and how the physical body relates to the mind. So that is what they were working on. But they were caught in the trap of *dualism* that I attempt to dispel in the *ninth essay* in this series. Needless to say, they did not solve the problem and posit the solution into *consensus reality*. Detailed discussion of Enlightenment philosophy surrounding these issues is beyond the scope of these essays.[24]

I eventually realized that the *internal observer*—the *cameraman* that I mentioned above—is the same mental capability that enables an individual to gather sensory perceptions of the world that is *outside* the individual—the

Thou(s) and *It(s)*. *Individual consciousness* must deal with both the *internal* and the *external* world of the individual in order to enable the individual to function in the biosphere. Individuals, mind and body, deal directly with the biosphere that produced them. If I am right, that solves the problem that the aforementioned philosophers were concerned with, but I will just develop my theories, particularly in *essays four*, *eight*, and *nine*, without trying to discuss their theories in these essays!

After thinking and studying about *consciousness* in great depth, I realized that it is not at all likely that the human brain *produces* consciousness, nor is it likely that consciousness is something *physical* as many scientists and philosophers contend. But it is quite clear that individual human organisms (like other sentient organisms in the biosphere) *participate in consciousness*. *Consciousness* is something *much more comprehensive* than a mere *physical function* that *evolved* within the human *organism* or other sentient beings. It is a *system* that is essential to the *operation of the biosphere*. That is the central thesis that I develop in this series of essays. The *eighth essay* focuses specifically on that thesis.

It finally became clear to me that the concept that I was trying to capture is *individual participation,* by the *individual human organism* (and other sentient organisms), in the *consciousness* that *systematically runs the biosphere.* So, the term *individual consciousness* fits for the description. It conducts introspection. *Individual consciousness* does not endow individuals with the *totality of consciousness,* but simply enables individuals to *participate meaningfully in the consciousness* that operates the biosphere. Individual human *participation in consciousness* is *subjective and imperfect*. Humans do not see perfectly, hear perfectly, or think perfectly, and likewise, they do not *participate in consciousness* perfectly. As a matter of fact, seeing, hearing, and thinking are all integral parts of *individual participation in consciousness*. But even though human *participation in consciousness* is imperfect and incomplete, *individual consciousness* enables individual humans to participate effectively in the biosphere.

Individual consciousness is totally *subjective*. No doubt, the *capacity* for individual *participation in consciousness* is transmitted through *genes*, and its evolution started a long time ago. *Individual consciousness* establishes, and is the essence of *individual identity*, and I will develop that concept further in the next essay in this series, where I will explain how faith creates *individual identity*. Throughout these essays, I use the phrase *individual consciousness* in the special sense described here, and usually use italics and bold print to differentiate *individual consciousness* from the concept of *consciousness* and the full *system of consciousness itself*, which I usually call either the *consciousness system* or the *system that is consciousness*.

An individual's *faith* is created by and resides in *individual consciousness*. The faith that resides in *individual consciousness* enables each individual to size up and conceptualize, mentally organize, and become prepared to deal with everything that exists outside of what he or she identifies as part of himself or herself. *Individual consciousness* receives and processes the data collected by the senses about the world *outside* the individual. This is not to be construed to mean that *individual consciousness* deals only with "*representations*" of the outside world. It deals directly with the outside world. It *directly perceives* the outside world via the *senses*. It and the outside world exist as parts of the *interdependent biosphere*. It enables the individual to participate in the *biosphere*. Within the individual, it constructs *representations* for *memory* and use in *language*. It *interprets perceptions*, in light of its storehouse of knowledge. It creates the individual beliefs about what Fowler called the *ultimate environment*, and I have called *ultimate reality*. *Individual consciousness* organizes the data collected by the senses about the biosphere that exists outside the organism and differentiates it from the organism itself. It uses the data about both the *self* and *other-than-self* to create an understanding of what it believes to be *reality*. The internalized image of *reality* is the understanding that the individual derives from (1) *direct perception* and (2) *consensus reality*. As Vygotsky pointed out, *language* is a major tool for *internalization* of information maintained by the culture that I call *consensus reality*. The *complete reality* that individuals search for, but can't fully apprehend, is what James Fowler called the *ultimate environment*.[25] *Individual consciousness* creates and engages an individual's understanding of *reality* to the extent necessary to enable the individual to satisfy his or her needs using the resources found in the *biosphere*.

Individual consciousness also collects and stores information about the individual that it serves, and in doing so, creates the *personal identity* of that individual. That *participation in consciousness* is unique to the individual, and that vantage point is not available to anyone else. I will explore the *establishment of personal identity* more completely in the next essay in this series, which is a continuation of the analysis started here. The process of building *personal identity* begins when the individual differentiates himself or herself from the surrounding environment, as I am describing here. The immediately surrounding environment, particularly including the immediately surrounding *social* components of the biosphere, exerts a major influence in shaping *individual identity*, including cultural identity. Each individual has a unique relationship with the biosphere, which gives rise to a *unique individual identity*.

From the vantage point of *individual consciousness*, everything in the *biosphere* can be categorized using Martin Buber's categories: *I, Thou,* or *It. Everything* fits in one of these three categories. What humans perceive is either a part of one's *self,* (including one's own body) or something other than one's self—a *Thou* or an *It.* The *I* interacts with *Thou(s)* and *It(s)* to satisfy needs. That is the way *life* in the *biosphere* works. Differentiation and interaction are important functions of human *participation in consciousness* in dealing with the biosphere. The *I* participates in *consciousness* and acts on the faith—*knowledge about the biosphere*—that his or her *individual consciousness* has collected, to satisfy the individual's needs in the biosphere.

In *essay two*, I described the environment in which faith arises. I explained that all matter in the biosphere is, has been, or can become alive by being or becoming a part of a living organism. Putting aside for the moment the universe beyond the earth, *I*, *Thou*, and *It* are all components of the *biosphere*. Everything in the biosphere (and that necessarily includes the sun as the energy source for the biosphere) is a part of a *single, interdependent system* that functions as an operating whole. All *I(s), Thou(s), and It(s)* are parts of it, and every part is dependent on other parts. Individual humans are no exception. The biosphere is encompassed by a comprehensive *consciousness system* that is essential to its entire operation. The *Thou(s)* and *It(s)* of the *biosphere* appear and *present themselves* to its sentient organisms, a matter that I will discuss in depth in the *eighth essay*. That is how the *consciousness system* works. Each sentient organism *senses* the other components of the biosphere from the unique viewpoint of its own *individual consciousness* and deals with it in accordance with its own needs. But the biosphere itself operates as one big system, and *consciousness* is at the heart of its operations.

Faith organizes human beliefs about *Thou(s)* and *It(s)*. What we really believe about the universe, the biosphere, ourselves, and other people, and about how the universe and biosphere came into being with all of their complexity, is our *faith*. *Faith systems* are maintained by human cultures, but *faith* is also very much a part of the *inner world* of every individual, in the form of *individual beliefs*. Of course, much of the *content* of individual faith is *internalized* from other individuals and groups in the immediately surrounding culture.

The suggestion that faith is the basis for human action is not new. St. James suggested that what a person *does* shows what that person *believes*. "I will show you my *faith* by my *works*."[26] And, "*Faith*, if it hath not *works*, is dead."[27] Whether faith is religious or nonreligious, it governs behavior. It channels the energy of *life force*. Jesus expressed that same idea when he said, "You shall know them by their fruits."[28] *Fruit*, in this context, means *works* or *actions*. People who participate in Christian faith will produce *good fruit*, according to Jesus. However, there is an ominous other side to the fact that faith produces works. Jesus also said, "Are grapes gathered of thorns or figs of thistles?"[29] If a person's faith is not sound and does not include the right principles, then that person's work will not be good. Jesus illustrated the point by his actions. He zapped a *fruitless* fig tree, because it had no fruit.[30]

The fact that good trees produce good fruit, and sound faith produces good works, is totally consistent with the dynamics that brought about *cultural evolution*. Ideas that work effectively will likely keep on working, but mistaken ideas just won't work and will pass out of existence. Humans develop *faith*, and build *consensus reality*, by continuing to use *ideas that work* and storing them linguistically, in memory, in writing, and electronically for future use. The noosphere had been evolving for a long time when the Bible described the *evolutionary idea* that *sound faith* produces *good works*. From that point in time forward, the fact that Christians *believed* this Scripture promoted that important truth that supports social evolution in the noosphere. The thought is deeply embedded in Western culture and was probably embedded in Charles Darwin's faith. He likely internalized it somewhere in the course of his mental development as he trained for theology.

FAITH ENGAGES THE BIOSPHERE

It is a very short step from differentiating the *I* from the *Thou(s)* or *It(s)* of the biosphere to understanding how faith affects decisions about individual actions. The *Thou(s)* and *It(s) are the biosphere*, the environment in which faith develops. Individual faith develops for the purpose of providing information that enables the individual to make decisions about what actions to take in the biosphere. Faith contains the knowledge about the biosphere and the individual's society that enables individuals to satisfy their needs. Humans *act* on what they *believe* concerning the biosphere in order to satisfy *needs*. Human needs—the things that the *I* needs—can only be satisfied by *Thou(s)* and/or *It(s)*. The human need for food, clothing, shelter, companionship, praise, love, sex, and everything else that Maslow suggested that humans need can only be satisfied by *Thou(s)* or *It(s)* that are in the biosphere. *I(s)* do not and cannot exist independently of *Thou(s)* and *It(s)*. Interdependence—symbiosis—is the way life in the biosphere works. Everyone knows that plants use carbon dioxide and make oxygen; animals use oxygen and make carbon dioxide. But the interdependence of *everything* that exists in the biosphere penetrates far deeper than that simple illustration. The *Thou(s)* and *It(s)* are part of the larger *consciousness system* that operates the biosphere. They *present* themselves—make themselves available—to the *individual consciousness* of the *I(s)* that need them. I will develop this line of thought more fully in the *eighth essay*.

Impersonal *It(s)* satisfy human needs. *It(s)* include food, water, air, plants, and everything else that is not *I* or *Thou*. But remember that the *It(s)* are, for the most part, *living matter*, or *potentially living* matter, and the biosphere is all about life. *It(s)* are the components of the living *ecosystems* of the biosphere. *Individual consciousness* directly experiences *objects—Thou(s)* and *It(s)*—that the organism needs in order to survive. When humans eat meat and vegetables, life is supporting life! The objects needed for survival exist within the biosphere and can be identified by *individual consciousness*. *Participation in consciousness* enables individual sentient organisms to decide what to do to get what they need. The biosphere, including other humans in the biosphere, satisfies human needs. Participation of sentient organisms in the *consciousness system* is an essential part of how the biosphere works.

For humans, the *human social environment* is the most important part of the biosphere. Other people who are part of that social environment—*Thou(s)*—provide satisfaction for most human *needs*. Through the economic system, *other people* provide many of the *It(s)* that satisfy an individual's needs: clothing, food, education, medical services, electricity, gasoline, food, transportation, energy, etc. But other humans supply much more than impersonal *It(s)*. They provide friendship, security, companionship, and other social and emotional needs. One of the basic needs that Maslow identified was the need for sex. *Thou(s)* satisfy that need. But sex serves a human purpose beyond the satisfaction of immediate individual needs. It perpetuates the *group* and assures human continuity in the biosphere. It is at one and the same time the most intense *individual* activity and the most important *social* activity of humans. The bonding of sexual partners is the ultimate human intimacy. It is the ultimate *sense of feeling* in consciousness. It involves the emotions. Like other human activity, this activity accomplishes *individual*, *social*, and *cultural* objectives all at the same time in the system that operates the biosphere. If God had endowed all his commandments with the energy that backed his direction to Adam and Eve to, "Go out and replenish the earth,"[31] the world would be a mighty fine place!

The crowning achievement of the *biosphere* is human *participation in linguistic consciousness*, which established the *noosphere* and accelerated cultural evolution. With language, *groups of humans* were able to develop *social systems* for meeting the *needs* of individuals as we will discuss in the *fifth essay* in this series that deals with *social systems* and *institutionalization*. The *Thou(s)* of the biosphere, each of them trying to satisfy his or her own needs, form and energize the *social systems*. *Social systems* are much more efficient for meeting needs of individuals than individual effort would be. *Religion, morality, law, economics, education, politics*, and *government* are all *systems* that help humans to *satisfy each other's needs*. *Social systems and institutions* invoke a *higher level of use of consciousness* than is available to individuals. Individuals participate in that larger *system* of problem-solving intelligence, without necessarily understanding how the systems operate. Usually, individuals are not even aware that they are participating in a system.

They expend their individual motivational energy to support these systems, although they are simply working to **satisfy their own needs**. *I*, *Thou*, and *It* are all constituent parts of the large, complicated system that is the biosphere. The **consciousness system** encompasses the entire biosphere, operates it, and unifies it. Human societies are integral parts of the biospheric system.

For cultures to function, cultural groups must motivate individuals to meet the needs of other individuals, so that the cultural groups can accomplish their purposes. Cultural groups become **institutionalized**, and thereby become **"things"** that individuals experience as part of **reality**. Some, such as **corporations** and other **business organizations** are legally recognized as "persons," but many others, like the **social systems**, and loosely organized groups, are more nebulous. Although they are nebulous, for most individuals they a unquestioned parts of **reality**. But the point is that these **"things"**—these cultural groups—**must have** the supportive activities of individuals in order to exist as groups. Group faith creates **work ethic** to make the **economic system** work, and it creates **morality** to assure orderliness. These **social systems** (**economics and morality**) capture individual motivational force that enables the systems to satisfy needs of its members. Individuals work to earn a living, and their work supplies the needs of other members of society. Individuals must **behave themselves** in keeping with the requirements of their groups and perform tasks needed by the group. That is how **morality** comes into being. Groups **need** that good behavior and the beneficial work effort from their members. They must have cooperative effort of members in order to get all the work done that is required to meet individual needs of group members! Individuals will eventually and inevitably die, but the **institutionalized group** lives on, and consciousness lives on in it. That is how the biosphere works.

Moral behavior is more than a **rational decision** to please others in order to get something for ourselves. Humans **need** the acceptance and support in their groups, so they behave themselves in keeping with the requirements of the group and supply support for the group in order to get the acceptance and support that they need themselves. They *need* love and appreciation. Moral behavior *supports need satisfaction* and survival of cultural groups. Individual *emotions* and *self-esteem* are shaped by acceptance in the *groups*.

The capacity of groups to satisfy human needs and promote survival—the capacity of humanity to satisfy needs *using social systems*—took a major step forward when the human capacity for *linguistic participation in consciousness* and *language* evolved. The *groups themselves* began to participate directly in *consciousness*. Cultural evolution and the capacity to satisfy human needs for survival escalated at an increasingly rapid rate from that point forward. Whatever the need, it helps to be able to talk about it! Or assign numbers. Or write about it. Or put it on TV and the internet. The *motivational energy* utilized by all *social systems* is derived from efforts of individuals to satisfy their own needs, but *language, symbol recognition*, and *electronic participation in consciousness* enabled individuals to work together in groups with continually increasing efficiency to satisfy those needs.

THE ULTIMATE NEED

In this examination of needs that propel human motivation, I suggest that the *quest for meaning* is the activity that addresses the ultimate human need. The quest, or *need for meaning*, invokes religious *faith* and is a very real and powerful motivating force. Religion is a *system* that satisfies a human need. *Spiritual participation in consciousness* asserts itself in the lives of individuals. The effort to understand the ultimate environment and its meaning is a constant challenge. The *quest for meaning* is an important part of the motivational force that sustains us. It keeps us going. Psychologist Victor Frankl described how *faith* and *purpose* provided the strength he needed to survive a Nazi concentration camp.[32] Other needs keep us occupied temporarily, but absence of *meaning* and *purpose* results in *disillusionment, inactivity,* and *dissolution.*

Abraham Maslow identified the *ultimate need*—the apex of the hierarchy of needs—as *self-actualization.* Certainly, differentiation of the *self* from the environment and successful establishment of a meaningful and fulfilling *self-concept* and *personal identity* are very important. Achieving a comfortable level of equanimity and satisfaction with one's levels of achievement may be the most important thing that an individual can accomplish. But the fact that people do what they do to get what they need, and strive for *self-actualization,* does not mean that people always act *selfishly* as the terminology listing *self-actualization* as the ultimate need might suggest. Everyone depends on *other people* for the things that they need for themselves. To satisfy his or her own needs, an individual must satisfy the needs of others. Everyone is dependent on his or her social groups and must work with those groups. Working with those groups is necessary for survival. Indeed, each individual is dependent on his or her entire culture and its social institutions. Failure to fulfill social responsibilities can be disastrous for an individual.

Of course, that does not mean that everyone always acts unselfishly. Many people act selfishly most of the time. But at a very basic level, we all depend on others for satisfaction of our own needs. To satisfy our own needs, including the needs for self-esteem and the social needs that Maslow identified, we must do things that benefit other people. Jesus said, "If anyone desires to be first, he shall be last of all and *servant of all*,"[33] and this principle is embedded deeply in our *social systems.* Service to others is critical, both for personal development and for the welfare of the group. So, the fact that people do what they do to get what they need is not an endorsement or validation of either *selfishness* or *individualism.* On the contrary, because everyone depends on others, they must serve others to accomplish their own goals and satisfy their own needs. This truth does not *depend on* or *arise from*

Scripture, but is consistent with Scripture. Jesus *recognized* an important *truth* and helped to plant it into the faith system of Western culture. It works.

Although Maslow described the apex of needs as *self-actualization*, I believe that the term *quest for meaning* better describes the highest form of individual motivation. Beliefs that give meaning to our lives are critical to our well-being. Beliefs concerning the purpose of our being sustain our emotional life. The *quest for meaning* leads individuals to *religious faith*. The quest never ends. *Self-actualization*—fulfillment of the *quest for meaning*—is an ongoing process and is never fully achieved. As long as we humans "see through a glass darkly," we will continue to need to seek more of life's meaning, because the ultimate goal eludes us and keeps moving ahead of us. Intuition tells us that *reality*—the *whole of consciousness*—exists, and we strive to master it. But although our human *participation in consciousness* can expand and continually *achieve greater participation*, it can *never achieve* total perfection and knowledge.

The question of meaning inevitably asserts itself to every human being. Why are *we* here? Why am *I* here? What is the meaning of all of this? The *quest for meaning*, the search for answers, seeks satisfaction of the ultimate need. The *quest for meaning* invokes *spiritual participation in consciousness*, and engagement with unseen, *nonphysical essences*, ever striving for deeper understanding. The *quest for meaning* and Maslow's concept of *self-actualization* overlap. *Self-actualization* results from the *quest for meaning*. My dissatisfaction with the term *self-actualization* to describe the *ultimate human need* is its seeming endorsement of *individualism*, at the expense of the importance of *group function*. Maslow used the term *self-actualization* in his earliest articulation of his theory. His theory was brilliant, and gave him wide-spread recognition. He was one of the founders of the *Humanistic Psychology*. Humanistic psychology believes that *human nature* is *basically good*. But Humanistic Psychology is quite *subjective*, and many of Maslow's personal ideas about what it means to be a *good, successful individual* found their way into his concept of *self-actualization*. He sought to generalize and further explain *self-actualization* in a 1968 book, *Toward a Psychology of Being*. In the preface he wrote, concerning the term *self-actualization*, "However, besides being clumsy from a literary point of view, this term has proven to have the unforeseen shortcomings of appearing a) to *imply selfishness rather than altruism*..." (Emphasis mine) So, I was not the first to note this problem. But even with Maslow's attempt to clarify the intended meaning, the term still appears to be a rather subjective opinion about the highest human possibilities, and it is not entirely clear what one must do to arrive at *self-actualization*. One would think that Maslow's *self-actualization* would correspond completely with the *sixth stage of faith* described by Fowler, who dug deeply into psychology in his work, but it is not at all clear that the two are the same. The difficulty may arise from the fact that different individuals may be born into the biosphere for different purposes. Fulfillment of the *quest for meaning* might reach different destinations for different people. And I suspect that Maslow would have agreed with that assessment.

Ironically, *self-denial* is the ultimate form of *self-actualization*, as James Fowler showed us in his description of the stages of faith, and can be better understood as part of the *quest for meaning*. The *quest for meaning* is a *journey*, not a *destination*. I doubt that anyone is ever totally *actualized*; everyone is always engaged in the *quest*. And everyone is part of the larger system that is the *biosphere* and everyone *participates* in the larger *consciousness system*. All meaning stems from that *participation*.

An ironic aspect of Maslow's *self-actualization* is that one can only achieve *self-actualization* in the context of a *group*. The irony is deep: without the group, individuals wouldn't even know that they *have*, or *are*, a *self!* The *self* could not be identified by *individual consciousness* as an object in the absence of a group. And the highest individual needs must somehow be reconciled with the needs of the group. *Self-actualization* can only be achieved in self-sacrificing service to others. The *quest for meaning* always converges with efforts to support survival of one's groups. Jesus gave his life for the salvation of humanity. Mahatma Gandhi and Dr. Martin Luther King, Jr., sacrificed themselves for the greater good of society and their people. Hobbes and Butler, enlightenment philosophers who asserted that *self-preservation* is the first law of nature, were wrong! Preservation of *one's group,* not *self-preservation,* is the *first law of nature.* If that weren't the case, bravery would never have been considered a virtue. In the twenty-first century, the relevant *group* for everyone includes all of humanity. I know, and have known, many good people who have given their lives, not in a single magnificent or disastrous event, but one day at a time in service of humanity.

The *quest for meaning* reflects the greatest of all needs. Cultural evolution in the noosphere provides an ever-increasing understanding of *ultimate reality*. Our *quest for meaning* pulls us toward an understanding of that *ultimate reality*. It pulls us toward the realization of *complete consciousness*, beyond mere participation. Religions organize the *quest for meaning* that seeks *ultimate reality*. To be successful, religions must bring about *spiritual participation in consciousness. Individual consciousness,* including *linguistic participation in consciousness,* and its *symbol-related* progeny, is our only tool in the *quest for meaning.* Consciousness, perception by sentient beings in the *eternal now,* remains a deep mystery, and *ultimate reality* eludes us, and we are relegated to faith—a *leap to faith*[34] in the often-quoted words of Soren Kierkegaard. We just jump, grab, and hang on as best we can!

4) FAITH AND INDIVIDUAL IDENTITY

FAITH IS NOT JUST BELIEFS about the *external world* that presents itself to *individual consciousness*. Faith includes *what individuals believe about themselves*. As I suggested in the preceding essay that deals with *human motivation* and the relationship of individuals to the biosphere, the spark of consciousness in which individuals participate is the *internal observer* that establishes *self-identity*. It enables the individual to establish beliefs about the *self*. This is how faith establishes *individual identity*. Faith also establishes *character* that is based on the *quality* of the individual's beliefs. The faith that establishes *identity* and *character* includes critical elements of *self-perception*—what the individual believes about herself or himself. It necessarily includes what the individual believes about human beings and human nature *in general*. The *self* is a concept maintained by *individual consciousness* as an *object*. An individual cannot fully develop a concept of the *self* as an *object* until he or she (1) begins to think *abstractly* in concepts, and (2) has developed the concept of *human beings*.

Individual *participation in consciousness* enables each individual to collect personal information and construct an identifying personal story. Ironically, *language,* a group function, plays a significant role in individual *self-identification. Individual consciousness* creates a personal myth at what James Fowler identified as the *third stage* of faith, the period of puberty. The personal myth is largely constructed with words. Self-identification produces what the individual knows and recognizes as *"I."* So, when an individual says *"I,"* exactly what *is* she or he talking about? That question is what this essay is about. The description of how faith defines *self-identity* in the current essay continues the discussion about *individual differentiation* from the remainder of the biosphere that began in the preceding essay.

INDIVIDUAL CONSCIOUSNESS

As indicated in the preceding essay that dealt with faith and *human motivation, individual consciousness* enables individuals to identify themselves *objectively* as human beings, and at the same time distinguish themselves from the *It(s)* and *Thou(s)* (which includes other human beings) of the biosphere. That *identification* and *differentiation* is the first step toward establishing *personal identity*. It distinguishes *I* and what *individual consciousness* identifies as the *self* from everything else in the biosphere. That differentiation enables the individual to deal with the rest of the biosphere to satisfy his or her needs. But *differentiation* from everything else in the biosphere does not, in and of itself, establish *personal identity*. Much more is involved in the establishment of *identity*. The separation from the biosphere only differentiates what *I am* from what *I am not*. After that differentiation, *individual consciousness* begins to construct a *positive* personal identity for the individual. The *I* begins to imagine *what I am*, as opposed to what *I am not*.

Individual consciousness is aware of itself and includes all of the mental capacity required for individual participation in *linguistic, musical, spiritual, symbol recognition, mathematical*, and *electronic participation in consciousness*. It is the central part of individual personality and identity. Examination of *personal identity* starts with the identification of this *mysterious attribute*—this unexplained *self-awareness*. First, *individual consciousness* must distinguish the individual that it serves from the rest of the biosphere. Then it begins to identify that person as a *human being*, and establishes *beliefs* about the individual human being that is the *self-concept*. Did you notice the Descartes did not say, "I am, and therefore I am a *human being*?" But in order to be *thinking*, he had to first *internalize concepts*! The *individual consciousness* that is at the center of *individual identity* and is the *individual*, has functional power to do the *believing*. As we have seen, *faith* is involved in the *internalization* of *concepts* that form the basis for abstract thinking. *Individual consciousness* is where *faith resides*. *Individual consciousness* and what it believes about the individual in which it resides is what a person is really talking about when he or she says *"I."*

Individuals introspect, or look inside themselves, to seek personal identity. *Individual consciousness* does the looking. But the *individual consciousness* that conducts that *examination* is not what *individual consciousness* sees: it cannot see itself. As noted in the essay about the role of faith in *human motivation, individual consciousness* is the *observer*—not the *observed*. *Individual consciousness*, with all its imperfections, is the crystal of *consciousness* within the *human organism* that collects and builds a personality—a *personal identity*—around itself. It *internalizes language* and *concepts* that are included in language, that are available in the surrounding culture, and it collects *individual experience* and builds an identifying *personal story*.

Hereditary structures provide the *mental capabilities* that allow *participation in consciousness*. The human capabilities that support participation in the *consciousness system evolved*. But the *consciousness* in which humans participate *did not evolve. Participation in consciousness*—the awareness that enables humans to share *reality*—the *biosphere*—that is also perceived by other humans—is a profound mystery. I suggest, metaphorically, that it is the *Divine breath* breathed into humanity in the biblical story of *Adam*, who symbolizes *humankind.* The *capacity for individual partici-pation in consciousness* is transmitted by genes. It has been in development for ages. It does not appear in the current generation out of nothingness. We have to simply accept both *consciousness* and the *awareness of our own consciousness* (or self-consciousness) at face value.

Life and animal *participation in consciousness* are very closely linked, if not totally inseparable. *Individual participation in consciousness* is the essence of *individual human life*. When death permanently asserts its hold, the nucleus of *consciousness* that accumulated the experience of *personal identity* departs the matter that composes the body. Without preservatives, decomposition of the physical body ensues, and the physical elements that compose the body return to the biosphere. *Participation in consciousness* obviously occurs within the physical body of human beings and other sen-tient organisms, but only if that physical matter is *participating in life*. The connection between human consciousness and life has important implica-tions that I will explore further in the *eighth essay*

We cannot answer all of the questions about the *origins* and *nature of consciousness* or *self-consciousness.* But we can understand that *faith,* empowered by *individual consciousness*, establishes *personal identity.* What we *can't* understand is what *individual consciousness is* and where it came from. The part of us that has faith—the part that does the believ-ing—seems to arise from *inscrutable depths of consciousness* that *includes what we call unconscious* and invests itself in the individual. We don't know, and can't explain, how or why that happens. It is clear that consciousness is associated with *life*, and that the human *capacity* to *participate in con-sciousness* is transmitted from generation to generation via DNA. DNA carries the blueprint for the physical human structures that actually deal with consciousness—whatever it is—and enable the individual to function in the biosphere. But that does not explain the existence of the consciousness that the physical human body participates in. Consciousness is *just there*, and we don't know what it is or where it comes from. Consciousness itself somehow appears out of a *fathomless abyss of unconsciousness*. Perhaps the Bible describes its origin best, when it talks about *darkness* that "*covered the face of the deep*" before God said "*let there be light*" or "*breathed the breath of life*" into Adam's nostrils. Although we don't yet know what it is, or how we participate in it, what we believe about the *nature* of *consciousness* itself impacts who or what we think we are. As stated above, *I* believe that *individual participation in consciousness* is a *spark of the Divine* and that it establishes *personal identity*.

DEVELOPMENT OF THE PERSONAL MYTH

James Fowler described the process of developing *personal identity.* According to Fowler, *personal identity* develops during his *third stage* of faith development. It occurs during the puberty years. Obviously, the individual's personal *story* starts developing before that stage, but at that stage, *identity* crystalizes into an enduring form. During that stage, the individual comes to grips with the world beyond the family. Concerning this *third stage*, Fowler says, "Faith must synthesize values and information; it must provide a basis for *identity* and outlook." At this stage, associated with *adolescence*, *individual consciousness* forms a personal *myth*, "*the myth of one's own becoming in identity and faith*." The personal myth incorporates "one's past and anticipated future in an image of *ultimate environment* unified by characteristics of personality," and entails "*the creation of the myth of our personal existence*." Applying Fowler's theory to my description of the role played by consciousness, it is *individual consciousness* that establishes *identity* for the individual that is no longer tied as closely to family. It moves the individual toward independence as an adult.

Individual consciousness constructs the *story* that it believes about the individual, and that story establishes the individual's *personal identity*. *Individual consciousness* believes the story that it constructs. The story uses words but is not totally word dependent; it includes feeling—intense feeling. It is part of *individual faith*. The Bible affirms, "For as he thinketh in his heart, so is he."[35] *Individual consciousness* guides and directs the *self* as the individual continues acting out the story of the person the individual aspires to be. *Individual consciousness* does not, for the most part, *intentionally create* a *story* in order to establish personal identity. The individual may try to live up to an *ego-ideal self* and in that way affect the unfolding story. But in the final analysis, the actions that one takes to cope in the biosphere *create a personal story that reveals itself to individual consciousness* based on actual experience and interaction with the surrounding environment as a part of the developmental process. *Individual consciousness* just *experiences* the events that enter into the personal story. *Faith* embraces the story, and that produces personal identity. *Individual consciousness* doesn't just make up the story. It is a historian or biographer, not a fiction writer. It constructs the story from actual experience.

What *individual consciousness* believes about the individual's *potential* is an important part of the personal myth. We contain our own future. The *ideal image* of our self—the identity we desire, the one we are not but for which we have potential, the *ideal self* that is our *superego*—is also maintained and managed by *individual consciousness*. The Bible reports, "Faith is the substance of *things hoped for*, the evidence of *things not seen*."[36] Our *hopes* are a part of the personal myth, and, as indicated in the previous paragraph, can affect the unfolding story.

THE LIFE STORY

So, how does *individual consciousness* go about establishing individual identity? *Individual consciousness* uses the concepts created by humanity's *participation in language* to assemble the life story of the individual. It uses words maintained by the immediately surrounding culture. When someone asks me who I am, of course I do not say, "I am my *individual consciousness*, a spark of the Divine." Instead, I tell my story. I share what my *individual consciousness* remembers and believes about *me*. *Individual consciousness* creates identity by maintaining *beliefs* that are my *personal story*. "I am Dale Segrest from Tallassee, Alabama." Symbols created by *symbol recognition participation in consciousness* can be used for identification. Identification that calls for *symbols* might include an address, email address, a telephone number, a fax number, or a social security number, the information you provide when you "sign in" somewhere. Telling the story, I might give details about my family. "Yes, I've been married to Betty for over fifty-seven years. She was a Menefee, and had two sisters, Gussie and Suanne, and a brother, Ervin." At a checkout counter, I provide my driver's license or personal ID. At a hospital, I produce insurance cards and must remember my birthday. At a United Methodist meeting, I might identify my local Church.

We identify ourselves in many ways. I am identified by Emma, Kate, Steele, Forrest, and Fischer as *Paw-Paw, Mimi's husband.* I'm Philip and Mike's *daddy.* Occupation can be an important identifier: *lawyer, judge, retired*, and *still practicing law of counsel.* I have had many identifying roles, such as American, Christian, Methodist, Rotarian, son, brother, father, grandfather, retired judge. All these roles are represented by an arsenal of words that are maintained in *consensus reality*, that I did not create but internalized.

To identify myself, I might say, "I was born in rural Macon County, Alabama, in 1942. My parents were Forrest and Ella Segrest. My brother, Wade, four years older than me, taught at the Montgomery Academy for many years and served as headmaster there for a number of years. He is retired. My brother, Chan, is four years younger than me. He retired after a long career with the telephone company, and now he raises hay and cows." Because **Segrest** is a common surname in Macon County, Alabama, I might distinguish myself from other branches of the family, or identify my own branch.

Genealogy helps establish identity. In the United States, *surnames* usually provide some indication of *paternal family* identity. In biblical times, genealogies enabled individuals to identify with a group, and that information helped to identify them to others. The lengthy paternal genealogies found in the Old Testament helped Israelites create their identity and understand who they were. Think about it: they had practically no other way to identify themselves, either for outsiders, or within their own group. In modern times, people are much more likely to mention their *community, nation*, or *state* than to mention a *tribe or remote ancestry* to identify themselves. But ancestry can still be an important identifier. Alex Haley's book *Roots* attracted attention to the genealogy of Black people in America and underscored the importance of *genealogy* in establishing identity.[37] In Alabama, the United States Government recognized the Poarch Band of Creek Indians as a tribe in 1984. To establish tribal identity, and identity within the tribe, the Poarch Creek Indians had to conduct meticulous *genealogical research*.

Education is a part of the identifying story. My story includes "Shorter High School," "Huntingdon College," "University of Alabama Law School," "University of Nevada at Reno and the National Judicial College," "Judicial education," "Master of Judicial Studies." If any of that strikes a common chord in a get-acquainted conversation, more details might follow; "in law school at the University when Joe Namath played football there"; "two national football championships in my three years of law school." Identifying myself at a *church gathering*, in addition to identifying my local church, I might add "… attended Bradford's Chapel while growing up," and "lay speaker"; "conference lay leader" and "attended several general conferences." If any of that strikes a chord, I can add more details. All of this is the kind of information we use when we try to *identify* ourselves.

We identify with the **groups** to which we belong. **Groups** are a part of our personal **story**. What we believe about **our groups** has a strong impact on who we think we are. Obviously, some groups have more impact than others on the way we think of ourselves. Groups of which we are a part play a role in how we **identify** ourselves. **Race** and **sex identity** are obviously important personal identifying factors. They penetrate to the core of **individual consciousness** of one's self, and shape the faith that builds the personal story.

When we apply for a job, we provide a **resume**. The resume is our story: an outline or narrative of work experience, education, and training. The **personal story** that we use to identify ourselves always consists of information that **individual consciousness** has stored and believes about **personal identity**. The fact that we use the **personal story** when we try to identify ourselves shows that we **believe** that the personal story is our **identity**. Faith establishes identity.

But what is an individual's **core identity**? What makes me, **me**? Theologians talk about a **soul**, and I have mentioned the numerous **roles** that each of us plays. Do any of the many **roles** that I have mentioned establish or define what is really **me**? These roles are **personas**. A **persona** was a mask used in Greek plays to establish an actor's role. Today, the term signifies a role that a person plays that is not his or her **core** personality or identity. We all play many roles in life. **Personas** are important. They are all **parts of the story**, maintained by **individual consciousness**, that we use to identify ourselves, and we use them when trying to tell **others** who we are. But if we pull off all the masks, what would be left? Nothing but **individual consciousness**.

But the real story by which **we** identify **ourselves to ourselves** is very **internal**. We know things about ourselves that we **don't** tell. Ultimately, **individual consciousness** and the **story** that it actually **believes**—the personal information it has collected—is as close as we can come to our **core identity**. That is the story that most strongly impacts our behavior and self-image. Although words play a key role in establishing identity, identity entails more than just words—emotions and feelings that connect to memories play a part. What we believe about ourselves is *faith*, and it establishes identity! So, in one sense, my *identity* is what I *believe* about *myself*. But even more basically, I am the thing that does the believing: *individual consciousness*.

When we *tell* our story, we tend to focus on *external, public events*. We select events to project the image that we *want* to display. But any story that we tell is *only a story*. *The story* does not *recreate* the *actual events* of our lives. As with any "history," the story we tell is selective, and necessarily omits many details. Events unfold in the *eternal now*, and *now* is immeasurably complex, and memory records only the infinitesimally small part of it that our *individual consciousness* registers as significant. But what is remembered composes what we believe to be our story. The story we tell is composed of *words and sentences*. The words and sentences are *not* the *actual events* that they attempt to describe. They are *mental*. They are memories that are an interpretation of an irretrievable past. If we are honest, we will not lie. However, the words we use for our story *never* recreate the past events, even though we honestly describe the events.

A deep irony for the Western *ideology* of *individualism* is that at least since the development of *language*, the *words and concepts* that individuals use to compose the story to describe, and even to understand their own identity, both internally and externally, are actually maintained by the *cultural group*. *Linguistic participation in consciousness* and *language* are deeply involved in the creation of the personal story, but they are social phenomena. The *words and language* that we use to identify ourselves are maintained by the group at the group level. That is not the way my dog, Deuce, identifies himself. He just barks or growls to make his presence known or assert his existence! But beyond *individual consciousness* itself, human identity is almost completely composed of *concepts* that are maintained by *individual consciousness*, that have been internalized by the individual from *the individual's cultural group.* Ironically, the *self* is only a concept—an *object of experience.*

The irony of the use of socially maintained concepts to establish personal identity is not as strange as it first appears to a *culture of individualism.* The very *existence* of every individual is totally enclosed in and surrounded by a *cultural environment.* Without the conceptual components—the internalized concepts maintained by the groups that surround us—there is little content for *individual consciousness* to deal with. We exist as part of our cultural environment *in the biosphere*, and that is what enables us to "know" about ourselves. Without that knowledge of ourselves that is empowered by concepts maintained by our cultural groups, I suppose, like Deuce, we would just bark and growl!

Individual consciousness works with the *superego* to take the best parts of the personal story and create the best image that it can present to others in our cultural group, and then tries to propel us into activities consistent with that image. That is how the superego works. But if *individual consciousness* looks at the entire story (in the unedited, internal form) and the story is not very pretty then the individual will have *low self-esteem.* Ultimately, what makes me *me* is that completely subjective *individual consciousness*, making choices about what to do in the biosphere, based on sense data augmented by knowledge retained in its collected faith, and thereby writing the personal story, always in the moving instant of the *eternal now.*

UNDERSTANDING THE PERSONAL STORY

We use words and sentences to tell the personal story that identifies us. But we can use many different arrangements of words and sentences to describe the events that we include in the story. We can tell our personal story in many different ways, without lying. After all, as pointed out above, the *story* is not the actual event and *cannot recreate* the actual event. Events, in and of themselves are very ambiguous, and can be interpreted with many different meanings. When telling our personal story, a bad experience can be a *disaster*, a *turning point*, a *warning*, a *joke on me*, or an *opportunity to do better*. Defining events of our lives can be notoriously ambiguous. They often have *meanings* for us that they do not have for anyone else, and we worry and fret over the meaning of the details.

The adversarial practice of law capitalizes on the fact that lawyers can tell stories in more than one way, without lying. An important skill for a lawyer is the ability to truthfully narrate a story in a way that produces inferences favorable to his or her client. Every set of facts—a single event on a former stage of the *eternal now*—gives rise to multiple *epiphanies.* Understanding this fact and the possibilities that it creates is an important part of understanding how *individual consciousness* deals with identifying concepts. An *epiphany* is the sudden realization or comprehension of the essence or meaning of something. Lawyers (and everyone else) can conceptualize particular facts in many different ways. The single fact might be, "He pulled the trigger." But a resulting death can be a *murder*, an *accident*, a *manslaughter*, or a *justified homicide*. In large measure, the distinction between these legal concepts focuses on *unobservable mental elements*. Lawyers on opposite sides of a case try to evoke different *epiphanies* that arise from the same facts to present the case most favorable to their client, without lying. Likewise, individuals can tell their personal stories in many different ways, without misrepresentation. Underlying events, always in the past, are always too complicated, too unique, and have too many details, for words to completely recapture. When an event is over, it is over, and neither words nor images can reconstruct it, change it, or create a perfect image or representation of it. As Omar Khayyam taught us, "The moving finger writes, and having writ moves on."

We need to understand both the importance and the weakness of the *personal myth* which *individual consciousness* uses to identify us. We are aware of both the presentation of our story to others and our introspective understanding of it. Regardless of the meaning that we assign to our stories, others may assign a different meaning. How others interpret our story, or an event in which we have been involved, is important to us. **Feedback** from others affects what **individual consciousness** tells us about who we are. It affects our behavior. Feedback from others is like looking in a mirror. **Individual consciousness,** working with the ego and superego, is concerned about what other people think. Feedback is complex. It is not just what someone **tells you.** It includes the feelings that are created when someone **ignores you,** or **changes the subject** when you are talking about something that you are passionate about, or just the way someone **looks at you.**

It is one thing if strangers have a version of our story that differs from our own, but quite another if friends and family see the story differently from the way we see it. There is no way to really know what other people believe about us, and that can be a major source of anxiety, if we let it. We do not really know what **"they"** know or think.

The personal story is always inherently **ambiguous,** and we can **tell** it to others in many different ways. But it is much more difficult for us to manipulate the **inside story,** the one **individual consciousness** harbors in our heart and that we see and feel through introspection. The understanding that we harbor in our hearts about ourselves—the one built into **individual consciousness**—is very difficult to change. It is relentless. The story that we tell to identify ourselves to other people is not necessarily the "story" that forms the basis for our actions, although that story may actually affect our actions by causing us to try to maintain the image we want to maintain. But the story that **individual consciousness** maintains **internally** is the identity from which we **act.** **That** is who we **think** we are. The **inside story** is the most significant understanding of our own **identity.** It includes the parts that we don't choose to tell, although we believe them. Bedrock belief about our own personal narrative—the story our **individual consciousness** creates and maintains—is the nearest we come to understanding our *core identity*. It is an important part of our *faith*. And it is very difficult to change what we believe about ourselves. *Individual consciousness* clings tenaciously to what it believes about *everything,* particularly the *personal story*.

The story built into *individual consciousness* is constructed from *past events*, and it is always ambiguous. The reason that our *individual consciousness* builds it is to anticipate and deal with future events. The very purpose of *consciousness* is to allow us to make decisions about *what to do*. Those decisions always involve *now* and *the future*, never the *past*. It is important to remember that behavior, governed by *individual consciousness,* only occurs in the narrow, cutting-edge slice of time called *now*. The behavior that occurs in that fleeting instant is a building block that creates the *identity* that will evolve into our future recapitulation of events. Living positively in the *present moment* requires self-discipline, but the present moment is where we build our story. We don't usually do the things that we do in the present moment to build our story; we do what we do to get what we need. But nevertheless, what we do in that moment builds the story. And if we *need to* change our personal story to create a more positive self-image, we can try to find ways reconstruct the story. The story evolves. And we *can try* to do things to improve it!

MANAGING THE PERSONAL STORY

Under certain circumstances, it may be desirable for an individual to *reconstruct* the personal myth that is his or her identity. The story may need to be rewritten. He or she may want to alter that story to make it more positive. According to James Fowler, *recapitulation* of the stages can be an important aspect of development of our faith. Because of the ambiguities about the personal story that I have described, recapitulation can in fact bring *reconstruction*. And in many instances, it may be desirable for an individual to *re-envision* his or her story. Reconstruction can be particularly useful if there are negative parts of the story that weigh an individual down and limit opportunities. The individual might need to use roles, events, and characters in a narrative that differ from those on which she or he previously focused. He or she may need a new vision—a new image—for the *future self.*

Theoretically it is possible to reconstruct the personal story, to build a story that is equally true but more positive than the current version that our *individual consciousness* maintains. If the individual focuses on negative roles and/or depressing events (such as alcoholic, drug addict, mentally ill, got fired, got busted, got knocked up, got locked up, failed the test), the resulting self-image may not be good. A new narrative can focus on roles or events that are more desirable. Although they must be accurate and believable, they can focus on different events from the past and create new themes that the individual *lives into* in the ever-flowing *NOW*. An individual may want to assume a new role. He or she may want to **become a Christian**, or *complete an education*, or *overcome an addiction*, or change some undesirable trait. If anyone wants to change his or her life, it is important to focus on the future, rather than the past, and remember that one actually *lives* only in the cutting edge of time—*now*. One can plan for the future, regret, or be proud of the past, but can *act* only *now*. We sometimes need to embrace the possibility of a fresh start—*a new beginning.* That can only start *now*.

There are strong advocates for *positive thinking*. Bishop Norman Vincent Peale wrote a book popular during the mid-twentieth century titled *The Power of Positive Thinking*, (1952). We may think our life journey is moving in a negative direction although it is moving in a different, more positive direction. By thinking positive thoughts, one can create a more positive future. James Allen wrote a thought-provoking book, *As a Man Thinketh* (1903). Like Peale, he advocated self-improvement through the power of positive thoughts. Napoleon Hill wrote the perennially popular *Think and Grow Rich* (1937), published near the end of the Great Depression, showing how positive thought can change lives and produce wealth. So, why doesn't everyone just think positive thoughts and constantly improve themselves? If we do not like the personal story, why not just rewrite the story, with a more positive slant, and live into it? There are strong advocates, but significant obstacles.

OBSTACLES TO SELF-RECONSTRUCTION

Let's identify the obstacles to reconstructing the personal story. As we have seen, *individual faith* establishes *personal identity*. The greatest difficulty in reconstructing the personal story is that it is never easy to produce a new belief or change a belief about anything through the exercise of volition. Belief resides in *individual consciousness*. *Volition* does not usually control the work of *individual consciousness* in such matters. Volition is usually governed by *individual consciousness*, in that it acts consistently with the conceptual content of *individual consciousness*. We cannot "change our minds" about ourselves or anything else just because we want to. Jesus told Nicodemus that to see the Kingdom of God one must be *"born again."*[38]

There is an important reason for the fact that a new way of seeing reality is not easy: stability is important. *Individual consciousness* does not easily accept a rewrite of one's *faith*. If we could easily change our core beliefs, the resulting *instability* would often create intense problems. After a person has lived into an *identity*, it is not at all a light and easy thing to "live out" of it. Personal faith—what an individual thinks he or she knows, including his or her *personal story*—is strongly entrenched. *Individual consciousness* believes what it believes very firmly. That belief provides a strong stabilizing influence for the individual. *Individual consciousness uses life experience to protect us*. If core beliefs were easily changed, we would not be stable.

We really believe what we really believe. That's what we think we know. Like Jesus, most of us would not jump off the pinnacle of the Temple to attract attention to our mission, just because the devil uses Scripture to assure us that we can fly. That is because *individual consciousness* really believes in the law of gravity. Jumping off the temple was the devil's idea, and it would have brought a quick end to Jesus' ministry! In our right minds, we are not going to jump. We cannot change what we really believe that easily. So, if my *individual consciousness* thinks I am a sorry, no-good scoundrel but in a self-improvement effort, I try to tell a more positive personal story, even if the events that I include in the new story are true, *individual consciousness* is in the background, whispering, "Liar, liar," reinforcing the entrenched negative conviction. It *knows* who I am! It *is* my innermost being. It is *me*!

A law similar to the scientific principle of inertia governs faith. The principle of inertia is that "a body at rest tends to remain at rest, and a body in motion tends to remain in motion in a straight line, *unless acted upon by an outside force*." Similarly, if *individual consciousness* believes something, it keeps on believing it. If it does not believe something, it keeps on disbelieving it. The thought "unless acted upon by an outside force" suggests *conversion*, an important concept of Christianity. An outside force *is* involved in conversion to Christianity. In conversion, the communal Holy Spirit takes control of *individual consciousness*. It is no longer *I* who live, *but Christ who lives in me*.[39] But without an *outside force*, what we believe, especially the personal story that we believe about ourselves, is not likely to change just because we want to change it.

For these reasons, intentional effort to change one's mind, even staunch resolution, standing alone, especially in an effort to re-envision one's *personal story*, has a poor chance of success. *Doubts* arise because of what we *don't* believe. They are an integral part of *faith*. The disbelief that we push out the door comes crawling back in through the window of *individual consciousness* in the dark night of doubt. In another sense, we *doubt* because we really believe differently. If you doubt that you are a good person, it is because you have a negative self-image and have low self-esteem. Therefore, you think that there are no opportunities for success for anyone like you. It will not be easy to change those beliefs. An **outside force** is necessary. **Experience** can be an outside force that brings change. In the words of the cliché, some experiences, good or bad, can "make a believer out of you." **Education** can be an outside force that brings a change in beliefs. Other people can be an outside force. A strong support group is probably the greatest possible ally in self-improvement, which is quite consistent with what we learned in **essay two** about the peer group.

A **new, believable vision** is the key to successfully revamping what one believes about herself or himself. In the Scripture about **conversion** and being **born again**, Jesus was talking about how to **see** the Kingdom of God. He was talking about **vision**, which is a strong metaphor. "Truly, Truly, I say to you, unless one is born again, he **cannot see the kingdom of God**."[40] A new **vision** is essential to a positive change. The new image must be a **vision** that we can and do **believe.** We must **see** the world differently, the way that a child whose identifying story is still malleable sees it. Otherwise, we will see what we have come to expect to see. Successful change must be **goal oriented.** Somehow, **confidence** in the **new self-image** must find its way into **individual consciousness. Internalization** is the tool for change, and the support group can play a significant role. Fortunately, **reality** and consciousness that embraces it are not merely products of individual brains. As we will see in the **eighth essay** that describes the **consciousness system**, the consciousness that operates the biosphere is very broad and inclusive, but **individual participation** in the totality of consciousness is limited. Nevertheless, with effort, **individual consciousness** can improve its **participation in consciousness.** Unfortunately, like New Year's resolutions that volition seldom keeps, individual beliefs remain the same regardless of **shallow** individual volitional efforts to change them. Conversion, as Jesus told Nicodemus, is like being **born again**! Volitional effort alone is seldom adequate to bring about major personality change. Even though we philosophically believe that thin is better than fat, as a practical matter, we believe even more strongly that vanilla wafers are good in banana pudding.

ZERO AND NOTHING

Consider this story. Joe, a successful New York businessman, is flying with a group of business people over the South Pacific. His wife, parents, and children are back home. The plane crashes. He is the sole survivor and suffers total amnesia. He is washed ashore on an island. Although physically intact and conscious, he has no identifying objects in his possession. He is greeted by friendly islanders, who try to ask him who he is. Of course, he can't tell them.

This story provides insight into *individual consciousness* and personal identity: If our *story* is taken away, who are we? *Individual consciousness* is empty. The "nothingness" of Joe's lack of memory is very significant. There is great significance to the *zero* in mathematical theory. It is part of the basis for computer technology. Likewise, there is great significance to the *nothing* that is pure *individual consciousness*, devoid of content. The essence of the *zero* in mathematics is difficult to envision. It is even more difficult to envision, let alone analyze, the ground zero, the *nothing*, of individual existence. The ground zero, or nothing, for an individual identity is an *empty individual consciousness* in a physically intact, healthy body. So, the man who was "Joe" is obviously somebody, but who? Back in New York, he might still be Joe. But who is he on the island? Every child that is born has the opportunity to write his or her personal story on a clean slate, but society supplies the chalk and suggests a lot of the words.

This is an *existentialist* approach to identity. The importance of *nothingness* was described by the phenomenologist, Martin Heidegger, and further developed by the existentialist, Jean-Paul Sartre. But the illustrative story is mine, not theirs. Their descriptions of *nothingness* are quite complicated, and am no doubt leaving out a lot. But even so, the point that I have just described about the *nothingness of individual consciousness* is worth thinking about. The Taoists contemplated the usefulness of *nothingness*: What is useful about a spoon? It is not the wood or metal that composes the spoon, but the empty space that holds stuff.

At a time not long ago, the best minds thought that space was filled with *ether*. That theory was discredited, and for a time, space was just space: *nothing*. But in 2013, physicists confirmed the existence of Higgs boson, a minute sub-atomic particle. The Higgs *field* may fully occupy the space of the cosmos, if *occupy* is the right word. Higgs boson has a very interesting property. It causes other particles either to *exhibit mass* or exist *without mass*. Are particles without mass physical? Are they something or nothing? The concept of *nothing* has important implications for the existence of the *nonphysical* whose existence I am advocating.

Back to the story. Joe lives among the islanders, who befriend him. A beautiful young island lady becomes particularly fond of him, and nature takes its course. He is welcomed into the group. He learns to work among the islanders. He learns their language. They call him Mr. Blanc. Who is he? Who are his island children?

INTROSPECTION

Introspection is an important function of *individual consciousness*. Introspection reveals matters that are internal to the individual, to which other individuals do not have access. It reveals the *personal story* that establishes identity, as we have now discussed in detail. But it reveals other things, that we may need to distinguish from *core identity*.

An individual's *recollected experience* is only available to the *individual consciousness* of that individual. Sigmund Freud described some of the things we might see when we introspect. He described the *ego*, the *superego*, and the *id*. The *ego* is roughly equivalent to the *self*—it is what *I* usually identify as *me*. *I* am *aware* of my ego. But *individual consciousness* is the center of *awareness*, and cannot examine itself, and is always *completely subjective*. It can examine the *ego*, but cannot examine itself. I am *aware* that I am *aware*, but even that conclusion is actually based on inference, and I can penetrate no further into the phenomenon of my awareness. *Ego*, like the *self* is a *concept* established within *individual consciousness*.

The *superego* is the *conscience*—the internalized image and commands of parents—an *ideal self*. Freud, like Vygotsky, understood the importance of *internalization*, but he did not understand and describe the *process of internalization* nearly as fully as Vygotsky explained it. The *superego*, like the *ego*, is a *concept* maintained within *individual consciousness*. Both the *ego* and the *superego*, and even the *id* can be envisioned or conceptualized as *components* of the self. They have functional *emotional* roles, and their emotional activities enable *individual consciousness* to identify them as conceptual *objects* internally. The *id*, according to Freud, is the conscience-less "*seething cauldron*" of *energy* that impels us into self-serving *activity*. The *id* is very self-serving, or selfish, always seeking to satisfy selfish needs, according to Freud. The *id* may be the same as Bergson's *vital force*. The *id*, too is *conceptualized* within *individual consciousness*, but its function would be present, whether we conceptualized it or not. We can identify these structures of the mind that Freud described when we "look" inside ourselves. We believe that other humans have such psychological structures and that we can see the effect that these structures have in the behavior of other humans. Our observation of the behavior of others may help explain what we think we are seeing inside ourselves. The *id*, *ego*, and *superego* have no *physical* existence. They are *mental* or *logical constructs*. They are things *individual consciousness* "*sees*" only with the *mind's eye* and are "*objective*" only as theoretical constructs based on the behavior they produce.

In the present discussion however, I am not trying to develop a complete understanding of the *ego, superego* and *id*. My concern is to clearly identity and describe *individual consciousness*—the thing inside us that does the *looking* when we introspect—the totally subjective *I*, and to distinguish it from the *ego, superego* and the *id*. The internal observer—*individual consciousness*—is not the *ego, superego* or the *id*. We can never actually "see" *what does the looking*. "Seeing" the thing that is doing the looking in the process of introspection would involve an infinite regress. As we sort out the meaning of *I*, we must consider, but distinguish, these structures that may be "seen" by introspection. We cannot "see" *individual consciousness*. The ability to know that it is there is implicit, and very subtle. The inference arises from the simple fact that we *know* that we *know*. To *know* that we *know*, something has to do the *knowing!* And that gives rise to the inferences of *participation in consciousness* and personal existence. *Individual consciousness* does the *knowing*, so we know it is there!

Individual consciousness is the function of the individual human organism that actively *participates* in consciousness. But its *participation in consciousness* is not perfect. *Individual consciousness* does not contain and participate in the *whole of consciousness* and individuals do not have *all* of consciousness at their disposal. In the biosphere, consciousness seems to be reality's awareness of itself, and that includes everything! But even though humans can only *participate* imperfectly in consciousness, that imperfect participation is precisely what makes each individual an *I*. As we will see in the *ninth essay*, Descartes led the philosophical world into dualism by saying, "*I* think, and therefore *I* am." He was right about the thinking part doing the thinking and establishing his identity. Like him, we *know* that we *know*. But there were some aspects of *knowing* that he did not consider, but I will defer further discussion of the problems with his theory for the *eighth* and *ninth* *essays* and the discussion of *dualism*.

Individual consciousness is the *observer* that conducts introspection, but that is not all that *individual consciousness* does to establish personal identity. *Individual consciousness* collects *personal experience* in *individual memory.* Personal memory is only available to the individual. *Individual consciousness* integrates information collected by the senses from both *inside* and *outside* the individual. That integrated information, that understanding of the world, enables the individual to function in the biosphere, as we saw in the preceding essay. It also establishes *personal identity*, which plays an important role in individual human participation in the physical and social biosphere.

The *self* is an *image* created by *individual consciousness.* It is not the *operating unit* of the personality. It is the *image* that *individual consciousness* creates based on actual experience and feedback from other people. That *self-image* merges and commingles with the *ego. Individual consciousness* also conceptualizes the *superego—the internalized images and commands of parents that become a part of self-identity*—and which can arouse emotions if someone makes a disparaging remark about me, or if something embarrasses me. So, the *self*, the *ego*, and the *superego* are not the seat of *individual consciousness.* They are actually conceptualized by *individual consciousness.* The ambiguous pronoun *I* may sometimes refer vaguely to any of these, but they are *logical constructs* created, *seen*, or *imagined* by *individual consciousness.* The real *I—an individual's core essence*—is *individual consciousness. Individual consciousness* is aware of its *awareness*, and identifies the information that it collects about the organism that it serves as *I*, but cannot further *examine itself.* As indicated in the preceding essay on human motivation, *individual consciousness* is *always behind the camera*, not in front of it. It is the cameraman! It is always the *subject*, never the *object. Individual consciousness*—being the *essence* of the individual's *participation in consciousness*—can never see itself. Although I can't see my own eyes, I know that I have eyes! I can infer the existence of my eyes from the fact that I can see. And I see the eyes of other people, and what they seem to be doing with their eyes. In the same way, and for similar reasons, I, like Descartes, know that I have *individual consciousness*. It is me. But I can't *examine* it for the same reason that I can't examine my own eye without a mirror. And if I had never experienced other humans, I would have no idea what I am.

As indicated earlier, *individual consciousness constructs* both the *ego* and *superego*. I believe that what Vygotsky had explained about internalization of language and concepts shows that *language* is involved in the construction of *ego* and *superego* by *individual consciousness*. But *individual consciousness itself* is the real *I*. *It* is in charge of what the *"I" believes* about its own identity. *Individual consciousness* often unites force with the *id*. Unlike the *ego* and *superego*, *individual consciousness* did not construct the *id*, although it can identify the *id*. The *id* was already in place when language developed. Individual consciousness recognizes the *id* as a *concept*, but has little to do with its creation. The *id* may be indistinguishable from Henri Bergson's *vital force* at work in the individual human personality. It operates independently of, but interacts with, *individual consciousness* at a very basic level, as it likely worked with *primary consciousness* before humans developed the capacity for *linguistic participation in consciousness*, the same way that nonhuman creatures *participate in consciousness*. The *id* and *sexual interest*, and maybe other parts of the human mental components that are involved in motivation operate at a very basic, primitive level of *individual consciousness*. *Individual consciousness* is certainly *not unconscious* when it works with the *id*. It *knows* what it is doing! However, sometimes it does things to satisfy *those very basic motives*, like looking around the room to see if *he* or *she* is there, and looking back. My point is simply that *individual consciousness* actually plays a role in those kinds of activities. Understanding that *individual consciousness* does not always control, but often works with the *id* explains why we sometimes don't do the right thing, even if we know we should.

In the final analysis, *individual consciousness*, guides the operations of the individual in the biosphere in the *eternal now*, and continually writes the *personal story* with its activities in that instant. The creation of that very personal story differentiates individuals as *units* of activity and experience. *Individual consciousness* is not the *self*; the self is a *concept* maintained by *individual consciousness*—an *object* recognized by *individual consciousness*. The story that *individual consciousness* writes, while guiding the operations of the individual in the biosphere, is the closest we can come to *personal identity*, but that story is only the "tracks" made by the real person.

WE ARE WHAT WE BELIEVE

This essay has shown that *faith* maintained by *individual consciousness* establishes *personal identity*. It has focused attention on the *personal myth*— what we believe about our*selves*. Our story—what we believe about ourselves—is very important and is the means by which faith *creates identity*.

However, *individual consciousness* and the *faith* it maintains, establishes our identity—our basic character—in another very direct and important way. Our identity is established not just by what we believe **about** ourselves, but by what we *believe*. *Individual consciousness* does all the *believing*. If a person believes that there is not any such thing as truth, that person will display that belief in his or her actions. But if he or she is committed to the value and necessity of truth, that too will show up in behavior. If an individual believes that the requirements of morality do not apply, and that anyone can do whatever she or he can get away with, that belief will show up in that individual's behavior. But if sound moral formation occurs the person will conduct himself or herself accordingly. If an individual believes that science and its focus on the material world is the only approach to truth, and that science has a monopoly on truth, those beliefs will show up in that individual's actions. But if he or she understands that normative force and its support of morality and law are indispensable for successful human life together, and that science did not establish them and cannot "measure" them, that too will be reflected in behavior. If an individual believes that education is unimportant, that individual will not pursue education, and faith is not likely to progress beyond the lowest stages. But if he or she understands the importance of education and self-improvement, the resulting behavior will produce greater personal fulfillment. *Essay three* that dealt with human motivation showed that our *actions* are based on our faith. Our actions draw upon *all that we believe*—not just *what we believe about ourselves*. Our *beliefs establish* our *character*. They *are* our character.

But the *actions* that result from our *character write* the *personal story*. Our actions are based on what we believe. So, our character governs our actions, and writes the story. *Individual consciousness records* the story, and the recorded story is an important *part* of our faith, because it establishes *personal identity*, but other parts of individual faith play a major role in *writing* the story that establishes personal identity. What we believe *about ourselves* does not equip us to cope in the biosphere. Intense faith *about the external world*, including *society* and its *social systems*, including *religion*, *morals* and *law*, is essential to enable the individual to cope successfully in the biosphere. That is the faith that establishes character. If faith is sound and character is good, appropriate activity that brings personal fulfillment is likely to result, and the personal story is likely to be positive.

5) FAITH, SOCIAL SYSTEMS AND INSTITUTIONS

THIS ESSAY FOCUSES ON THE *evolution* of *social systems* and the *institution-alization* of *social structures*. Humans do not operate in the biosphere just as *individuals*. Humans are very social beings. Humanity exists in *societies* and societies have an organic life their own. Society has created a large number of *social constructs* that are indispensable to human existence in the modern world. These *social constructs* require *collective human faith* for their existence.

In this essay, I will focus on two different categories of *social con-structs*. I will identify *primary social systems*, that emerged naturally after the evolution of the human capacity for language. Those systems were not intentionally created by society. They resulted naturally as a result of human interactions, in which individuals did the things that they did in order to get what they needed as individuals. Even though these systems emerged automatically, they came to be *institutionalized* by human faith. The second category of *social constructs* on which the essay focuses is *social systems* and *social entities* that humans intentionally *institutionalized.* When humans realized that by working together, they could accomplish more than individuals could accomplish acting alone, they began to *intentionally* create entities to take advantage of corporate activity and the division of labor.

These social activities involved *human participation in consciousness* in groups. To fully understand these two categories, it will be helpful to look back at the evolution of human *participation in consciousness* as discussed in the preceding essays. As I have noted repeatedly, *language* is a *group thing.* Individuals did not create *language* individually. Society was involved. *The first, and most important social construct was language itself.* Society was involved in the evolution of human *participation in consciousness* from the evolution of language forward. As we have seen, after *social groups* created language, individuals were able to *internalize* the concepts *imbedded in language*, and use them in individual abstract thinking. That was the major step forward for human *participation in consciousness.* Participation in language, a social function, resulted in the evolution of *consensus reality.* I have mentioned *consensus reality* in earlier essays, and will fully develop the concept in the next essay, *essay six.* Like language, *consensus reality* is a *social construct.* It is important to understand that *consensus reality* contains the *abstractions* of *institutionalized social constructs* that we deal with in the current essay.

As we have seen from earlier essays, the second major step forward for human *participation in consciousness* was the development of *writing.* The development of writing ushered in the *Axial Age.* Writing significantly contributed to the ability of society to *institutionalize social systems and entities.* I will describe those developments in this essay.

THE EVOLUTION OF PRIMARY SOCIAL SYSTEMS AND INSTITUTIONALIZATION

The *primary social systems* to which I am referring include *family*, *religion*, *morality*, law, and *economics*. *The primary social systems* arose naturally. In fact, *all social systems* arise naturally, and are *faith dependent*. When I say that the primary social systems "arose naturally," what I mean is that the earliest *social systems* came into being without *intentional human effort* to create them as systems. Individuals just interacted with other people to meet their own needs, and the *social systems* arose *naturally* as the result of the interaction of individuals.

These *primary systems* evolved somewhat sequentially. I will describe these systems and their sequential evolution in greater detail later in this essay. As mentioned above, *language* itself was socially constructed. It is a *primary social system*, and was a prerequisite to the other *social systems*. But I have focused on *language* and its role in human *participation in consciousness* throughout these essays so there is no need to further discuss its role as a *social system* in the current essay.

As individuals go about their activities, they encounter *society itself* as part of the *environment* that surrounds them. Society exists for *individuals* as part of *reality* that is *external* to their *individual consciousness*. For individuals, society consists of the *Thou(s)* that they differentiated themselves from to establish personal identity, as discussed in *essays three* and *four*. Although society is composed of individuals, and every individual is a member of society and an integral part of it, *individual consciousness* of each individual experiences *society* and its *systems* and *entities* as *external reality*. It is not a part of the individual's *self*.

Of course, the *physical environment* also presents itself to *individual consciousness* as something *external* to the *individual*. In the *faith system* that evolved in the biosphere, as we have seen, *society* identified and abstracted *nonphysical essences* of *physical objects*. The *abstraction* of *physical objects* became *concepts* that individuals internalized for *talking* and *abstract thinking*. Those *abstractions* are stored in *consensus reality*. But society also *institutionalized social systems* and *entities*, that enabled individuals to work together more effectively in the biosphere as groups. Individuals experience these *systems* and *entities* as *real things external* to themselves. Society created *language* that *abstracted* the *social systems* and *entities*, and deposited them into *consensus reality* along with *abstractions* of *physical objects*. Society assigned words to represent those institutionalized systems and entities. For individuals, they are just as much a part of *reality* as are *physical objects*. The purpose of this essay is to explore not only the *social systems* and *entities* themselves, but to show that individuals consciously experience them as *real things*.

Groups of individuals, acting in concert, *institutionalize* many useful *social systems* and *entities*. In the modern world, these entities include *corporations*, *cities*, *nations*, *political parties*, *schools*, and many, many others. *Government* is often involved in the institutionalization of such entities. Society assigns *categories* and *names* to these structures. Please take a moment to contemplate the *immensity* of the *social structure* that I am describing: California, New York City, India, Australia, Russia, Washington D.C., IBM, any bank you can name, any State you can name, any city you can name, etc., etc., etc. Needless to say, when I refer to these *entities* as *social structures*, I am referring to their existence as *operating social organisms*, not as *places* and *buildings*. All of these are examples of *socially created structures* that *individual consciousness* experiences as *real things*. Individuals experience them as real things, external to themselves. Humanity cannot exist without these *social structures* that are *created by society*. Sociology calls the social process that creates these structures *institutionalization*. It is not a formal process; it occurs naturally as the result of collective *faith*. Peter Berger and Thomas Luckman described the process of *institutionalization* in a wonderful book, *The Social Construction of Reality: A Treatise in the Sociology of Knowledge*. As the subtitle suggests, the book also describes how these *sociological institutions* become a part of *accepted reality*, and are added to the collection of human *knowledge*. Like Lev Vygotsky, Berger and Luckman recognized that society *creates knowledge* that individuals *internalize* and use in their mental processes. The immense *institutionalized reality* that society has created is an important part of what I have called *consensus reality*. Individuals *internalize* the *concepts*, including the *social constructs* that society creates, and those concepts are *accepted reality* for the *individuals*, just as real as *physical reality*.

MORE ABOUT INSTITUTIONALIZATION

Institutionalization establishes a *"thingness"* for the socially constructed entity or system. The social group recognizes an *essence* that represents the *entity* or *system* and assigns it a *word* or *name*. The word or name is the *abstraction* of the *entity* or *system*, and individuals *internalize* the *abstraction* from language for use in *individual thinking*. It works. For instance, if I say the word *city*, you immediately know the kind of *institution* I mean. That *category* has been *institutionalized*. If I say *Los Angeles,* you know what and where it is; that it is a *city*, in *California*. The words *city*, *California*, and *Los Angeles* all represent examples of *institutionalized social constructs*. Our *recognition* and *knowing* result from the *institutionalization* of these *categories* and specific *institutions*. Individuals have internalized these *concepts* and *categories*. They are *real things*. *Social constructs* are an indispensable part of our *collective knowledge*. A tremendous amount of the knowledge in our *consensus reality* consists of *social constructs* and *social structure* that came into being through the process of *institutionalization*.

Institutionalization establishes many *structures* and they are *not physical*. The role of society in human *participation in consciousness* is immense. As mentioned above, *language* itself, and all the *words and concepts* it has developed are *social constructs*. In *essay six*, I will fully develop the concept of *consensus reality* that I have introduced in earlier essays. In that essay, I will show how *faith* creates *social concepts* like *Wednesday* and *Thursday*. Society itself created and maintains *consensus reality* and all its concepts that individuals use in *conceptual thinking.*

John R Searle, a great physicalist philosopher of the mind, wrote an interesting book, *The Construction of Social Reality*, that deals with the issue of *institutionalization* that we are now discussing. The *title* of his book is very similar to the title of the earlier book of sociologists Luckman and Berger mentioned in the previous section. The terminology that Searle used in his book is also quite similar to the sociological terminology that Luckman and Berger used. In short, Searle's book appears to reflect knowledge of the work of Luckman and Berger, although he does not mention them or their book. Searle recognized that *institutionalization* appears to create *social concepts* that seemingly have no basis other than *human faith and consensus.* He tried, *quite unsuccessfully*, to show that the many *nonphysical* social concepts created by *institutionalization* necessarily have some *physical* basis. He used examples like *money* and the *monetary system.* Although I agree that *money* and the *monetary system* are good examples of *nonphysical social constructs* that were built by society using the process of *institutionaliza-tion*, they do not have any *physical basis.* Searle argued that there is *always a physical* basis for such *social constructs*, but I suggest that they are supported purely by *faith* as a part of *consensus reality*, and that they do not have or require a physical basis. The *physical* bases suggested by Searle play no role in establishing such entities as *real things.*

Social systems and *social structures* that are *institutionalized* were built on *collective faith.* Faith is a necessary part of the process of *institu-tionalization.* Of course, it is not difficult at all to believe that particular cities that can be identified as "places" are *real things*, although their essences as *social organisms* are totally *nonphysical.* But there are many other *social constructs* that, unlike cities, can't be identified as "places." For instance, as I show in the *sixth essay*, we believe very strongly in *days of the week*, like *Wednesday* and *Thursday*, although they are quite invisible and have no location. Concerning cities, consider this: I believe in *London*, *Paris* and *Rome*, although I have never been to any of them, but I *know* about them. Faith is *knowledge*. It is *conceptual*, not *perceptual*. An even better illustration of the role that *collective faith* plays in *institutionalization* might be the operation of the *monetary system* that Searle mentioned! *Money* and the *monetary system* are backed by *nothing but* our *societal faith*.

Mythology and elementary forms of religions began to develop early and played a significant role in the expanding participation in *language*, *faith development*, and expansion of *consensus reality*. The *primary social systems* and other *cooperative human efforts* probably had to evolve to a certain level and actually work before the advantages of the process of *institutionalization* could be *recognized* and intentional *institutionalization* could evolve. Groups of people saw individuals accomplishing things by working together that were mutually beneficial, and more effective than individuals could achieve acting alone. An important element of their success was division of labor. By sorting out the tasks, groups were able to get more done. For instance, there was probably a division of labor between men and women. The groups gradually realized that the *social process* works, and that they could intentionally take advantage of it. But creation of new *systems* and *entities* required *creative thinking* and invocation of *faith*.

It is important to note that *institutionalization* initially evolved from *naturally occurring human interactions*. Individuals were just interacting with each other in an effort to satisfy their individual needs. But humans gradually realized that they could *intentionally institutionalize* social cooperation. They could intentionally create social structure, if they could *habituate the practice* and invoke the necessary faith. At first, they probably didn't *conceptualize* the systems and entities. They just saw social processes work over a period of time, and replicated them for different tasks. In their early efforts to intentionally establish systems and entities, the desired systems and entities were probably attributed to gods, and that helped to induce the necessary *faith* in the systems and entities. I am not suggesting that the attribution to the gods was *insincere* or that attribution was a *requirement* for *institutionalization*. We have our ways of *invoking faith*, and they had theirs. Theirs were *mythological*, and our methods can also be described as *mythological*.

Let's look at the involvement of human *motivational force* in the *systems* and *institutions*. We fully discussed individual motivation in *essay three*. As might be expected from our examination of individual motivation, all *social systems* evolve as a result of humans doing what they do to get what they need! The distinction between *primary social systems* that are automatically *institutionalized* and systems that were *intentionally institutionalized* promotes an understanding of the necessary role of individual *motivational force* that is involved in all *social systems*. To get what they need, individuals interact with *other people*. They do not do so in an effort to establish the *primary social systems*. The systems just arose naturally from human interactions. Humans did not *believe* what they believed in order to establish a *faith system, marry* to establish society's *family system*, engage in *religious worship* to establish society's *religions*, or become indignant about the misconduct of others or feel embarrassed about their own misconduct to establish society's *normative force for morality and law*. Humans just did what they did to get what they needed, as we discussed in the *third essay*, and *social systems* arose and were *energized* by the effort. The *primary systems* were not first thought out as *concepts*, and then put into practice. Their *institutionalization evolved* from the simple fact that *social systems work*, and help to *meet human needs*. But once it was *recognized* that the *humans can produce good results by working together, creative thinking* could utilize *intentionality* to *institutionalize systems, institutions* and *entities* of a *nonphysical nature*, just as it had in producing *tools* in the *physical nature*. The advent of writing greatly facilitated the use of *intentionality*.

INTENTIONAL INSTITUTIONALIZATION

As a result of the *Axial Age*—the shift from the *oral stage* to *writing*—that occurred with the advent of *symbol recognition participation in consciousness, institutionalization* took a giant step forward. The *Axial Age* made possible more *intentional* human activity directed to the express purpose of *institutionalization*. The ability to *record* and *store* knowledge *symbolically* and *external to all individuals* greatly aided the ability to *induce belief*. Writing committed authority figures themselves to positions they had taken; they were less likely to change their minds after committing in writing. Their writings were *external things*. Although it is just the symbolic representation of oral speech, writing has a certain *"thingness"* about it.

Writing enhanced *authenticity*. For instance, the *Ten Commandments* were *written in stone*. They were identifiable external *things*. All of the great religions used *writing*. Scripture was *canonized*. The writings were *things*. Jews, Christians and Muslims are *people of the Book*. Other great religions had their writings. Kings and priests were *institutionalized*. Their com*mands, decrees* and *declarations* were put in *writing*. The writings became identifiable external *things. Even today we have a strong tendency to believe what we read!*

From the *Axial Age* onward, *social systems* that evolved often involved more *intentional* planning. *Institutional structure* had to be *intentionally* created for *political* systems, *governmental* systems and *educational* systems. Unlike *primary social systems*, more complex *institutionalized systems* such as *education, politics*, and *government* do not arise automatically as *byproducts* of naturally occurring human activities carried out for purposes other than creating the systems. They were *intentionally* created.

That does not make them "unnatural." But humans had to be motivated to create them, and had to engage *creative thinking* about how to create them and how to operate them. But they too had to be *energized by individual motivational force.* And they were and are created to *serve human needs.* Religion and law that were initially *institutionalized* as *primary social systems* without intentional effort expanded greatly with the benefit of writing and intentional efforts at *institutionalization* during and after the *Axial Age.*

The *intentional institutionalization* of these social systems introduced, or emphasized, a *new element* in *social motivation. Leadership* is implicit in the intentional creation of social structure. The *leadership roles* themselves had to be *institutionalized.* The leaders had to be *institutionally* accepted for the roles that they play. The *archetypal imagery* of mythology and Jungian psychology played a role in the authentication process. Priests, *kings, judges* and other *authority figures* derive their authority from the *institutionalization* of their *roles.* Again, in the days of outright mythology, and in the early days of writing, the people had their ways of authenticating roles; and now we have ours. Ours could be described as a form of *numerology.* We *count votes,* and somehow that invokes faith. We count votes to authenticate roles, and the authenticated decision makers often count votes to authenticate their decisions. The pageantry of court and legislative proceedings are profoundly mythological—almost an attempt to *institutionalize* the intrinsic power of what I am describing as *consensus reality*! Our methods, like ancient methods, invoke archetypal imagery.

So, we now understand how *social systems* and *social structures* come to be accepted as part of *reality.* They are *institutionalized* in the ways described by Peter Berger and Thomas Luckman. After these systems and structures enter *consensus reality,* the *faith system* accepts them as *things* that exist, just as much as *physical objects exist.* In order for words to be assigned to these "things" so that they can enter *consensus reality,* as I use that concept, there has to be a *nonphysical essence* that represents them.

Berger and Luckman do not use the term *consensus reality* that I coined, but the process that they described helps explain how *consensus reality* that includes *nonphysical social constructs* came into being. They did not treat *language itself*—the thing that empowered *consensus reality*—as a social structure, but it was obviously *constructed socially*. Understanding that language is socially constructed shows how their description of the *social construction* of *reality* connects with the theory of *consensus reality* that I am advancing. They do not discuss the role of *essences* in the creation of *social systems* and *entities* that are *institutionalized*, but those *entities* and *systems* are themselves based on *nonphysical ideas* that must be dealt with by *consciousness*. They do discuss *internalization* and to be internalized, they had to be abstracted and conceptualized. In short, society is part of *external reality* for individuals, and it, and the systems and entities that it creates *present themselves* as *phenomena* to human minds. Our earlier discussions make it clear that these *social constructs* must be represented by *phenomena* that must be presented to collective human minds in order to be *abstracted* as words and enter *consensus reality*. But social constructs are *very real*, and humans can conceive of *nonphysical essences* that represent them because they *exist* as possibilities.

INCREASING COMPLEXITY AND INTERACTION OF SYSTEMS

Social systems have evolved to increasing levels of *complexity* as society itself has moved to higher degrees of *participation in consciousness*, and as the human population has increased. As discussed in *essay one* that describes the *faith environment*, and *essay two* that describes *stages and sources of faith*, society uses the *education* system *to install its faith* into individuals. All the *social systems* work together. *Education* is an *institutionalized social system* that is *intentionally* created. It trains individuals for all of the tasks that society requires, and plays a critical role in maintaining and expanding *consensus reality*. Society uses the *economic* system *to call individuals to specific assignments.* Many aspects of the *economic system* including *corporations, industrial systems*, the *monetary system*, the *banking system, retirement systems, markets*, and more exist and have reality because they have been *institutionalized. Law* results in large measure from the *institutionalization* of *morality. Government itself,* is, in a sense, the *institutionalization* of law. But morality itself has much force and effect independently of law. *Morality* has been *institutionalized* in many different settings. It is the *motivational force* that energizes all *ethics* and *ethical theories,* and there are many applications. Every profession has its own set of *ethical principles.*

There are many *social systems* that I have not mentioned. Those that I have mentioned are illustrative and play central roles in human survival in the biosphere. Both *primary* and *intentionally created institutionalized social systems* evolved *to serve human needs.* They are *functions of faith.* The important concepts and ideas that they use for their operation are *nonphysical. Creative thinking* extracts these important *nonphysical essences* from a realm of *pure possibility* and uses them to create needed *social systems* and *entities* that are not products of *scientific effort* as such, and are not susceptible to examination and improvement with use of the tools that science uses for its work that deals with the *physical world.*

The *moral, legal, social,* and *religious principles* on which *social systems* and *social institutions* depend for their operation did not result from efforts of science, and can't be measured or evaluated by science. But these systems are indispensable to human welfare. Modern humanity cannot exist without them. They are more than *compilations* of *individual* mental and physical activities. They operate corporately and holistically as *social organisms.* They result from the way that society itself *participates in consciousness* at a *higher level* than individuals can participate, in order to satisfy human needs. Society itself, as Émile Durkheim argued, operates as an *independent organism,* composed of individuals that are analogous to cells.

In this essay, I am focusing on the **social systems** and **entities** that society has **institutionalized** and uses in its corporate life. These **social systems** and **entities** utilize individual **participation in consciousness**, and harness individual **energy and emotions**, to cause things to happen that **satisfy** the **needs** of society and its members. Using an analogy to a computer, **language** and **consensus reality** are **software**, and **social systems** are the **operating systems**. The operations of these naturally occurring systems are quite **intelligent**, although not under the direct control of the mind of any **one individual**. That is because the **groups** involved are functionally capable of **participating in consciousness** and are in fact **participating in consciousness**. The **individual consciousnesses** of the **individuals** that are involved in the systems overlap with each other. The consciousness of one individual picks up where that of another leaves off. **Society** as an **organizational whole** is actually utilizing **consciousness**, although no individual is "consciously" directing the entire operation. The individuals involved may not even realize they are operating parts of a system. **Primary social systems** are generated by **collective faith** and operate at an **unconscious** level, so far as many of the **individuals** who are participating in them are concerned. What I mean is that individuals are largely unaware of the fact that **social systems** are **using the output of their individual energy** to serve the needs of society. But that unconsciously captured energy effectively operates the **social systems**. Although individuals are conscious of **what they are doing**, they are not fully aware of what the ultimate social results of their efforts will be and what the **social system itself is doing** as the result of the individual efforts.

THE SEQUENTIAL EVOLUTION OF SOCIAL SYSTEMS

In the remainder of this essay, I will focus on **social systems**. The **social systems** provide **organizational force**, and were instrumental in calling the **social entities** into existence. The **primary social systems** evolved sequentially, and after **language** and **faith** evolved, each new social system depended on systems that had already evolved. *Law*—recognition and enforcement of contract and property rights—was a prerequisite for *modern economics*. Modern economics cannot function without enforceable property and contract rights. *Morality* was a prerequisite for *law*. The same *normative force* that energizes morality also energizes law. *Religion*—collective belief and homogeneity of emotions—was a prerequisite for *morality*. *Faith* was a prerequisite for *religion*, and for all the *social systems*. *Language* and *abstraction* were requirements for *faith*. The *family* (or its predecessors) preceded and is involved in all the *primary social systems*. So, there is a natural progression in the development of *primary social systems*. The progression begins with *family* and *faith* and proceeds to *language*, then to *religion*, then to *morality*, then to *law*, and then to modern *economics*. *All institutionalized* systems draw on and depend on the *primary* systems. *Educational* systems, *political* systems, and *governmental* systems depend on primary *social systems*. A common core of *faith* permeates all of the *social systems*. All of the *social entities* play functional roles in the *social systems*. The *social systems* organize the activities and efforts of *individuals* and *socially created entities*.

This discussion of *social systems* and *constructs* is about *social phenomena*—not individual psychology and development. When I use the phrase *social*, I am referring to dynamics that only occur when people *interact with each other*. *Social systems* and *entities* have evolved in *complexity* and *functionality* to accommodate the progress and increasing needs of humans. Once all the *primary social systems* evolved, and became *institutionalized*, they began interacting with each other and affected, changed, and supported each other in the processes of *social or cultural evolution*. They depend on each other. Each culture has its own versions of the various *social systems*. Cultures—larger, more comprehensive systems—involving all of these *social systems* and *entities*—and more—evolved, and continue to evolve.

The evolution of *social systems* was made possible by the appearance of *linguistic participation in consciousness* that empowered functional *group participation in consciousness*. That participation and the capability of supporting *institutionalized systems* were greatly expanded by *symbol recognition participation in consciousness* and the advent of reading and writing. The evolution from *linguistic participation in consciousness* to *symbol recognition participation in consciousness* ushered in Karl Jaspers' *Axial Age* that laid the groundwork for modern *institutional* structures of the *social systems and entities* that provide the needs of the modern world. The transition from *linguistic participation in consciousness* to *symbol recognition participation in consciousness* was what caused the *Axial Age* to happen. The advent of writing greatly facilitated *institutionalization* of *social systems* and *social structures*. No doubt, the *electronic axial age* that we are now experiencing will again dramatically impact the evolution of social *institutionalization*.

I will now examine *primary social systems*, attempting to retrace the sequence in which they likely evolved. I am focusing on these *primary social systems* because the strong social forces that brought them into being are still very much in existence, and are *maintaining the systems* and *guiding their continuing evolution*.

FAMILY

Before humans evolved the capability for *linguistic participation in consciousness*, our biological ancestors obviously raised children. After language emerged, *faith* developed *around* and *within the family structure*. The large human brain, with all its capabilities, was likely a prerequisite for *linguistic participation in consciousness* by humans. Both parents were needed for the long course of development required for maturation of human children with their *large brains* that supported language. Parents are involved in teaching children their language. So, family was deeply involved in the processes of *social evolution* that began with *linguistic participation in consciousness.* Cultural evolution *incorporated* the *primal forces* of family into its processes. The relationships that exist in a family satisfy powerful *individual needs* of the husband, wife, and children. And as Maslow taught us, people do what they do to get what they need.

Starting with primordial family functions, social evolution forged the *family unit*, and *extended family*, as we know it today. Family, as it now exists in Western culture, is a *social system*. It is thoroughly *institutionalized*. It has played a role in cultural evolution that is quite special. When humans began *linguistic participation in consciousness*, family, in some form, was involved in the tasks that I have described in other essays concerning the development and perpetuation of *language, faith*, and *conceptual thinking*. Of course, the family's *primary biological* functions arose from the fact that *humans are animals*, and their basic *animal functions* were not *created* by faith, as I have defined that term, nor were they created by what I have described as *cultural evolution.* However, *faith* and *cultural evolution* was involved in creating *social norms* that set standards for the very necessary continuing biological functions of family, to the point that organization of the modern family is grounded in the *faith* system. We maintain *strong beliefs* about family and how it should operate. There are significant variations around the world in the understanding of *how family operates* and how the biological functions should be dealt with. These essays focus to some extent on the faith of the *Western* world concerning family. Although there may be considerable variation in the traditions of family in different parts of Europe and America, there are also significant similarities throughout the Western world.

In Western culture, the family is the *basic unit of social organization.* As we mentioned previously, Sigmund Freud described the role of the *authoritative father* and the *nurturing mother* in the moral development of children. He recognized the important role that *internalization* of *commands* and *images* of parents plays in the development of children.

The traditional family provides the template for *moral formation* and the perpetuation of the system of morals in Western culture. *Religious beliefs* have interacted with beliefs about family in the course of *cultural evolution*. The surrounding culture with its morality *reinforces* the role that the family plays. *Morality* imposes expectations on the individuals who occupy the archetypal roles of father and mother. Culture has adapted the role of the family to its purposes, and has used family to perpetuate cultural faith. The family is the first teacher of *language.* As the teacher of language, its role is critical for the perpetuation of *faith.* The *concepts* reflected in *language*, first learned in the family, are *internalized* for *abstract thinking* in the ways that Vygotsky described.

RELIGION

Religion, a *social system* closely associated with *faith*, was likely the *first social system* to arise after humans evolved the capacity for *linguistic participation in consciousness*. In the *second essay* that dealt with the *faith environment*, and other essays as well, I describe the revolutionary irruption of *linguistic participation in consciousness*, *language*, and *abstraction.* For language to work, the participants must believe in the *symbolic representation* of *objects* and *nonphysical essences* by orally created sound! The very process by which the *sound of a voice* in speech successfully represents *objects* and *ideas* in *individual consciousness* requires *faith*. Faith goes to the heart of *religion.* After language evolved, it played a major role in the development of religion. Those early, creative religions, now identified as *mythology*, played a critical role in human cultural and social development during the *oral stage* of *societal faith.*[41]

Development of language enabled humans to create *narratives*. The meaning that can be conveyed by a *story* far exceeds the meaning of *individual words* that may represent *concepts*. *Narratives* were important in the establishment of *consensus reality*. Stories capture meaning and can be easily remembered. The ability to tell stories empowered *creative imagination* to use stories to explain *origins* and other mysteries. Telling the stories—the *myths*—would have been an occasion for the *gathering of groups*. That is probably how myths originated. And the gatherings would have been occasions for *music*. The *music* and *storytelling* evoked awe and collective psychological involvement. *Worship* was born.

Spiritual participation in consciousness is an integral part of *individual consciousness*. Individual minds have the ability to penetrate into the mysterious *nonphysical* world of *essences*. Somehow, *individual consciousness* connects to the mysterious realm of consciousness in which *phenomena* that match *nonphysical essences* exist. That includes the *spiritual world*. It is also the realm of emotions: feeling that is not conceptual, as Friedrich Schleiermacher realized.[42] *Spiritual participation in consciousness* is the part of consciousness that enables individuals to evoke the kinds of elementary religious experiences that Émile Durkheim described in his book *The Elementary Forms of the Religious Life*, (1912). The human capacity for *spiritual participation in consciousness* probably evolved shortly after or even before the capacity for language evolved.

Mythologies had powerful influence throughout the oral period of *linguistic participation in consciousness*. Karl Jaspers' *Axial Age* saw major developments in religion. The *Axial Age* was the beginning point of all of the *world's major religions*, and I have attributed that development to *symbol recognition participation in consciousness*—writing and reading. The *Axial Age* involved widespread *intentional institutionalization* of religion. With writing, particular religions could be much more widely recognized. Religions *intentionally* developed *institutional* social structures. Religions have continued to exercise major roles in *collective* and *individual faith* into modern times.

I have identified the *quest for meaning* as one of the basic human needs. The *quest for meaning* is the motivational force that propels humans into *religious activity*. Like all basic needs of individuals, human nature provides the *quest for meaning* with the *energy* that it needs to accomplish its purposes. And like other needs, the *quest for meaning* compels action. It leads to religion and ultimately to *religious organizations*. Religious groups garner the energy for their group effort from the *individual participants*. The individual *quest for meaning* energizes *religion at the group level*, just as individual human motivation provides energy for other *social systems*. The transfer and contribution of individual energy into *collective activities* played an important part in primordial religious functions. As Durkheim explained, individual minds acting in concert produced powerful *collective representations,* which helps to explain the role of society in the production of *concepts*. *Concepts* provide the basis for *meaning*.

Although subtler than other needs, the *need for meaning* is very real and affects individual behavior. If an individual does not participate in an organized religion as such, or if he or she does not find meaning in organized religion, he or she will *seek meaning* in other activities that meet the primordial spiritual/psychological requirements of religion in order to satisfy the unavoidable *quest for meaning*. The *quest for meaning* engages *spiritual participation in consciousness* to search and probe into the mysterious unseen realms of consciousness itself, to try to extract significance for *individual existence* from among the invisible essences.

Dealing with *nonphysical essences* is an important traditional responsibility for religion, philosophy, and the general faith system. Although science necessarily *uses nonphysical essences* in its work, it cannot deal with *nonphysical essences* in the same way that it measures and observes physical *objects*. But scientific work itself can satisfy the *quest for meaning*, and its success in doing so has been rewarded by strong allegiance by its adherents. The *quest for meaning* is a motivating force for *science*. Scientific work can *take the place of religious work* in the *quest for meaning*. But science, although extremely effective when focused on the *physical*, is really not a good substitute for *religion*, with its focus on the *nonphysical*. And *philosophy* needs to actively engage and develop the *nonphysical* on its own merits, and not try to engage science on the turf of *science* and the *physical* when dealing with the *nonphysical*.

Religion is practiced in organized groups. Typically, individuals do not choose a religion; they accept the religion that their family or the immediately surrounding culture hands out to them. So, the individual choice as to which religion to join is usually determined—or perhaps a better word would be perpetuated—by the family and/or the culture into which the individual is born. Religious indoctrination often begins at an early age.

No *description* of the practice of religion can convey the actual impact of the *experience*. Mere *descriptive* words cannot *recreate* the feelings of comfort, security, and purpose that arise from true worship as a part of religious faith. I have explained that the *quest for meaning* impels humans into religious activity or its equivalent, but understanding that religions arise from the *quest for meaning* does not come close to describing the *actual experience* of religion. Religious *meaning* arises from *satisfaction* of emotional and spiritual needs. William James provided a powerful analogy: eating one raisin is more nourishing than reading the entire menu![43] Friedrich Schleiermacher contended that religious *experience* does not involve *concepts*, but consists wholly in *feeling* that is *nonconceptual*. To *experience* real worship, one must actually *engage* in real worship, and that doesn't mean merely attending church services. And participating in real worship has meaning that cannot be acquired by *learning* the theological concepts of Christianity or any other religion. The successful function of religion as a *social system* totally depends on the *actual participation* of devotees in the *actual experience*. In these essays, I argue that faith is what one *actually believes*. That principle applies to *religious faith itself*. Religious faith cannot work, either individually or corporately, if its adherents do not actually believe in the experience.

But confidence that the *object of worship exists* in the mysterious, unseen realm of *nonphysical* existence, but transcends, into one's very being, is a powerful *source of meaning*. If we *believe* that *we can trust the mysterious power that called us into being* from the dust of the earth and breathed into our nostrils the mysterious breath of life so that we became living souls, and are here for a purpose, *those beliefs* help satisfy the *quest for meaning*. Although we do not *understand how it happens*, through faith, we can *feel* our way into the unfathomable mystery.

This intellectual discussion of worship, and description of religious faith, cannot capture the intense emotional and *spiritual* significance of religious belief. Significant *feelings* are deeply attached to core beliefs and values. Those *feelings* are difficult to capture in words. But everyone has experienced something of these feelings in some context. If you search your memory and experience, and you can probably recall an experience that evoked the kind of *feelings* that I am referring to. Your recollection may be an actual *religious experience*. But if not, you have likely had some other deeply moving experience that helped satisfy your *quest for meaning*. Perhaps it was a wedding, a funeral, the Kennedy funeral procession, the raising of a flag at a Fourth of July celebration, the bugle or trumpet call of taps as a soldier or veteran was laid to rest, or hearing the eloquent words of Dr. Billy Graham, John F. Kennedy, Dr. Martin Luther King, Jr., Franklin Roosevelt, or Winston Churchill. Perhaps it was Atticus Finch[44] in *To Kill a Mocking Bird*, saying to the jury, "In the name of God, do your duty." Whatever elicits the intense *emotional response* that I am describing draws on intense *faith or feeling*. The practice of religion is not merely an *intellectual* experience; it involves *intense emotional, spiritual commitment.* It is *spiritual participation in consciousness.* Psychologist Dacher Keltner used the word *awe* in an effort to describe such experiences.[45] All words fall short and fail to express the *feeling* of true religious experience. But that experience, *shared communally,* though not "*communicated*" like a classroom lecture or an email message, has played an essential role in the evolution of the noosphere. Only the social unity inherent in the unified *commitment to ultimate values* backed by this type of emotional commitment could produce the *morality* and *normative force* that enables society to function. Religion has played a unique and indispensable role in cultural evolution!

An important part of the belief system produced by the religious background of Christianity in Western culture is our *commitment to transcendent values*. Important parts of that belief system have been incorporated into the beliefs of secular society. Almost everyone believes that truth exists in the universe, separate and apart from the particular factual circumstances that we encounter. *Law* depends on our *faith in transcendent truth*. We believe that there is *justice worth contending* for, even if justice does not occur in a *particular* case governed by our all too human legal and judicial systems. *Science* itself depends on faith in *transcendent truth*. We believe that the laws of physics are present and operational in the farthest parts of the universe. I submit that all of this *operating faith* in *transcendent values* is rooted historically in the fountainhead of *religious* faith. The fact that morality grew out of religion and that the normative force of morality is essential to the operation of law is not inconsistent with the principle that requires separation of *church* and *state as institutions*.

This faith in *transcendent truth, morality, law*, and *justice* arose from many generations of belief under the influence of the *Judeo-Christian religion*. Whether Christian or not, we believe that "*truth endureth forever*."[46] Faith in transcendent truth sustains our commitment for an unending search for accurate solutions to problems. *A thousand years of Platonism* in the medieval church produced a significant faith in *transcendent values* that now passes unconsciously from generation to generation, independently of church and religious connections, despite questions raised by physicalists. It *works* because it is *real*. It is *institutionalized*. The *faith in transcendent values* is so subtle, so omnipresent, that most people are not even consciously aware of it. For them, it is just a part of *reality*.

MORALS ROOTED IN RELIGION

The preceding discussion of *religion* leads quite naturally into the discussion of *morality*. Morality enables groups of humans to live and work together for their common good. It is the *sinew* of social function. The *moral beliefs* found in *Western culture* are strongly rooted in the Judeo-Christian heritage; Western morality did not evolve separate and apart from religion. Religion provided the passionate common belief system that was a prerequisite for *morality*. The Roman *pater familias* could, with impunity, leave a deformed baby on the hillside to die. Science can't prove that the Roman practice was *wrong* or *evil*, but *it was* wrong and evil. It was murder. Our strong conviction that it was wrong and evil grew out of our religious heritage. In the absence of the passion of religion, there is no *emotional force* that binds the group to the requirements of morality. Debate about the merit or lack of merit of a particular value, or system of values, would never bring the *commitment* and *consensus* into a system of morality that is essential for its operation. *Arguments* produce division and discord, not *consensus*. To produce moral values, there must be *consensus* and there must be *commitment*. Without *consensus* and *commitment* deeply embedded in human society, the moral system will not work. First, there must be *consensus*. There must be a *common belief*. Neither scholarly debate nor any other kind of debate led to the consensus that was required for morality to work. *Religion* provided the *prerequisite* commitment and consensus for our system of morality. And it was not the *arguments* among Church leaders and theologians, but the *faith of believers* that laid the foundation for what we believe about morality. And there must be *commitment*—true belief and commitment of *emotional energy*, collective emotional energy—that will *require compliance,* in order for the system of morality to work. Religion provided both *consensus* and *commitment*.

But morality does not exist *just* because individuals believe *something*; the faith that evokes and supports morality must have *content*, and connect to something *real*. Needless to say, morality works because we believe in it. However, it does not work *just because* we believe in it; it works because its contents reflect *transcendent truth*. The principles of morality are *real*. Ultimately, that is *why* we believe in it. It is *real* because its practice by the cultural group that *institutionalized* it promoted the welfare of humanity. It *preserves life* and *promotes human survival*. Its ability to do that existed before humanity articulated its principles, or arrived at a consensus about them. But for morality to work for humanity, and systematically affect human belief and behavior, *consensus* was necessary. The consensus must be founded in *reality*—the *ultimate environment*. Morality has to *participate* in *truth* if it is to work. Real morality *always* promotes the welfare of humanity.

In Western culture, whose origins were deeply rooted in Christianity, the philosophical moorings that began in *Platonism* continue to be an important element in our beliefs about moral values. We believe that there is *transcendent truth* that supports *moral values*. We believe that there is a real and significant difference between right and wrong that transcends any particular incident. We believe that some answers are right and better than other answers. That faith is neither a *mere accident* nor the *product of human creativity*. It reflects the *rightness* that is built into the universe that includes human society. Faith in *transcendent truth*—the belief that *moral principles* are based on *transcendent truth*—is the foundation of our system of morals. Dr. Martin Luther King, Jr., clearly recognized the necessary connection of *just laws* to transcendent *truth* in his "Letter from the Birmingham City Jail". That letter was the most profound exposition of *natural law* written in the twentieth century. The proof of validity of moral principle is the extent to which morality *works*, the extent to which it promotes *survival* and the *fulfillment* of humanity.

Morality depends on *normative force*. Normative force arises from the *processes* of individual moral formation, which, as I have pointed out, are an integral part of *faith* formation. *Normative force* in the group results from the *collective force of individual moral convictions*. Even though the immediate sources of moral formation are parents and the peer group in the Western world, parents and peer group are shaped and surrounded by a culture that has been deeply affected by the Judeo-Christian heritage.

Actions and *feelings* of individuals combine in society to produce the *moral system*. But individuals do not engage in those actions and feelings in order to create a moral system. Individuals simply seek the security and acceptance that they need and adjust their own behavior to meet the expectations of others. When other individuals do not adjust their behavior in a similar way, the complying individuals as a group are *indignant*, and the individual who is not in compliance encounters *disapproval*. Often the fear of disapproval itself brings *compliance*. So, the moral system works *naturally*. A large panorama of *human interactions* evokes natural *feelings* and *reactions* that energize the moral system. The system is self-activated and self-perpetuating. But it is thoroughly *institutionalized*.

As I have indicated, religion was a *precursor* of morality. But once the *system of morality* evolved, supported by *human motivational forces* that had originated in religious faith, morality took on a *reality of its own*. It became *institutionalized* as a *social system*. It was no longer tied to religious faith as such. It had been *institutionalized* as a separate "thing." It was simply seen and understood as a part of *reality*, on its own, and scholars could deal with it as such, independently of religion. The faith system had posited all of the concepts necessary for its existence into *consensus reality*. So, as a *system*, the *system of morality* now exists independently of its *religious* origins. It has been absorbed into the *secular belief system*. But it remains very *faith dependent*. It works because people *believe in it*. But it is important to know that in the West, morality evolved from religion. Understanding that point may have important implications in this *electronic axial age* in the search for a workable common faith within the biosphere that can work for human preservation and fulfillment throughout the biosphere.

LAW AND NORMATIVE FORCE

Law derives its *power* from collective faith. Its power arises and evolves from the same social forces that produced religion and then morality. Law depends on *normative force* as the ultimate source for its power. Many legal philosophers underestimate the important role that *normative force* plays in the operation of law. Law that does not ultimately receive the backing of *normative force* will not work over the long haul. It cannot sustain the *basis in faith* that is required for its existence without that backing. Law provides the functional authority for government itself, and the governmental *enactment* or *pronouncement* of law is merely its *formal authentication*. As indicated earlier, there is a sense in which *law* arises from the *institutionalization* of *morality*, and in which *government* itself arises from *institutionalization* of *law*. It is *institutionalized* in order to *authenticate* and *enforce* laws. What we now recognize as both law and government were *institutionalized* and began to evolve as *social systems* as the result of Karl Jaspers' *Axial Age*, when oral traditions were being put into writing. They were powerfully reinforced by *symbol recognition participation in consciousness*. Physical, written *expression* helped to *institutionalize religion*, *law* and *government*. They evolved as the result of the *mythological* approach to truth and reality, not the scientific approach. The *mythological approach* to truth that produces *consensus reality* is extremely important. Although law is *articulated* by humans, and *authenticated by formal governmental processes*, as I described in *Conscience and Command* (1994), it draws on Platonic *faith* in *transcendent values* and the normative force that I described in the preceding section for its driving force. In *Conscience and Command*, I developed the concept that *normative force* of morality does not differ from the *normative force* that is necessary in order for law to work. I developed the idea that for law to work, it must be backed by *motive force*. People must experience the *need* and be attracted to the *tasks* that are essential to operate the legal system. The *motive force* that produces *morality* provides the central core for the *societal energy* that is required for *law to be effective*.

The *Axial Age*, when religions were expanding their social power based on the availability of writing, also marks the point at which *law* evolved from its background in religion and morality. Law was *institutionalized*. Stories of the *gift of law* by gods were quite common. Belief that law was a gift of gods played an important role in the *authentication* of law in the *faith system*. But the *physical writing* contributed significantly to the *process of authentication*. It is interesting to note that in the Biblical account, the *gift of law* preceded the *naming of a king*. Law was *not* exactly the *"command of the sovereign"* which modern legal positivism contends to be the basis for law. The king was subject to the law. These Biblical events were reduced to writing in their final form during the *Axial Age*. The *Axial Age* marked the beginning of human understanding of law. During the *Axial Age*, writing provided a way to *record* law *outside the human mind* so that it could be *remembered and known*. Law and its supporting social structure were *institutionalized*. Principles that are *in writing, external* to any human being, are somehow *more believable*. Law came to be recognized in the faith system as a *real thing*. As I described in detail in *Conscience and Command*, the processes by which law is *authenticated* are still well within the realm of *mythological* approach to truth. The use of the *mythological* approach to *truth* has continued to evolve and plays important roles in the *institutionalization* of *social systems*. For instance, appellate courts write opinions to explain their decisions, and in the Anglo-American legal system, legal *precedents* are considered *law*. Every opinion could begin, "Once upon a time there was a (man or woman) who....": pure *mythological method*. And they wear robes—and even wigs!

St. Thomas Aquinas described the basis for *natural law* in *human nature* in the thirteenth century. Law arises from the nature of humans as social beings. You realize, of course, that the nature of humans as *social beings* plays an important role in the things that I have been describing throughout this series of essays. Society is a *real thing* in the biosphere, *external* to individuals, and society produces the *normative force* essential for law. It is *real*. Aquinas' description of *natural law* was a huge development. International law schools came into being in the High Middle Ages. Elements of Roman law were rediscovered. Law in its purest form was not at that time regarded as a mere creation of the *nation state* as is believed by modern *legal positivists*. Indeed, without widespread faith in the *transcendent existence of law*, nation states may have never come into being. As suggested earlier, there is a sense in which *government* is the *institutionalization of law*. It is *institutionalization* for the *processes* for *authenticating* and *enforcing* law. In the modern world with its *international economy*, and international problems like *global warming, pollution, destruction of rain forests*, and *nuclear proliferation*, nation states operating like businesses competing for scarce resources and commodities may get us all killed!

Law, as we know it in Western civilization, probably could not have evolved and emerged in any faith environment other than that of Western civilization, with its faith in *transcendency* and *transcendent values*. As with morality, the *normative force* that energizes law is founded in our *faith* system. It is embedded in the Platonic belief in *transcendent justice* that was instilled into the faith system of Western culture by Christianity. We believe that principles of law *transcend* particular incidents and that justice requires *right* answers. That belief gives law its force. Our faith in *transcendent truth* and *transcendent justice* is essential to the Western concept of law. Faith in *justice* is firmly attached to belief in *transcendent truth*. The only *"proof"* of the *reality* of law as a concept is that it *works* by promoting the *survival* and *fulfillment* of humanity. The legal system functions because of the *feelings* and *commitment* of the people, not the rationalistic *arguments* of legal philosophers. *Faith*—commonly held belief—adds the *fervor* that is required for the *enforcement* of law. People require it; they demand it. They invest their *motivational energy* in it.

In the relatively recent past, after modern nation states had emerged, legal theorists developed the concept that law is nothing more than the "*command of the sovereign.*"[47] This theory differs significantly from the *natural law* theory described by Aquinas. According to these modern theorists, law is, at best, the rational solution to problems of human conflict and, at worst, the exercise of *raw power*. The *governments of nation states create* and *enforce law* according to these theorists. But *faith in law* was likely a prerequisite to the formation of *nation states* as we know them. But law is not merely a product of the *human mind*, although it is maintained in *consensus reality*. It is founded in *transcendent principles* that support *human survival* and *fulfillment*, that must *exist* before they can be *articulated*.

Legal positivism dominates the thinking of modern legal philosophy. *Legal positivism* asserts that the *nation states* make law. Law is produced by human minds. *Select* humans with *institutionalized* positions just decide what is best and agree on it. *Substantive content* is not a factor in establishing the reality of law for legal positivists. Positivism does not recognize the obvious fact that moral *normative force* lies at the heart of law's *motive force* and defines and limits its *functional capability*. Normative force is a requirement if law is to be effective. The earlier theory of natural law recognized the strong affinity between law and *morals*, even though Aquinas did not have access to the modern understanding of how *moral formation* occurs and the *dynamics it produces*. It recognized the connection of authentic law to human welfare and human nature. The partial *loss of recognition* of the role of *moral force*, brought about by wide acceptance of *legal positivism*, may lie at the heart of many of our *law enforcement* and societal issues. While *consensus* may be produced *provisionally* by legislative enactments or judicial pronouncements, ultimately the *quality* of the principle (or *lack of quality*) will assert itself. *Bad ideas won't work; good ideas will work.* Good ideas have a *natural origin*, and only good ideas that work will bring desirable social evolution and human fulfillment. Modern legal *scholars* and *philosophers* often *scoff* at the notion of *finding correct legal principles.* They are *wrong. Essences* precede *articulation*, and must be found. We must *search* for right legal principles.

Legal positivists have defined law as *what a court does* or *is likely to do.* This is a mistake, in so far as the reality of law is concerned. Law, particularly criminal law, seems to measure its effectiveness by the number of cases successfully prosecuted. But prosecutions actually represent instances in which criminal law has failed to produce the desired results. A representative from the Center for Disease Control once testified in my court. After she had testified, and off the record, I had the opportunity to ask if her agency had produced a computer model to measure its success by calculating the number of illnesses that *do not occur* because of her agency's efforts. I explained that I would like to see such a model to measure the successful operation of law by crimes that are not committed. She knew of no model for measuring success for disease prevention, and I know of no such model to measure the successful operation of law. In the legal realm, prosecutors congratulate themselves on the number of convictions, that result in jail time, even though the United States, the "land of the free," has the highest rate of incarceration in the world. Our criminal law is not operating successfully. It is not achieving its purposes. There has to be a better measure of successful operation of law.

Nation states themselves are *social institutions* that evolved to meet human needs. They are *intentionally institutionalized social systems.* Unfortunately, they are proving less and less adequate to deal with challenges to human survival. The largest threats to humanity today are *international* in scope. Expansion of the role of law as a *naturally occurring social phenomenon* in the noosphere will be a part of the solution to the expanding international problems that threaten humanity.

I have described law as a primary social system and government as an intentionally institutionalized social system. The nonexclusive primary social systems that I have identified (family, religion, morality, law, and economics) are not the objective or purpose of the human actions and motives that produce them. People do not do the things that they do to intentionally create these systems; they do what they do to get what they need, and these systems emerge. But some of the institutionalized social systems, including government, are intentionally and consciously created. The framers of the Constitution were intentionally creating a nation state. Normative force, a critical component of law, is not created by mere legislative action, or by mere declarations of courts, but arises from human interactions. The social institutionalization of law and government entrusted law to legislative bodies and courts, but it is incumbent on those legislative bodies and courts to find principles that are, or can be, backed by normative force based on principles that support human fulfillment. Normative force is the essence of the concept of law that I am focusing on and describing as an essential component for the ultimate reality of law. Let's hope that cultural evolution has not come to an end, and that biospheric solutions involving law at a new level of understanding will evolve!

MODERN ECONOMICS AND LAW

Economics is one of our foremost *social systems*. At its most basic level, here is how economics works: something that you have is more valuable to me than to you. Something I have is more valuable to you than to me. So, we trade, and we are both better off. Because of the exchange, the items that we exchanged can better satisfy our needs. When all of the individuals in a group watch for opportunities to make such exchanges, *economic value is created* that benefits the group. Every available asset will be used to its maximum advantage for the welfare of the members of the group. That is the way *economic exchange* serves **human needs**. Economic exchanges increase the value and usefulness of the assets of the group, and create **economic growth**. The assets that are available better serve the needs of society if they come into the hands of the person or entity that has the highest and best use for them. Economics is a *primary social system*. The system arose because of the trades and exchanges that people and entities make. People and entities do not make trades and exchanges in order to create an economic system but to get what they want or need. The *economic system* arose as a byproduct of the *motivation* that brings about the trades and exchanges. Although economics originated as a *primary system*, as suggested earlier it has spawned many *institutionalized social systems* and *social entities* that engage in economic activity and serve human needs.

What most individuals provide for society is *service*. Diverse tasks performed by individuals in diverse occupations working for diverse social entities serve the needs of society. Most individuals are paid salaries for their work, and that cost is passed on to the ultimate consumer, so society *pays* for the needed services. The *economic system* is essential in the *division of labor* in society. It calls individuals to the *diverse occupations* to perform all the needed tasks. It calls individuals to specific occupations to satisfy specific needs of *society* and its individual members. And it provides individuals with a livelihood.

Economics is a *social system* that plays a significant role in the satisfaction of individual needs. The system engages *individual motive force* very naturally. No doubt, from the earliest beginnings of *linguistic participation in consciousness*, and maybe before that, humans *exchanged goods and services*, and the exchanges were mutually beneficial. In its earliest development, *mere possession* of physical objects was probably all that individuals needed in order to effect exchanges. The use of *language* tremendously enhanced their ability to exchange goods and made economics as a *social system* possible. Humans could make trades using language, without the *physical objects* that were being exchanged necessarily being present. The new difficulties of *trust* that this kind of trade created are very obvious. A new *layer of complexity* was added.

One of the great benefits that *law* provides is clarification of *property rights*. Law also supports the *formation of contracts* for exchanges. These developments were prerequisites for *modern economics*. So, although the same human *motive forces* that *cause exchanges* that gave rise to economics as a *social system* do not give rise to law as such, both *law* and *morality* are *prerequisites* for the complex *modern economic system*. Law defines the *property rights*, and *governs* the *exchanges*. The *motive force* that connects law to economics is the *need for security* for the parties to the exchanges, which is part of the motivational force that underlies law generally, and is included in Maslow's hierarchy of needs.

Not only does law define *property rights* and create the *contractual basis for exchanges*, it enforces those *rights*. The benefits produced by elementary economics were further enhanced by participation in *symbol recognition participation in consciousness, mathematical participation in consciousness*, and *electronic participation in consciousness.* But as economic processes became more complicated, the misunderstandings and outright treachery in the exchanges became ominous possibilities. The *enforcement* power of law became an increasingly necessary requirement to assure that property rights were respected, and that transactions of exchanges were performed as agreed. Every textbook for a beginner's course in economics lays out certain *prerequisites* for economics. *Law* is one of those *prerequisites.* Modern economics would not work without a *system of law that establishes and enforces property and contract rights.* In order for the *system of exchange* to work and become the complex system of economics capable of supporting the expanding human population in the biosphere, there had to be enforceable *contract and property rights.* Law *defines* those rights and usually has to do nothing else for the economic system to work. Law is most effective in its support for economics when it accomplishes its purposes simply by defining rights, and without the necessity for any form of legal action for enforcement. The economic system usually manages itself naturally if well-understood property and contract rights are in the background. When that happens, law is also fulfilling its highest functional possibilities. Commerce *can* proceed without intervention of the *court system*, and is most effective when it does so. But even in the absence of court involvement, law is there providing the necessary social structure for economics to work. Most business transactions proceed very smoothly without any need for court involvement. But if there is disagreement, law *must provide the capability for enforcement of* property and contract rights through established procedures. There must be *dependable* property and contract rights that are enforceable if there are to be dependable *exchanges* so that society can reap the benefits that attend the most effective allocation of resources. But there must be a fist inside the glove!

Morality is also a *prerequisite* for economics. Successful commerce requires that people keep their promises. As already noted, people usually keep their promises without the necessity for legal action, because it is in their best interest to do so. The truth is that the legal system *could not* enforce every contract if people did not usually keep their promises. The whole system would break down. Usually, the court system doesn't have to intervene. If courts were required to routinely intervene in every exchange of goods, the economic system would not work. The *transaction costs* of *legal enforcement* through the court system quickly eliminates the economic advantage of exchanges that go amuck and require legal action. People must do what they promise to do if the economic system is to work. Once the system of contract rights and property rights is in place, backed by moral commitment, society *can create* economic value by exchanging property, and law does not usually have to intervene. When the legal system is performing at is best, and *normative force* is *fully operative*, and the law *morality* and *law* that rely on normative force are *indistinguishable*.[48]

EDUCATION AND FAITH

We have examined *economics, law, morality*, and *religion* as *primary social systems*, and now I will briefly examine one intentionally *institutionalized system*, for illustrative purposes. Education is a very important, intentionally *institutionalized system* that plays a major role in *faith development*. Its creation required creative imagination. Of course, not all *institutionalized social systems* are intentionally created, but many are. As we have seen, there are a very large number of intentionally *institutionalized social systems and institutions*, but I will analyze only this one important example that is deeply involved in the *faith system*. In the *second essay* in this series, I discussed *education* as a *source of faith*. Now I am focusing on the *education system* as a *social system*.

There is a strong sense in which the *education system* naturally evolved in response to the needs of the *primary social systems* that I have described and other institutionalized *social systems* and entities to which I have alluded. The workers for the many tasks created by the *division of labor* in the *economic system* require training. Business and political leadership require training. The education system now provides much of the training that is needed in every walk of life. The whole purpose of education is *teaching* and *learning*. All of the *primary social systems* that we discussed are prerequisites for the *education* system and other *institutionalized systems*, such as *politics* and *government*. But in the not-too-distant past, children often followed the occupation of their parents or entered into an apprenticeship to learn a trade or business. The young simply learned from their elders. The industrial revolution and the ultimate futility of subsistence living through farming brought changes. The parents (and often the kids) worked in the factories or on the farm. If education was going to happen on the scale needed for the expanding population and economy, *schools* were needed. With the growing complexity of the modern world, and growing population, more complex *mental operations* were required for the tasks at hand. The evolution of the noosphere required greater and greater knowledge and skills for the tasks required for the work at hand and human survival. Education was no longer an option but a necessity. So, the *education system* was called into existence by *natural social forces*. But *schools* do not just arise naturally, in same way that religion, morality, law, and economics evolved. Schools require structure that had to be deliberately created. That is often, but not always a part of the process of *institutionalization*. While *intentionality* is not always required for *institutionalization* of *social systems, faith* is always required to maintain them. A broad-based educational system evolved, with intentional planning and leadership..

The *education system* intentionally undertook the task of preparing youth for the *myriad skills* that society requires. In the process, of course, the education system also *collects and stores the knowledge and information* that the youth need to learn and pass on. In *essay two*, I identified education as one of the main *sources* of faith. Lev Vygotsky recognized it as the primary source of *higher mental processes*. The *education system* plays a critical role in the *development* and *preservation* of the faith that exists in civilization as we know it. In addition to its teaching mission, it is often the incubator for research and development of new information and *expansion* of faith. The modern education system is a much more efficient system for developing and taking advantage of talent than any previously existing systems for preparing human beings to exist in the biosphere.

Education became the cutting edge for *cultural evolution* and growth of the noosphere. As the result of schools, learning was no longer limited to the *privileged classes*. Upward social mobility was facilitated by educational opportunity for people of all classes. The very existence of schools brought social changes that were not necessarily the purpose for which the schools were established. Much more widespread human *participation in consciousness* has been made possible, and greatly enhanced by modern education.

Education, political systems, and *governmental* systems are all *social systems* that satisfy human needs. Because they satisfy needs, individuals contribute the *motivational force* to operate them. But unlike religion, morality, law, and economics, *intentional effort* and planning is required to establish these systems. But they, too, ultimately rely on *faith*.

Now that I have *illustrated* primary *social systems* and *intentionally institutionalized social systems* and their relationship to *faith* and *consciousness*, I do not believe that further discussion of the *political* and *governmental* systems as *intentionally institutionalized social systems* will further the discussion of *faith and consciousness* that is the focus of these essays.

A CONCLUDING SUMMARY

Consensus reality is the vast collection of human knowledge created by human *participation in conscious* that is the content of faith. I will discuss *consensus reality* in detail in the next essay. It is the software that operates society. *Society* is deeply involved in building *consensus reality*. Society builds the *social structure* that humans require for their existence. That *social structure* is contained within, and gives structure to *consensus reality*. Society uses *language* to install that software into individuals and thereby perpetuates *consensus reality* and *social systems*. Society operates as a *corporate unit*, with individuals called to diverse tasks by the *economic* system, trained by the *education* system to perform those tasks to serve the needs of society, and taught to work cooperatively by *morality* and *normative force*.

A progression of powerful *social systems* serves the structure of societies in Western culture. They evolved sequentially. *Family* is in the background of all the systems, and was there from the beginning. *Language* gave rise to faith, and that made *religion* possible. *Religious faith* that arises from *spiritual participation in consciousness* preceded *morality*. It had the power to organize the emotions and give a moral orientation to the masses of people, and that orientation gave rise to the consensus and *moral force* necessary to sustain society. That communal religious and emotional bonding, in turn, was a prerequisite for the creation of the *normative force* required for *law*. *Law* must have the *normative force* of *morality* to energize its concepts and operation. Without that motive force, nothing would happen to enforce law. Both *law* and *morality* are *prerequisites* for *modern economics*. Modern economics must have the support of a legal system, and recognition of enforceable *property* and *contract rights* in order to function. But law alone could not provide the necessary support for economics without reinforcement from *morality*. *Faith in law* including the *property* and *contract rights* it defined, combined with its moral underpinning, is more influential than the *active enforcement* of law in providing a good environment for *economics*. Despite often quoted suggestions by *legal positivists* that "law is what a court does," or "law is a prediction of what a court will do," there is a strong sense in which law is working properly and producing its best results only if courts are not involved at all.

The *primary social systems* arose automatically from the activities of *individuals* and *socially institutionalized entities* interacting with each other in everyday tasks. They were just doing things to satisfy their own needs, with no plan to create *social systems*. The *primordial social forces* that brought them into being are *still* very much *in operation* and are *still* very *necessary components* of the modern *social systems*. But *primary social systems* led to the *institutionalization* of *social systems* and *entities*, so that human *intentionality* could be applied to the creation of *institutionalized social systems*, such as *education, politics* and *government*, as well as myriad other *institutionalized social entities* that are now involved in the operation of *society*. *Intentionality* is often required for development of *institutionalized social systems* and *entities*. *Primary social systems* laid necessary foundations for the evolution of institutionalized *social systems*. Once launched, *institutionalized systems* developed the capacities needed to operate as somewhat *independent* systems. But they continue to interact and evolve together, with each providing support and affecting the evolution of the others. Each of them is very *faith dependent*. Human faith has been instrumental in producing an immense *social structure* that has been received into and is maintained by *consensus reality*. All these systems and entities derive their *motivational force* from the exertions of individuals who are trying to get what they need. All are integral parts of the biosphere, participating in the *consciousness system* that runs the biosphere. They all arose from the *mythological* approach to truth, not the *scientific* approach. *Social systems* and social *entities* depended, and still depend, on the existence of *nonphysical essences* that present them as phenomena to the human mind, in order to enter the *consensus realities* of various cultures. They must be capable of *abstraction*. We have strong *faith* in these *social systems* and the *principles* that have evolved that support them. Our faith is essential to their operation. They serve essential human needs, and our complex cultures cannot operate without them. Continued survival of the vast human population that occupies the biosphere today depends on them.

6) FAITH AND CONSENSUS REALITY

I INTRODUCED THE CONCEPT OF *consensus reality* in the *introduction* and in the *first essay*, in the description of the *faith environment*, but I will dig much deeper into the concept in this essay. *Consensus reality* necessarily resides in and is maintained by *groups* and contains the *abstractions* (all of them) that arise from the language that individuals use for communication in a culture. Individuals also *internalize* the language for *conceptual thinking*. *Faith,* and the *consensus reality* it produces, play special roles in *human participation in consciousness*. In the current essay, I move the discussion of *consensus reality* to a new level. I begin to work my way more deeply into a discussion of *philosophy* and *consciousness* by developing the concept of *consensus reality* in greater depth. The discussion deals with *faith's relationship to reality*. *Consensus reality* is a *way-station*, maintained by society, occupying a position between *individual consciousness* and *ultimate reality*. In a sense, it is the *collective memory* of the culture or subculture that maintains it.

Before launching the detailed discussion of *consensus reality*, which is the focal point of this essay, it will be helpful for me to review the plan that I used for presenting these essays. First, I described *faith* as *what we really believe*—what we think we know—and identified the evolving biosphere as the *environment* in which human faith develops. Next, I described *stages* and *sources* of faith, which expanded the understanding of the environment in which faith arises, and showed how the environment shapes the faith of individuals. Then I described certain important functions of faith: 1) its role in *human motivation*, 2) the part it plays in establishing *individual identity*. I completed the focus on the *functions of faith* with a discussion of the important role that faith plays in *institutionalizing social systems*: religion, morality, law, and economics, and ultimately *education*, *politics*, and *government*. And I explained the important concept of *institutionalization* of *social entities* and *concepts*. A key theme in this whole series of essays is the importance of things that exist, but are *not physical*. Throughout, I refer to this part of reality as the *nonphysical*. I have suggested the importance of the *nonphysical* from the outset in these essays, but the concept and its importance continues to expand. For instance, the *essences* of *social systems* and the *principles* that operate them are largely *nonphysical*, and *social systems* are absolutely necessary for human survival.

Consensus reality is the collective storehouse of cultural knowledge. It is created and maintained at a *group* level. It *arises from linguistic participation in consciousness* and becomes the vehicle for *group participation in consciousness*. I did not discover Vygotsky's work dealing with the *internalization of language* as the basis for *higher mental functions* until 2020 and had already developed my thoughts fairly fully by that time. Vygotsky clearly understood that *reality* is *the ultimate basis for language*, and that *language* reflects culture's attempt to understand *reality*, although he did not dwell on that point in his writings. I try to develop that idea in this series of essays. Although Lev Vygotsky did not use either the term *consensus reality* or the concept it represents, he pointed out in the early twentieth century that *language* maintains and provides *abstractions* that *individuals* internalize for *abstract thinking*. *Consensus reality*, as I am using that term, contains *all* the abstractions maintained by humanity. It also includes the *narratives* that use those abstractions to preserve, communicate, and transmit *meaning*. Although multiple *consensus realities* have arisen in the multiple cultures and societies that exist in the biosphere, most of us believe that there is only *one reality*. The *consensus realities* constructed by various cultural groups all engage that same *reality*, each in its own way and from its own perspective.

Consensus realities that collective human minds put together are absolutely essential for humanity, although they are imperfect. As we have seen, societies operate as holistic systems. *Consensus reality* is the collective memory of the culture or cultural group that maintains it. The human mind cannot capture the *totality of consciousness*, nor can it completely comprehend *ultimate reality*. Individual humans, without language and the help of society, could extract from the biosphere very few of the essences that exist there. The *essences,* or *phenomena,* are what make the biosphere intelligible to humans. Acting in concert, *groups* of people have *abstracted* many essences found in the biosphere as *words* and assigned communicable *meaning* to the components of the biosphere. *Knowledge* requires *conceptualization. Ideas* are important. *Consensus reality*, with the meaning I have assigned to it, represents the cutting edge of human *knowledge* in the human quest for *reality*. The imperfect faith of every culture produces the *consensus reality* that imperfectly represents *reality* for that culture—*imperfect* but absolutely necessary for the very *existence* and *operation* of the culture. But the culture or subculture that maintains its own version of *consensus reality* does not necessarily understand that its *consensus reality* is only an incomplete and imperfect understanding of *ultimate reality*. Each culture tends to incorrectly believe that *its consensus* is *the ultimate reality* and that other cultures just have mistaken beliefs.

DIGGING INTO CONSENSUS REALITY: THE NONPHYSICAL

The *collections of knowledge* that cultures maintain as *consensus realities* consist of *abstractions*. Some abstractions almost seem to exist only because there is a *useful consensus* about them. Take the named days *Wednesday* and *Thursday* for instance. They are excellent examples of *institutionalized social constructs*, and I will discuss them in depth. The named days of the week take on useful reality because *we all believe in them*. I will deal with this example of *consensus reality* in detail for illustrative purposes.

When Constantine adopted the seven-day week, the days were given names. They were named for the sun, moon, and five planets known at the time. The planets themselves had been named for mythological Roman gods. There was mythological/astrological precedent for the naming scheme. The Babylonians were first to adopt a seven-day week, and they had named their seven days after the sun, moon and five known planets. The Greeks had adopted the same scheme, using the Greek names for heavenly bodies. Norse mythology recognized Woden (Wednesday) and Thor (Thursday), so when the time came to apply names to the seven days in Anglo-Saxon, those names, the counterparts of the names of corresponding Roman gods, were used. Whatever connection there was between gods and days was *purely mythological*. The West dropped Babylonian astrology, Woden, Thor and all *mythological* Babylonian, Greek, and Roman gods from its operating faith system long ago. However, we still strongly believe in the days of the week that were named in their honor. The named days of the week are deeply embedded in our collective faith.

Many important concepts that humanity shares in *consensus reality* can be traced to mythology. We do not have to return to the belief in Babylonian, Roman, or Norse mythology to use these concepts, but to understand the essential role of faith, it is helpful to understand the important role that *mythology* played in the evolution of useful concepts in our faith system.

These concepts are *important*, and they are not *scientific*. Many things that we discuss in this series of essays are important and not scientific. Many very important parts of the way we live and what we believe did not originate in science and technology and must be sustained by *faith* without scientific proof. The faith that *mythology* and the *Axial Age* produced is still quite strong, but it has discarded many of the original religious beliefs. We need to understand how *our faith*—the faith that produces the **consensus reality** on which we rely—evolved, and the hold that the *mythological approach* to truth still has on *our minds.* We no longer call our important *nonscientific* faith **mythology** and often speak disparagingly about earlier mythologies that culminated in the *Axial Age.* We don't really have a satisfactory word for the *nonscientific* approach to truth that is essential for matters that science cannot deal with. But we really still have our own *mythological* approach to truth, and it is very important! Many important beliefs that did not arise in and cannot be substantiated by science are still required in order for human life to have any quality or even to continue in existence.

We cannot look out the window and *see* Wednesday or Thursday. There is nothing *empirical* to identify them. There is nothing physical about them. They exist in the collective belief system of the culture. They *look* no different from any other day, like Saturn's day! The *reality* of Wednesday and Thursday exists in our minds—*all* our minds—our *collective mind.* They are thoroughly *institutionalized.* Our collective faith system—*our* mythology—*demands* that we believe in the named and numbered days. The functions of society require a system that organizes days of the week. Of course, days are real. Years are real. Days come one behind another, and there is repetition in the annual cycle of days. Those physical facts are observable. But social life requires organization. The *conceptualization* and *organization* of days was not produced by observation of the days themselves, but nevertheless is extremely useful. Those concepts provide understandable structure for *reality.* It enables us to deal with the days and seasons *linguistically* and with *communicable understanding.* The collective maintenance of structuring concepts like the days of the week is absolutely essential to every culture.

Why seven days? Of course, the Bible says that creation of the world occurred in seven days. That religious source may help explain the tenacious Western faith in the *seven*-day week. The *names* that our culture has assigned help us *keep up* with the days, but that doesn't explain the names themselves. The belief in a seven-day week evolved even *before* the writing of the biblical account. The Babylonian religion, from which Judaism's Genesis creation narrative may have been derived, used a seven-day week. Most historians apparently credit Babylonia with the creation of that organizational structure. Roman Emperor Constantine adopted the seven-day week during the 4th century. The mythology that produced our *consensus reality* evolved culturally. But the result is very useful.

But why *seven*? Here are some physical facts that may be involved. The moon rotates around the earth *about* every twenty-nine days. It is *about* fourteen days from a new moon to a full moon, and about fourteen more back to a new moon. But these time periods are only *approximate* multiples of seven. Maybe these numerical facts entered into the numbering of the days of the week. But that would have been based on mythology and astrology, not science. And solar and lunar events and the rotation of the earth do not provide an exact *mathematical* explanation for the way anyone *numbered and named* the days of the *week*. Lunar months will not reconcile mathematically with the 365 days plus a fraction (a year) that it takes the earth to orbit the sun. *Days* actually result from the *rotation of the earth*. Seven-day weeks will not reconcile mathematically with the twenty-nine-day *plus a fraction* cycle of the moon, and certainly not with the recognized months that *vary in length*. The rotation of the earth, the orbit of the earth around the sun, and the orbit of the moon around the earth simply do not provide tidy mathematical relationships. Nevertheless, these physical facts may have been involved in the *numbering* of the days, but there is no better explanation for the *naming* than that mythology and astrology recognized a sun, moon, and five planets when the naming occurred, and all of that can be traced back to Babylonia. There may be some explanation about how the days came to be identified with these astronomical entities, but I don't need that information to make my point. The real point here is that there is no real physical, experiential way to differentiate Wednesdays from Thursdays. They are purely *institutionalized social constructs*. But they are part of a system that is absolutely essential for human life in today's world, just as law, morality and religions are essential. They exemplify the entire *institutionalized social system* that keeps track of years, months, weeks and days.

The human faith system took untidy physical facts and created a very useful system of names, numbers, and sequences for days, weeks, months, and years. Regardless of the origins of the naming and numbering, the human *social need for organization* maintained the useful organization, because that social organization of time serves our *social* needs. The useful result allows human groups, *participating in consciousness*, to plan useful, cooperative events. It empowers individuals to plan their times for work, play, rest, worship, and whatever else is needed, in coordination with other individuals. Coordination of the social activities of multiple humans is the key to understanding the reason that this system was *institutionalized*. These faith products are very similar to the kinds of useful social products that Émile Durkheim described as *collective representations* arising within primitive religion in Australia.[49] The seven-day system is quite resistant to change. The French tried a ten-day week after their revolution. It lasted twelve years. The Russians tried a five- and then a six-day week after their 1917 revolution. By 1940, they were back on a seven-day cycle! There is no logical or scientific reason that these alternate schemes would not work, but the *faith system* that maintains *consensus reality* about nonphysical facts is very powerful. The seven-day week is thoroughly *institutionalized*.

Regardless of the origin, humans *need* a comprehensible system of days, weeks, months, and years, about which there is consensus, in order to organize their activities in the biosphere. The system satisfies *social needs*. Faith enforces it because it is necessary. It allows humans to plan life and their myriad activities, including religious activities. The association with gods may have induced belief and reinforced the *significance* of the belief. The *quest for meaning* entered the process, and the gods of the Indo-European language groups got into the naming process. The names were good mnemonic devices. The *internalization* of the system begins in the first grade or before. *Mythology* sought and found ways to "teach us to number our days."[50] Constantine's edict probably helped. He had converted to *Christianity* by the time he opted for the seven-day week. The system evolved in the *power of religious belief*. Culture has preserved the system because of the social benefits. The power of the beliefs reflects deeply embedded *nonphysical essences* that organize imprecise physical facts! They bring something that is *real* but not *physical* into the realm of *social existence*.

Human faith dissociated the belief in named and numbered *months* and days from the *moon* long ago. The length of the months are very imprecise, and have little or nothing to do with the length of actual lunar cycles. Nevertheless, faith still *vigorously* enforces beliefs about calendar *months* and the *days* of the *week*. There is more toleration for criminal activity than for standing outside the consensus about days, weeks, months, and years. We *must have* a system to number (i.e.,1066, 1215, 1775, 1863, 1865, 2021) years, and again the system was founded in religion. We can remember and have great faith in the reality of the numbers. Everyone *must* agree about *Wednesdays* and *Thursdays*, regardless of whether we can agree about other objects and essences! They are part of *reality*! A person is *out of touch with reality* if he or she thinks today (whenever you read this) is Friday, August 27th, 1984! A person who actually believes such a mistaken thing is "not properly oriented as to time." Human faith has successfully appended numbers and names to time and fixed them in *reality*. One can get locked away in a psych ward if he or she gets far enough "out of touch" with that *reality*. *So, what is reality?* Whatever it is, it is not just *physical*; it includes powerfully held thoughts and beliefs and they are very *nonphysical*! I will deal with the debate about *physicality* in the *eighth essay*.

Scientists do not go to work in the lab to *prove* whether or not it is *Monday*, and would have no tools to deal with that question. They go *because* it is *Monday*, and may have taken *Saturday* and *Sunday* off because that was the "*weekend!*" Despite the obvious *importance* of the consensus, *science* was not involved in the way humans organized days of the week. It did not create and does not maintain the strong belief system that underlies human faith in the system of names and numbers for days, years, and months. Science didn't do it.

Of course, keeping up with recurring seasons requires detailed respect for the solar year. Humans calculate the length of the *solar year*—the earth's annual trip around the sun—with as much mathematical precision as possible. Science *does* work on that and has produced very precise numbers for rotations, orbits, etc. But that is not what produced the *system* for *naming* and *numbering* days and months. And a part of the reason for that important scientific work is to keep everyone in sync in the mythologically created system! The recognized *names and numbering system* arose in, or against a background of, *mythology* and *religious belief* and are products of and maintained by *faith*. Collective belief creates, organizes, and maintains our system for keeping up with all these important concepts that mark *invisible* time. The *names* and *numbers* are not *physical,* but they are a necessary part of *group consciousness* and extremely necessary in order for *group consciousness* to work. They are a part of *social reality*.

I have discussed these ideas about the days of the week in great detail for *illustrative purposes*. The use of *Wednesday* and *Thursday* to illustrate the *reality* assembled by *consensus* is an infinitesimally small beginning point for appreciating *reality*, much of which is *nonphysical*, that society has recognized and now maintains. *Consensus reality* has produced many other *abstractions* that are equally essential to our existence. Continual collection of *abstractions* builds and increases our *perception of reality*. *Consensus reality* is the reality that humans engage in daily. It is the direct product of our collective faith. It is *not all,* and certainly not a *totally accurate* reflection, of *ultimate reality*. But it is useful, because it participates in, and is *an approach to, ultimate reality*. So far, I have focused on *nonphysical concepts* that are part of *consensus reality*. I did that because it almost appears that they are *created* by faith, and have no reality beyond the faith that maintains them. But that is not true.

CONSENSUS REALITY AND ULTIMATE REALITY

Consensus reality does not include all of *ultimate reality*, but *ultimate reality* includes all of *consensus reality*. It includes all *nonphysical essences* that humanity has unveiled. There are different categories of *nonphysical essences*: (1) *essences* that represent *physical objects*, (2) *numbers*, that may be implicit in the biosphere, (3) geometric shapes that are implicit in the biosphere; (4) what I will call *structural components* of *physical reality—time*, *space, matter, energy*, and *motion*, that may be implicit in the biosphere, but differently from numbers; (5) *institutionalized social constructs*, (6) subjective essences such as *beauty*, and, of course, there may be other categories. In the *biosphere*, the *consensus reality* maintained by humans that obviously contains these *nonphysical essences* plays a very significant role. The *lack* of *adequate development* of *knowledge* and *language* concerning *nonphysical reality* is demonstrated by the fact that there is only the term *"nonphysical essence"* to represent these *diverse categories*. And when these diverse *"nonphysical essences"* reach the human mind, they are (all) called *phenomena* by some philosophers. This word usage gave rise to the word *phenomenology*, as the name of a very important branch of philosophy. There is presently no clear linguistic way to describe and differentiate these diverse types of *nonphysical essences*. Knowledge and recognition must always precede expression in language. Lack of clear *understanding* of *concepts* about *nonphysical essences* is revealed by the lack of adequate *nomenclature* for expressing them. There is great need for further development of the understanding, concepts and language for an adequate *phenomenology*! But in the absence of better nomenclature, I will continue to use the term *nonphysical essences* for all these *phenomenological essences*.

Ultimate reality includes both the *physical* and the *nonphysical*, and it provides the basis for all the conscious operations and *shared consciousness* in which humanity collectively participates. The *human social system*—human *society* itself—is a part of *ultimate reality*. It is *external* to every individual although every individual is an infinitesimally small part of it. Its *institutions* are represented by *essences* drawn from *ultimate reality*, that humans have **utilized** and *internalized* in order to create the *institutions* necessary for the ongoing life of society. Once those *social institutions* have been *institutionalized*, abstracted, assigned words, and entered *consensus reality*, individuals can *internalize* them.

Utilizing the *consciousness system*, the noosphere has built up a huge body of *collective knowledge*. The collection of knowledge grows with each generation. The noosphere has assembled the *reality* in which we live, and the fact that the reality in which we believe works and allows us to live together in the biosphere in large numbers is the evidence that what we have assembled corresponds in some way to *ultimate reality*, although our participation in *ultimate reality* is not perfect. The creative processes of consciousness are still alive and extremely active! Just because some *social "things"* could have been done differently does not eliminate their necessity or reality. For instance, in America, we drive vehicles on the right side of the road. In England, they drive on the left. It can be done either way, but a system—one way or the other—is absolutely necessary. In other social matters, such as naming and numbering days of the week, there were *myriad possibilities*, but the necessity for society to *choose one* and *institutionalize* it was not *optional*. A system *had to be created*, and once the essence for it was adopted, and the system was *institutionalized*, it was very much a part of *reality*.

Humanity depends on myriad *objects* and *essences*. It would not be possible for humans to deal with those objects and essences effectively without the benefit of words that *name them*. Collective faith of humanity has *named* all the *physical objects* and *nonphysical essences* that culture has successfully identified and maintained, and stored the words and names in *consensus reality*. To do well, individuals must participate as fully as possible in *consensus reality*. *Consensus reality* is the shared living consciousness of the group. But it is also the basis for individual *conceptual thinking*. Maintenance of *consensus reality* is not *optional* for humans as a group. It is absolutely necessary. Society is *real*. It *must* make choices *as society* although there may be multiple options for *mandatory functions*. Whatever option it chooses becomes deeply embedded in reality and necessity. This is the way *cultural evolution* works in the biosphere, and as it happens, the *biosphere is evolving* something *new*. Society needs to find and choose the *best solution* to whatever problem it is dealing with. Then society has to find a way to *institutionalize* the essence that it selects from the many options available to it. Individuals are only temporary occupants of the biosphere and temporary participants in the ongoing *consensus reality*, but society lives on and makes choices that are real, and *binding on individual humans*.

Individuals cannot disassociate themselves from the *consensus reality* that is created by the faith system maintained by their culture. Collective faith and shared consciousness create conceptual *reality* for our minds that is shared by other individuals. We manage our lives in *consensus reality* that includes the *institutionalized* options that society has chosen. We seldom even think of the mysterious *consciousness* that connects us with the biosphere and with each other, and with *ultimate reality*, and enables us to maintain the consensus.

Individuals confirm *"reality"* by comparing their individual experience to the experience of other people. If almost everyone agrees about the reality of an *object* or *idea* then we believe that it is real. *Nonphysical reality* is implicit in the very existence of *language*—the way we share concepts. Human minds deal directly with *external reality* through consciousness. Individuals do not merely deal with *representations* of external reality. Individuals directly *participate* in it.

Groups use *language* to *successfully create abstractions* of *physical reality* in the form of words that enable individuals to share that reality in groups. Of course, the *sharing* of *concepts* by *groups* of humans involves the use of *representations*. But *individuals* participate *directly* in the biosphere, not *indirectly* through *"representations"* of the objects that compose biosphere. Consciousness is there for the purpose of allowing sentient beings, including humans, to deal directly with the biosphere. *Consensus reality* that allows humans to share concepts can be very inaccurate. Nevertheless, *consensus reality* and the *nonphysical database* that it maintains is essential to human *social* life. It provides *abstractions* and *concepts*, and enables individuals to participate in the biosphere much more fully and effectively than any individual could participate in the biosphere acting alone.

The *first essay* in this series dealt with the *faith environment*. In it, I suggested that the *scientific method* is a refined form of *consensus reality*. It does not accept the validity of an experiment that no one can repeat. Scientists must *communicate* the results of their experiments so other scientists can repeat the experiment with the same results. Repetition and communication produce *consensus* among scientists. Consensus in the scientific community operates the same way that consensus operates in society as a whole. It is a *search* for truth. After other scientists confirm a scientific experiment, we can believe in the *reality* of the proposition under investigation, at least until it is disproven or further refined. Science capitalizes on the fact that *objectivity* involves group participation in reaching a consensus. *Individual* perception, even for scientists, is always *subjective.*

Consensus reality is the entire collective human faith. It includes everything that we humans think that we know. It is easy to reach a consensus about simple *physical objects,* like tables, chairs, dogs, cats, and all the things we can touch, see, taste, hear, and feel. However, an equally important part of *consensus reality* relates to agreement about *abstractions* or *phenomena that do not represent physical objects.* The concepts of time and space are *nonphysical. Numbers* represent *nonphysical essences.* It is more difficult to understand how humans reached a consensus about these *nonphysical things* than how they reached consensus about *physical things,* but as I explained in the preceding sections of this essay, the consensus about the *nonphysical things* is very strong, and very necessary!

Individuals do not *consciously* and *intentionally* create the consensus that I am describing. The consensus arises in the *consciousness system* and exists *implicitly* in the *belief system* of *society.* It is not so much "Hey, I agree with you," as "Hey, I see that too." No vote or poll is involved in establishing it. Consensus just forms naturally. Individuals participate in it through *faith.* Individuals are not usually aware of the processes involved in consensus formation. It is a learning process. *Collective faith* creates and maintains *consensus reality. Consensus reality* reflects group effort to *capture and express ultimate reality.* Individuals are born into groups, and participate in groups. Participation in the groups that surround the individual instills the group's consensus about reality into the individual. Individual faith is the effort of an individual to grasp reality, and *consensus reality* plays an important part in creating *individual faith. Everyone* shares in *consensus reality* even if they personally don't agree with some aspect of it. Collective faith maintains *consensus reality* based on the *belief* of individual members of the *group* that what almost *everyone* in their group believes *is* reality. Even *nonbelief* in a concept confirms the existence of the concept in a strange way. What is it that the non-believer *does not believe?*

Much of the consensus we accept as *reality* existed in the minds of people in existence when we were born. And most of it, and more, is likely to be here in the minds of living people after we die. The working consensus evolves as humans gain knowledge or knowledge becomes obsolete. It becomes more accurate with each generation.

CONSENSUS AND PHYSICAL THINGS

It is easier for humans to reach a consensus about *physical objects* than to reach a consensus about *essences* that are *not physical,* because they can see physical objects and easily *share* abstractions of those objects. I can see a table or a horse, and you see the same table or horse. The *physical world* that all sentient beings share is the *common denominator* for consciousness. All humans share it. But *physical objects* actually present themselves to the human mind as *nonphysical phenomena. Words* are abstractions: they represent the *physical object.* They are the *name* that a *group* of humans has substituted for the *phenomenon* that presented the *physical object* to several human minds—the *representations* of physical objects that the eyes, ears and other senses presented to those human minds.

All of this is part of the *system that is consciousness.* The *essences*—the *phenomena*—presented to the mind by vision and hearing, etc. are *not physical,* or at least not completely physical. Essences that present physical objects are, in a sense, *pre-mental abstractions* of the physical objects. The *media* for transmission of the essences may have some relation to something physical— light, sound—right up to the point where *knowledge* appears, but the *gap between physical processes and ultimate thought processes is sizeable!* We use words to *represent* physical objects, but only after the *essences* of those objects have presented themselves to human minds, received names, and become concepts. The *words* that the group assigns to represent the physical objects in language—*the abstractions*—are *not physical,* nor are the *essences* or *phenomena* that present them to the mind. The *process of abstraction* is a part of what is involved in *linguistic participation in consciousness.*

Suppose we *have no language,* but you and I both see a dog at the same time, and I say "dog." You hear the sound of my voice, and you say "dog?" I nod my head and say "dog" again. We are on our way to creating a *word* that represents a *physical object.* The word stands for the animal, and later, we can communicate about that animal without seeing it. And we create *categories*: another dog comes by, and I say "dog," and you nod and smile and say "dog." A third dog comes by, and you say "dog" and I nod and clap my hands in celebration. We have created a *category.* But then it gets complicated. My dog comes by and I say "Deuce," and you look puzzled. I will not drag this illustration out, but after I say "Deuce," Deuce just wags his tail and doesn't say anything, even though he knows he is *Deuce.* He even wags to "old dog," but I don't think that he knows that he is *a* dog: he thinks he is *the dog,* as well as *Deuce.* But let's make one more quick point about the dog *concept.* The dog example just given will help to illustrate how *thought* originates. We assigned *meaning* to the oral sound, *"dog."* After we generate that word, I can *think* about the dog, and I have a matching *abstraction*—a *concept—dog*! I am *thinking abstractly.* If you reread the short dog narrative and think about it, you can easily see not only a *word,* but a *thought* developing.

But naming and abstraction are even more complicated than that. *Nothing* comes by and I don't say anything, or I actually *say the word "noth-ing."* When I say the word *"nothing"* you look puzzled. I won't even try to discuss the *conceptual complexity* here! No doubt, you can think your way through it! Please just pause and meditate on *"nothing"* and *"nothing comes by"* for a few seconds. It is easy to see how we get to a consensus about *phys-ical objects* like dogs, but not quite so easy to see how we get to a consensus about *nonphysical essences* such as *"nothing." Nonphysical* essences, such as *time, space,* and *numbers* are quite important. Somehow, *schemas* or *archetypes* enable us to identify *nonphysical essences* of *physical objects* and assign a *name* (like *dog*). At that level, the attachment of *meaning* to a *sound* seems pretty simple, even though the mental processes that are involved are really quite mysterious. But then when the process of attaching *essences* and *assigning words* is *extrapolated* to the *abstraction* of complex *nonphysical essences,* like *nothing* or *e=mc2,* the mystery is greatly compounded! We know where *physical objects* are when we see them, but *where does the nonphysical stuff come from,* and *where is it when we are not thinking about it?* The *nonphysical* does not seem to be *confined* by *time* and *space.*

Physical objects are the things that we can see, touch, taste, hear, or feel. We can measure them and deal with them mathematically. Science has done extremely well with them. But importantly, for the present discussion, we *name* them, and the *name* is an *abstraction* and *not* physical. It represents an *essence* of the *physical object* that presented itself to the human mind as a *phenomenon.* We have a strong consensus about many physical objects. The *consensus* actually involves both the *physical objects* and the *phenomena* that present them to the mind (or the *nonphysical essence* that the mind captures with use of the senses). *Linguistic participation in consciousness* lets humans substitute *words* for the *phenomena,* and then human groups can share concepts in language, but like other phenomena recognized by the mind, words are *nonphysical.* They are *abstractions.*

Humanity did not do much with the *process of abstraction* until it developed the ability to share knowledge by using *language.* To use language to share thoughts about a *physical object,* humanity *had to* assign the object a *name.* The name—a word that represents the *physical object*—must become a part of *language* if humans are to communicate and preserve knowledge about it. Physical objects had to be *abstracted* and represented by *words* before the human group could *share* knowledge about the object with language. The substitution of the *name* for the *phenomenon* that presents the object to human minds enables the group to include the abstraction of the *physical object* in *consensus reality*. The ability of the *group* to deal effectively with *physical objects* is greatly enhanced when they *abstract* them and include them in the shared *vocabulary*.

No doubt, the most important function of the *noosphere* for humans was the abstraction of physical objects. And no doubt, the creation of the very first word involved at least two humans, and a scenario like the one depicted in the "dog" story that I presented above. Language is social. But naming *physical objects* made it easier for humans to deal with physical objects. They could deal with them *mentally* and *identify them*, and share them abstractly with other humans, even if they were not looking at them. And they could deal with the *abstractions*. Words like *TIGER* and *SNAKE* probably caught on fast! Naming *physical objects* also made it easier to *exchange* the objects and made *systems of exchange*—rudimentary economics—more feasible. Abstraction, and the assigning of names to physical objects, made almost any task that required any kind of cooperative effort among humans that involved those objects easier to accomplish. Science can deal with *physical* objects but cannot deal with the *nonphysical ones* in the same way. And it can only deal as it does with the *physical objects* because it has *socially created words* and *language* that enable it to share the *nonphysical abstraction* and *concepts* of physical objects. Perhaps the relative ease with which humans can abstract physical objects entered into the decision of Galileo to choose *physical objects* for science to study. *Nonphysical essences* like the essences for *Wednesday* and *Thursday* whose reality are imbedded in the reality of society and its necessary operations are much more complicated to deal with.

It is important to note that the *very first human use of words* involved the *process of abstraction*. But now we need to take the discussion of *abstraction* to a different level. The *process of abstraction* and the *concept of abstraction* are two different things. The *process of abstraction* obviously had to be in use and recognized by humans before humans could develop the *concept of abstraction.* Humanity could not create a *concept of abstraction* until after it had developed the *process of abstraction* and *consensus reality. Abstraction* is not just an individual thing. It involves group sharing of concepts that *represent* objects. The *concept of abstraction* (that is, the *thing* represented by the word *abstraction*) is the *abstraction* of the *process of abstraction*. The *process* of abstraction can *operate* without anyone thinking about the *concept* of abstraction. My dog knows that *he* is *Deuce*[51] and is into the *process* of abstraction that far. But he doesn't know that the word *Deuce* is an *abstraction*. Although Deuce is *aware* that he is *Deuce,* he doesn't know that I abstracted him! When I named *Deuce, I knew* that I was giving him a name. I know that when I named him *Deuce,* I *used the process of abstraction to create an abstraction,* although I probably didn't think about it at the time I named him *Deuce!* Humans have given the *process of abstraction* a *name;* its *name* is *abstraction.* That word represents the *concept of abstraction.* I am not just entertaining you with a play on words; this analysis plays an important role in Western philosophy that I will discuss in the next essay.

We cannot separate our *individual mental life,* in which our brains are involved, from the *consensus reality* that exists in our *group faith system.* Individual mental life—*participation in consciousness*—when engaged in abstraction, uses the shared knowledge—the faith—of the group. We *use concepts—abstractions*—when we think. As Lev Vygotsky pointed out, we *internalize* our *concepts* from the language of our cultural group. We learn the words, believe them, and use them. So do other individuals. The *function of consciousness* is deeply affected by *language* and *faith. Individual consciousness* is greatly enhanced and *group consciousness* empowered by language and faith. For *physical reality,* in the absence of the *consensus reality* that the group maintains, there would be no words and abstractions. Without words and abstractions, people just see *things;* they don't see *"trees,"* and do not even know that trees are *"things!"* Much philosophical analysis of consciousness deals with *abstractions* and *words,* not *observations!* Human groups would be almost powerless to deal with the *physical* environment in the ways that human societies must deal with it in order to survive, in the absence of *nonphysical abstractions.*

Consensus reality includes abstractions of both *physical objects* and *nonphysical essences.*[52] Faith deals with *abstractions.* The world of *faith* is not *physical,* and *consensus reality* is the world that we actually *know.* It consists of abstractions—*ideas*—that represent many *physical objects,* and even more *ideas* that represent *nonphysical essences.* There is at least *one nonphysical idea*—the specific or generic name—for every *physical object* that exists in *consensus reality,* and many additional *nonphysical essences* that have no unique corresponding *physical object or genus.*

As indicated earlier, *unanimous* agreement about a concept is *not* a prerequisite for that concept to be a part of *consensus reality* in the sense in which I am using the phrase *consensus reality. Consensus* does not mean that *everyone* agrees on a *definition* for *every word.* Not every word has a perfect definition. The *consensus* that creates *consensus reality* arises from "agreement" at a *more basic level.* It is a collective *mental recognition* that an object or essence exists. Maybe a term like *"quasi-agreement"* would help to conjure up the meaning of *consensus* that I am trying to convey. Consensus is about *existence* and *meaning,* not technical definition. The fundamental agreement at that basic level consists of the widely shared belief that *the physical object or nonphysical essence exists.* After that basic level of agreement—the quasi-agreement—is achieved, there can be endless disagreements about the *meaning* of *words* that humans create to represent the *objects* or *essences.* There can be disagreement about whether the words chosen accurately represent the *object* or *nonphysical essence* under examination. This is particularly true of *nonphysical essences.* For instance, most people agree that there is such a thing as *morality.* They agree that morality exists. But there are endless disagreements about the particulars. A *consensus that something exists* is a prerequisite for the word that represents it to successfully enter language and *consensus reality*. An agreed upon *definition* is not *a prerequisite*, and even if there is a clear definition, *meanings* conveyed by the word can vary. Please note the difference between *definition* and *meaning*. Words can be used and can convey meaning, even without an agreed definition. But that also means that words do not always convey to the hearer the *meaning* intended by the speaker or writer.[53] And meaning can actually be conveyed by sounds that are not words. We are both looking at a beautiful sunset, and you say "Ooo." I immediately understand what you mean.

There are many books about language, the structure of language, the origins of language, the parts of speech and their functions, the physical and nonphysical prerequisites for human production of speech, and anything else that anyone knows or believes about language. I read a great deal of that kind of material in arriving at the thoughts I am describing in these essays, but trying to capsulize that vast domain of knowledge would not advance the purposes of these essays. I think that it may help for me to try to briefly illustrate, without fully developing, the difference between *word definitions*, as provided by dictionaries, and *meaning* that is conveyed by speech from one mind to another. I will use two examples. First, ambiguity begins at the level of the sounds made by the human voice. An identical sound by the human voice represents the words *to, two, and too.* I hardly need to provide dictionary definitions for those words to make the point that the ambiguity of meaning starts with the very sounds that represent words! Simply uttering the *sound* for *to*, or *too*, or *two*, without context or *other words* conveys *no meaning*. Second, let's consider the word *going*. I invite you to visit various dictionaries, all available online, for the definitions of *going*. Then consider the possible *meanings* of the following collections of words that include the word *going*: "*going* to France;" "*going* to jump;" "*going* to college;" "*going* to start classes" "*going* on a diet;" "prices are *going* up;" "*going* to jail;" "*going* to hell;" "things are *going* to hell in a handbasket;" "*going* crazy;" "time to get *going*," "that's the *going* thing." You can think of others. In combination with other words, the word *going* can convey a lot of very different meanings, and dictionary definitions are little help in unraveling some of those meanings! This demonstrates the fact that *individual words* convey little *meaning*. Sentences, paragraphs, narratives and other collections of words are involved in the use of language to convey meaning. *Meaning* for speech and language necessarily involves a collection of words, so *definitions* of words and the *meaning* that can be conveyed by language are quite different things. New words can create new and different *meaning*, and new words are sometimes needed, but more often the existing collection of words, in differing arrangements, are quite adequate to convey whatever meaning needs to be conveyed. *Consensus reality* contains not only words, but meanings that can be stored in a vast number of combinations of words. The valuable thing that *consensus reality* collects and passes from generation to generation is *meanings* and not just words.

CONSENSUS AND NONPHYSICAL THINGS

In the analysis that I am about to present, I distinguish *physical* things from *nonphysical* things. At this point, I need to make it clear that I am talking about *physical* and the *nonphysical* in the sense in which those two words are presently understood and used, and with the properties currently associated with them. I strongly suspect that the meanings of *physical* and *nonphysical* will change with the passage of time, and that the distinction between them will become blurred, as more is learned about subatomic particles such as the *Higgs boson*, which interacts with other particles so that they either have or don't have mass. In the analysis I am about to present, I also distinguish *consensus reality* from *non-consensus reality*. There is a consensus about many *physical objects* and *nonphysical essences*, but I believe that there are also many things, both *physical and nonphysical,* about which there is *no consensus*. I will try to clarify what I mean by *nonphysical* in the current section of this essay. I will also try to clarify what I mean by *non-consensus* in the next section. I believe that the meanings of *physical* and *consensus* are sufficiently clear for the analysis that I will present, so that they do not need clarification. But I will discuss the *nonphysical* and *non-consensus* and try to clarify their meanings before I proceed with the analysis.

So first, let's clarify what I mean by *nonphysical*. I can *think* about a horse without having a particular horse or breed of horses in mind. You and I can *talk* about horses, without having a particular horse or breed of horses in mind. The *nonphysical abstraction* of *horse* exists in *consensus reality*. A particular horse is *physical*, but the *abstraction* of the horse is not. It is easy to reach a consensus about the *concept* of a horse and arrive at an abstraction. A three-year-old can do it, and can recognize and even talk about a horse. But we don't usually realize that it is the *essence* of horse that presents itself to the mind as a *phenomenon*, and that the essence is *nonphysical* and forms the basis for *the abstraction* that culture created which is also *nonphysical*. *Physical media and structures* may be involved in transmitting sense data to the physical brain, but the *phenomenon* somehow becomes a *thought* when that data takes effect in the mind as an *abstraction*. And the *essence* or *phenomenon* that presents objects to the brain, inside the head, through physical media does not seem to be physical itself. The *abstractions* that the phenomena produce certainly do not seem to be physical.

Words and *names* that represent *nonphysical things* are also an important part of *consensus reality*. We have talked about the *days of the week*. There are many others, such as *time, space, truth, beauty, love, motion*, and *justice*. *Words and names*, including the names of *physical objects and genera*, are *nonphysical*. All *ideas* are actually nonphysical. *Numbers* are *abstractions* and are particularly important examples of *nonphysical ideas*. If I mention *ten*, I might be talking about fingers, dollars, ideas, numbers, or cucumbers. *Nonphysical* things are involved in both *thought* and in *communication*.

As I have stated, *abstractions* of *physical reality* are much easier to comprehend than *abstractions* of *nonphysical essences*. It is more difficult to reach a consensus about purely *nonphysical essences* such as *justice* or *beauty* than to reach a consensus about horses. But many *nonphysical essences* such as *time* and *space* and *numbers* that our *senses* cannot detect somehow present themselves to our minds as *phenomena*.

Words and language are the elements of *consensus reality*. *Words* themselves are *nonphysical*, and they represent both *physical objects* and *nonphysical essences*. Consensus about a *physical object* or *nonphysical essence* cannot enter *consensus reality* unless its *essence* presents itself as a *phenomenon* to multiple human minds and those minds come up with a *word* for the *phenomenon* to represent the *physical object* or *nonphysical essence*. Words and language, mathematical notations, musical notations, and other symbolism are important tools of *consensus reality*. They create concepts and narratives that express *all that humanity knows.* They have greatly expanded human *participation in consciousness*. Unless we can express things that we know in *words* or other *symbolic expression*, we cannot share them with other humans. Words and language *express* all that humanity knows about *reality*. They are prerequisites for most of the ways that humans can share knowledge. But *words themselves are also nonphysical reality.* The reality that words represent includes the reality *constructed* and *institutionalized* by society. As stated earlier, these social constructs are *not optional*, and they are very much a part of *reality*. They are just as *external* and *real* to *individuals* as the *physical world*. For the most part they are in the *biosphere* when individuals are *born*, and still there when the individual *dies*. They are absolutely essential for humans to live together in the biosphere. They are very important *nonphysical essences*.

Let me inject just a reminder about terminology surrounding *nonphysical essences*. *Physical objects* present themselves to the human mind as *nonphysical essences*. The word *phenomenon* is used to describe the *nonphysical essence* as it is presented to the *mind*. After a number of minds have encountered a *phenomenon*, they can create a *word* for it, and use it in language. By creating a word, they *abstract* the *physical object*. Other individuals then internalize the *word* into their minds, where it becomes an *abstraction* available for *abstract thinking*: an *idea* or a *concept*. Nonphysical essences that are *not associated* with *physical objects* can present themselves *directly* to human minds as *phenomena* and become words.

NON-CONSENSUS REALITY

Consensus reality does not capture *all of reality*. There are things that humanity doesn't know, or about which humanity has no working consensus. Consciousness includes and/or allows us to reach out for reality that the human consensus has not captured. *Non-consensus reality* is truth and reality about which humans do not know, and/or possibilities about which humans have no consensus. Humanity obviously has not named the *physical objects* and *nonphysical essences* in this unknown, *non-consensus reality*. Ironically, the present *discussion* must remain *within consensus reality* because *consensus reality* is prerequisite to all human *communication*. There are *no specific words* for the specific objects and essences in *non-consensus reality*. But we know that there is reality beyond our consensuses. So, I can point in the direction of *non-consensus reality* with absolute confidence that it is there. Humanity does have a consensus that there is truth and reality *that we do not know about*, and for which we lack definitive words. That is *non-consensus reality*. In some instances, we may know or suspect that something exists but have no consensus about it. Physicists suspected the existence of the Higgs boson for almost fifty years before they verified it by experiment. But in other instances, we may be completely unaware of the *physical object* or *nonphysical essence* that exists outside of consensus. There may even be subatomic particles like the Higgs boson that actually play a role in causing consciousness, but about which we know nothing. Ignorance has no way to plumb its own depths.

Traditionally, the words *transcendent* and *metaphysical* have been used in the kind of discussion I am now undertaking. But in the present analysis, I am about to contrast **consensus/non-consensus** reality with **physical/nonphysical** reality, and the words *transcendent* and *metaphysical* are not useful for this analysis because their meanings overlap. *Transcendent* has several meanings. In philosophy, the word *transcendent* is an opposite of the word *immanent*. The *immanent* is immediately present. The things we believe to be *physical* are often immediately present. They are often *immanent*. The *transcendent* is not immediately present. The *transcendent* might *surpass physical existence* or even commonly understood abstractions. The *concept* or **essence** of a particular physical object *transcends* the object itself. But that, unfortunately, is also what *metaphysics* is all about.

The term *transcend* also sometimes relates to things that *surpass the capacity of the human mind*. For instance, **God** is transcendent. No human concept expresses or ever can express God's **essence**. In a sense, the *metaphysical* represents *nonphysical* reality. Like transcendent, the metaphysical *surpasses or exceeds* the physical. But definitions of *metaphysical* often actually include the word *transcendent*. In other contexts, I can use the words *transcendent* and *metaphysical*, for their traditional meanings, but not in the present analysis. This is an example of the inadequacy of existing nomenclature for *nonphysical essences.* The nomenclature is inadequate because the *nonphysical* has been given inadequate scholarly attention, and, as I am trying to explain, until a *consensus* is reached about a *nonphysical essence*, it cannot be assigned a word and brought into *consensus reality*! The deficiency of vocabulary presented a real challenge for me in trying to describe some of the ideas advanced in this book! But, of course, that is why I am writing the book!

Science has made great progress in developing knowledge of the **physical**, and the nomenclature for physical reality has developed commensurately. But little progress has been made in a long time in the development of knowledge of the **nonphysical**, and because of this, adequate nomenclature for the nonphysical has simply not developed. As we saw earlier, we must develop the **knowledge** before we can develop the **language**, and there must be **consensus** before **words** can be assigned to create an **abstraction**. Ultimately, with continuing development of theories of relativity, quantum mechanics, and other theories, some theoretical connection between what we regard as **physical** and what we regard as **nonphysical** may develop, but until that occurs, and consensus is reached, and appropriate nomenclature evolves, we are stuck with the nomenclature and understanding of **physical** and **nonphysical**, and the distinction between them that exists in our current **consensus reality**. Until new knowledge develops, and is assigned words, we really can't talk about it. And the seeming digression in this and the preceding paragraph is no digression at all from the topic of **non-consensus reality**. In fact, it illustrates the inexpressibility of **non-consensus reality**. If and when humanity develops knowledge of the connection between what we presently understand to be **physical** and what we understand to be **nonphysical**, I suspect that the new understanding of the **"nonphysical"** will still not resemble what we presently understand to be **physical**, because it will still have properties not currently associated with the **physical**. But the human understanding of **physical** and **nonphysical** is likely to change dramatically in the **electronic axial age**, and the two may begin to merge. If some currently unknown subatomic particle, or particle that exists separate and apart from atoms, is discovered to be involved in **consciousness**, both the **physicalists** and **nonphysicalists** will claim a "victory," regardless of whether the particle has mass!

Non-consensus reality is not included in the **consensus** produced by **collective faith,** except as a generalization. But understanding that there is truth and reality beyond our present knowledge is important. Although we do not know the cause and cure for cancer, we keep looking for them, because we believe they exist and we can find them. And even if we cannot bridge the gap between *physical matter* and *knowledge* in our understanding of the biosphere, we will keep trying. *Truth* does not end at the edge of present human knowledge. Progress in the noosphere depends on our *faith* that there is truth and reality outside and beyond our present consensus. If the noosphere had not produced faith in truth beyond present knowledge, it could not have produced science. Scientific principles that we now know and understand were outside of *consensus reality* in the recent past. We know from history that *unknown reality* can crash through the existing human consensus. Copernicus, Kepler, Galileo, Leibniz, Newton, Descartes, Darwin, Vernadsky, Bergson, Vygotsky, Durkheim, Einstein, and many others gained insights into reality that differed greatly from previously existing beliefs.

Faith in *non-consensus reality* is belief in an open-ended concept of *possibility*. We believe in *possibility* without knowing what is possible. We have faith that *physical objects* and *nonphysical essences* exist that we do not know about *yet,* and/or may never learn. They could be principles, abstractions, concepts, essences, or even physical objects. If we did not have faith in the existence of *physical objects* and *nonphysical essences* beyond our immediate grasp, we would deal with the world very differently from the way that we deal with it now. Like nonhuman animals, we would deal only with the matter at hand. There would be no motive for trying to find solutions that lie beyond present knowledge. Knowledge comes in pairs, like hot and cold, dark and light. So, we do not just *know*. We *know* that we know. *Knowing* that we *know* causes us to know that *there are objects and nonphysical essences about which we do not know*. That knowledge engages human motivation to search for further information. We act on what we believe. Faith includes the belief that *there is reality that we do not yet know*. So, we continue the quest for additional knowledge.

AN ANALYSIS OF REALITY

I prepared the graph displayed below to illustrate the present analysis. It distinguishes *consensus reality* from *non-consensus reality*. *Together*, those two categories include *everything that exists*. Secondly, it distinguishes *physical objects* from *nonphysical essences*. *Together*, that pair *also* includes *everything that exists*. Each pair represents all of reality, but they divide reality in two very different ways.

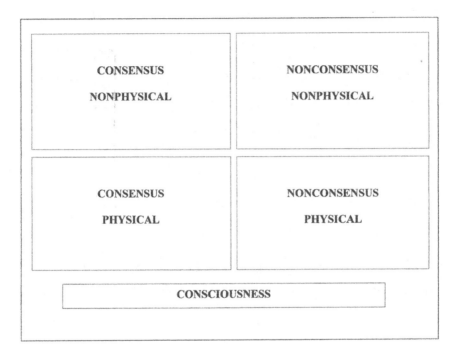

Physical reality is represented on the bottom of the graph below the horizontal line. *Nonphysical* reality is above the horizontal line. *Consensus reality* is to the left of the vertical line. *Non-consensus reality* is to the right of the vertical line. The *consciousness system embraces all*. Reality includes both *physical* and *nonphysical* objects and essences that actually exist in *the consciousness system*, as I will discuss in the *eighth essay* in this series.

The lower left quadrant represents *consensus physical reality*. *Consensus physical reality* includes tables, chairs, horses, trees, and all the physical objects that we know. It is the world of *physicalism* or *materialism*. It includes streets and bridges, houses and stores, cars, trains, and airplanes, the food we eat, the water we drink, and the air we breathe. It includes the *ecosystems* of the physical *biosphere* that provide all the physical ingredients necessary for human survival. It represents all of physical reality that we understand. However, *knowledge* of physical reality is not there. *Knowledge* is *not physical*; it is mental. *Knowledge* is in the upper left quadrant. Humans could hardly deal with the lower left quadrant without the upper left quadrant. Humans must have the *nonphysical* words and numbers—the *abstractions*—found in the upper left quadrant, in order to think and talk about *physical* objects in the lower left quadrant.

Consensus that is possible because of *linguistic human participation in consciousness* enables us to *conceptualize* the *physical objects* in the lower left quadrant. In the *consciousness system*, these physical objects *appear* to sentient organisms. Each is represented by a *nonphysical essence* that is in the upper left quadrant in our analysis. They appear to you and they appear to me, directly in our consciousness. But in order to share them with other humans or accurately remember them when not directly *perceiving* them, humans must *abstract* them and assign a word for the *phenomenon* presented by the physical object. Human groups create *words*, or *names*, to *represent* the *physical objects* that *present* themselves to the human mind, and then human groups can *talk* about them. Then these objects can become available to *individual consciousness* from a *non-perceptual* source. They are available *conceptually*. In the graph, *abstractions* are in the upper left quadrant. Our *individual consciousness* connects with that of others via the upper left quadrant through *language* and communication. Humans can deal with the *phenomena* that represent the *physical objects* of the lower left quadrant without directly perceiving them, once there is a *word* for the *object*. If my dog *Deuce* is not lying here next to the computer desk, keeping me company, I can ask my wife, Betty, where he is. Betty and I can also talk about Japan, because we have internalized the *institutionalized concept* of Japan, even though neither of us is there, nor have we ever been there.

Many of the things represented in the lower half of the graph were physically present in the biosphere before the human capacity for *linguistic participation consciousness* evolved in the noosphere. The lower right quadrant was very large, and the upper left quadrant very small back then. But then again, most of the *nonphysical essences* or *phenomena* now represented in the upper left quadrant were always in existence, but humans just didn't know about them, and had not assigned a word to represent them. For instance, I believe that the laws of physics existed before scientists found them and described them in words, and so did the quantum of light and the Higgs boson.

But back to the illustration. Modern society spends more time consciously dealing with the *nonphysical essences* in the upper left quadrant than with *physical objects* themselves. And there are obviously a lot more *nonphysical essences* to deal with than there were when language first came into being. Before *linguistic participation in consciousness* appeared, there was little, if anything, in the upper left quadrant (although the *phenomena* that relate to physical objects were in existence, waiting to be found, radiating from *physical objects*; and time, space, and force and other *nonphysical essences* were also in existence). Lots of *physical objects* and *nonphysical essences* were still on the right side of the graph because there was no consensus about them. But language empowered *consensus,* and for humanity, that changed almost everything about how they experience the biosphere.

In our everyday activities, *physical reality* that we *perceive directly,* and our *abstractions* of *physical reality* that exist in our memory, blend in *individual consciousness* so that we seldom think about the difference between *perception* and *conceptualization*. But in *human participation in consciousness, conceptualization* is just as important as *perception*. The *abstractions stored in memory* affect the identity that we assign to the things that we *perceive*. As I have mentioned, I do not directly perceive *tree*. The *word "tree"* is an *abstraction*. Although I directly perceive a *big green thing*, I have no word or concept to describe it as a *tree* (or even as a *big green thing*, for that matter) without the *abstractions* that I have internalized from *consensus reality*. *Tree, big, green, and thing* are *concepts—nonphysical essences—abstractions* stored in my *individual consciousness*, where I stored them after learning to talk and receiving them in my own mind as *concepts* from *consensus reality*. But in our day-to-day use of consciousness, we do not usually distinguish what we *sense* with our *sense organs* from what we *know in our minds*. We automatically use what we *know* to identify what we *sense*. Precisely because of this automatic use of *knowledge* in *perception*, *knowledge* actually sharpens sensory perception. Thus, faith and language enhance *individual consciousness*. When I think I see a big green tree, *direct perception, memory, and abstractions* are all involved in the *mental processes*. Individual *conceptual thinking* utilizes the content of the upper left quadrant of the graph, and *perception* invokes those meanings to interpret what it experiences. Of course, humans use the *words* and *abstractions* found there for communicating—for moving thoughts from one mind to another. But the concepts also *interpret* and *add meaning* to *direct perception*.

So, the upper left quadrant is the cutting edge—the *growth plate*—of the *noosphere*. As the noosphere evolved, it identified *phenomena* associated with the *physical objects* below the horizontal line of the graph, and *nonphysical essences* above the horizontal line of the graph. In the mystic realm of consciousness, the noosphere matched *phenomena* with *physical objects and nonphysical essences* and assigned *words* to represent them. Cultural groups reached a consensus about things that were right of the vertical line. Their actions established the existence of an increasing number of abstractions in the upper left quadrant. *Most* of them—the physical objects and nonphysical essences—probably already existed on the right side of the graph, *but* both biological and cultural *evolution* in the biosphere produces things that are *totally new*. This fact presents an interesting question, that I will not digress to discuss, but will at least mention: Did the *essences* of airplanes, submarines, computers, and automobiles exist on the right side of the graph before examples of the *physical objects* were produced? One cannot read Roger Bacon's prediction of airplanes and submarines in the thirteenth century without responding with a resounding *yes*. There is apparently *no limit* to the *nonphysical essences* that can be reached with *creative imagination*. There are plenty of unused ideas "out there." And science cannot prove that a damn one of them exists!

From the time that language developed, the pace at which humanity has matched *phenomena* with *physical objects* and *nonphysical essences*, and assigned *words* to them has steadily intensified as humanity moved from *oral* communication to manual *writing*, to the *Age of Print*, and now to the *electronic* stage in faith development and a new *axial age*. Likewise, creative thinking has reached into the storehouse of *essences* in the top right quadrant of the graph, and applied them to newly created *physical objects* for the bottom left quadrant of the graph, and recorded them in the consensus found in the upper left quadrant by giving names to the invented objects. In addition to *nonphysical essences* that represent *physical objects*, society has *institutionalized* many *nonphysical essences* in the creation of the *institutional structure* of society, as we have mentioned earlier, and assigned *words* for those structures. And then there are *nonphysical essences* such as *time, space, energy*, and *matter* that find their way into the *collective mind* and *language, consensus reality*, and *individual minds*.

Concepts of *physical objects* are in the upper left quadrant, but *physical objects* themselves are not there. Cultures and groups organize all of the *linguistic software* that allows them to function as cultures and groups in the upper left quadrant. By software, I mean the *nonphysical concepts* that empower the *thinking* of the culture. *Concepts* that empower our under-standing of *physical reality—time, space, matter, energy*, and *motion* all exist in the upper left quadrant. These *concepts* are not *physical* themselves. *Matter* is *physical* but the *nonphysical essence* that represents it in the mind is not. There are lots of *concepts* of *nonphysical essences*. We have men-tioned the days of the week. We can add months, and years, as *concepts* that exist because they have been *institutionalized*, and we all believe in them. *Numbers* and all *mathematical concepts* are there. Colors are there. Colors may relate in some ways to *physical reality*, but the *ideas*, the way that *we consciously experience* both *numbers* and *colors* are clearly different from *physical reality*. I can think about *red* without thinking about a red *object*. I can think and talk about *ten* without thinking about fingers, toes, or any other physical example. In short, all of the *ideas* with which we organize our understanding of the biosphere are in the upper left quadrant.

Words, language, essences, abstractions, and *phenomena* are *non-physical parts* of the all-encompassing reality. When we use *words*, one part of *reality* is describing or representing other parts of reality. Words some-times try to say not only what reality *is*; they try to say what it *is not*. However, *reality has no opposite*; it includes all opposites. Even *nothing* exists in the upper left quadrant! The addition of *zero* to the number system just a few hundred years ago empowered modern mathematics to help create modern technology. Like *zero*, the word *nothing* is a part of reality. What it represents is the *absence of anything*. So, it is obviously *nonphysical*. The very existence of the words *nothing* and *zero* and the reality they represent, demonstrates the fact that important parts of *consciousness* do not *inhere in the physical*. The *nothing* concept is *not physical* and does not exist below the horizontal line in our graph of reality. However, in the realm of words and thought in the upper left quadrant, the concept of *nothing* has a positive, useful exis-tence. It exists in *consciousness* like other *nonphysical essences*. Humans have not yet exploited *nothingness* in the *nonmathematical* noosphere to the extent that they have developed and utilized *zero* in the mathematical realm, even though Taoists at the beginning of the *Axial Age* realized its importance. Computer technology depends on *zero.* We cannot really imagine *nothingness*, but our minds can't encompass *consciousness* either. And we don't fully understand *zero*, do we? *Zero* and *nothing* have a lot in common. *Zero* has proven its worth in mathematics. Ironically, we are still struggling with *nothing.*

The *nothing* concept likely has analogous significance for *linguistic participation in consciousness* and its progeny that *zero* has had for *mathematical participation in consciousness*! I suggested its significance in the story of Joe, the amnesiac, in the essay dealing with establishment of identity. Let me suggest a possible application this understanding of nothingness in mental operations. *Zen* and *Yoga* recommend deep breathing and relaxation. The idea is to empty one's mind so that there is *nothing* in consciousness. One does not experience *nothing* by *thinking harder*, but by *thinking less*, and the result apparently has therapeutic effect! The beneficial effects are well recognized. *Zero* occupies a position between *positive* and *negative* numbers, and elsewhere is a *placeholder*. Perhaps *nothing* occupies a position between the *physical world* and *consciousness—empty consciousness*. Perhaps between *physical* and *nonphysical?* Does it have a role as a *placeholder* elsewhere?

Humans evolved the *capacity* to *think conceptually* as a prerequisite for *linguistic participation in consciousness.* The *capacity* is genetic. DNA contains the blueprint for the physical structures that *participate in consciousness.* But individuals actually *think conceptually* because collective human minds have extracted *essences* from the mysterious realm in which those essences exist, given them *names*, and posited and maintained them as *abstractions* in the upper left quadrant of the graph!

Then there is the lower right quadrant. There is not yet a consensus about everything physical. We have a consensus of sorts about tiny things like the Higgs boson, but it was difficult to reach that consensus, and there is still not a clear understanding of all implications. There may be other such particles. The consensus about great big stuff, like the universe measured in light years, and its myriad contents, has been difficult to reach, and there is likely more to develop. Is light a quantum or a wave? Light has no mass, so is it physical? Are there subatomic particles smaller than quarks? As mentioned above, human understanding of the *physical* and the *nonphysical* may eventually merge, but we are not there yet. We are limited to our understanding of the *present meaning* of those two words for discussion of what we think we know about the *physical* and the *nonphysical*, and those concepts are still useful. Before we knew about germs, there was no consensus about germs. Do red and blue exist as anything *physical* separately from *physical objects* that appear to be red or blue? Or separately from the impression they make on the mind? Are red and blue purely upper left quadrant stuff? So there is probably a lot of stuff that is physical about which we have no consensus.

The original *biological equipment* for human consciousness—unenhanced *biological senses*—did not enable humans to perceive a lot of the stuff that we believe to be in the lower right quadrant. But science developed mechanical tools, like microscopes and telescopes and much more, that expand human consciousness to discover a lot of the content of that quadrant. There are, no doubt, many other interesting things for science to explore that are still in that quadrant. What do we not yet know about subatomic particles? Do they have their own particles? Rattlesnakes and other animals allegedly sense their surroundings via heat or infrared wavelengths, butterflies use ultraviolet, and bats hear via high-pitched sound waves. What other types of *sensory equipment* are there in presently existing sentient beings in the biosphere that humans don't have and don't know about but might, in the future, find and create devices to utilize? Can sensory devices expand to utilize wavelengths that are not currently in use, as they have utilized radio, sonar, radar, X-rays, and other wavelengths that are currently used in human artifacts?

Perhaps the most interesting quadrant of all is the upper right quadrant. *No* consensus. *Not* physical. Purely *nonphysical* (both *metaphysical and transcendent*). Mere possibility. Potential concepts about which we do not have a clue. Like the next invention, or the next step in evolution; it's out there, but we don't know what it is. This murky quadrant is extremely important to our *faith system*. It contains *nonphysical reality* that we know is there or might possibly evolve, but we have no consensus—or do not even know about. The undiscovered. The unknown. Unknown scientific principles; mathematical theories that have not yet been worked out. Social institutions not yet imagined. Everything that is possible, but unknown. The upper right quadrant overawes us. Horror movies capitalize on the *emotions* evoked by our faith that the upper right quadrant is there, and the awe that it kindles. We obviously believe in it: horror movies scare us! Alfred Hitchcock and Rod Serling took full advantage of the upper right quadrant in their creative work. There may be theories and principles hidden in the upper right quadrant that are important to human survival. The upper right quadrant possibly holds many important *things unseen.*

ALL-ENCOMPASSING REALITY

The reality that I am analyzing—*physical and nonphysical, consensus and non-consensus*—encompasses everything that exists. Even if we could say what reality is not, (which we cannot do), that would not help define what reality *is*. As mentioned before, *reality has no opposite*. If we say that something is *unreal* that simply expands our understanding of what is real. The *unreal* is part of our *larger conception of reality*. Dinosaurs, unicorns, and passenger pigeons do not exist today in the lower left quadrant of the graph, but they exist in the upper left quadrant along with the zombies that philosophers of consciousness are fond of. Even dragons that look like dinosaurs populate collective human mythological memory and exist in the upper left quadrant. When we say that something does not *exist,* we are talking about *physical existence* and mean that it does not currently exist in the lower half of the graph. The beautiful ambiguity of the sentence, "*Nothing* exists in the upper left quadrant," may actually help to explain the mistake of the physicalists! Not only the *existence* but also the *linguistic expression* of *nonphysical* reality is a difficult to comprehend.

PLURALISTIC CONSENSUS REALITIES

Every culture has its own *consensus reality*, so there are multiple *consensus realities*. The Hindu worldview is not the same as the Christian worldview. The worldview of the French is not the same as that of Americans. Even within particular cultures, or religions, or countries, diverse racial and other groups have different *consensus realities*. African Americans have a *consensus reality* drawn from their unique cultural experience. Even Baptists and Methodists don't see things exactly the same way! During the course of cultural evolution, differing viewpoints, or mindsets, evolved for different groups and diverse cultures emerged. Groups located in different geographic locations, separated by insurmountable geographic barriers, including oceans, mountains, and sheer distances, developed different *faith systems*, and each developed its own *consensus reality*.

Let's explore the problem presented *pluralistic consensus realities*. Earlier, I suggested that the Biblical story of the *Tower of Babel* provides a good analogy. But what if there are two different groups: A and B. Group A calls the black-and-white striped animal *zebra* and Group B calls it *horse*. No problem. They get together and call it one or the other. Somebody says, "Just call it *pig*." But a group C calls something else *pig* and does not think anyone should eat pigs. I love BBQ but do not knowingly eat horses, dogs, or cats, although I understand that some people do eat them. Group D thinks zebras are holy, and Group E believes in reincarnation and thinks no one should eat the flesh of *any* animal. Group B does not think that Group C, a different ethnic group, is even composed of human beings.

This discussion, though flippant, illustrates the complexity of pluralistic *consensus realities* and the chaotic problems that they present. People in differing cultures take the differences very seriously. Challenges presented by pluralism—multiple *consensus realities*—are formidable. *Pluralistic consensus realities* are matters of *great concern* for the *electronic axial age* in which we now find ourselves. The differences in a pluralistic world about *nonphysical concepts* like *truth, virtue,* and *justice* are mind boggling. Concepts that are fundamental to the continued existence of the human race may be at great risk in an *intolerant* pluralistic world. *Faith* that will unify the world does not exist in and cannot be derived from the *consensus reality* of the *Western* world alone. Other cultures have been in existence for a long time, and *their consensus realities* contain very important elements of truth. All *consensus realities* are *approximations of reality*, seeking the same, *ultimate reality*. A common approach is vital, and is one of the toughest challenges facing the *electronic axial age*.

CONCLUDING COMMENTS

This essay focused on humanity's efforts to capture *ultimate reality* in *language, words* and *symbols*. Humanity's efforts have produced multiple *consensus realities*. When *linguistic participation in consciousness* first appeared, distance and geographical barriers already divided humanity around the globe, and humanity continued to migrate and spread. Physical division caused differing *faith systems* to develop. Modern means of *transportation* and *electronic participation in consciousness* have connected humanity worldwide for the first time ever. It is exciting to live in the *electronic axial age*, in which all humanity can be fully connected, but all is not well at humanity's family reunion! Widely divergent pluralistic views encounter each other very directly, and broad cultural differences conflict with each other. As long as humanity remained geographically divided with the diverse cultures and groups located in different parts of the earth, pluralistic faith systems could easily coexist. Now that they are in close contact, coexistence without conflict is not so easy. With intentional tolerance, they still can coexist until a common, unifying, faith evolves. Common faith will evolve eventually, one way or another. Humanity's challenge is to search for a common, unifying, faith, and to find ways to peacefully coexist until that faith evolves. For everyone to honestly seek truth is all that is required. *Religions* should intentionally work to forge a consensus among plural *consensus realities* by seeking *truth* in the sense of a more accurate understanding of *reality*. The effort must produce a consensus that will work globally. Understanding a lot more about *nonphysical essences* will play an important part in reaching the needed *global consensus*. I believe that *converging faiths* can produce a powerful, growing consensus and elicit even higher levels of human *participation in consciousness*!

7) TRADITIONAL VIEWS
OF REALITY

THE STUDY OF FAITH THAT I commenced many years ago led me inexorably into the *mystery of consciousness*. The exploration of *consciousness* further led inexorably to an attempt to explore human efforts to discern *reality*. The *reality* that produced, surrounds and supports humanity is the *biosphere*. Profound *philosophical questions* that I first encountered in the core curriculum of Huntingdon College, a church-related liberal arts college, pushed their way back to the front of my mind as I began to explore the nature of reality.

As a retired rural judge and retired general practitioner in the practice of law, I am familiar with both the advantages and disadvantages of a being a generalist. As a generalist in law practice, it was exhilarating to occasionally compete with experts. But it was difficult. Specialized knowledge has advantages. The advantage of a generalist, if any, is the ability to see the big picture more clearly, but the disadvantage is in the myriad details. Specialization gives greater opportunity to master the details of a narrow discipline. Education in that small liberal arts college instilled in me a love of philosophy, but did not make me an expert! Over the years, I have returned to philosophy frequently in my reading and thinking. Because I think that the issues that I am exploring in these essays are important, I cannot avoid a discussion of Greek philosophy, even though I know that I am a generalist, not trained in Greek or Latin, and that there are experts in Greek philosophy. Law is my chosen field. My interest in the *philosophy of law* led me into related disciplines, including general philosophy, psychology, anthropology, and sociology. I found that the cross-disciplinary study was very valuable for my understanding of law itself. And that study led to the thoughts expressed in these essays. So, with fear and trembling, I share my insights into general philosophy.

In the preceding essay, I showed that the effort of diverse collective *faiths* to find reality results in multiple *consensus realities.* Language empowered every human culture to compile its knowledge and pass it from person to person and generation to generation. Each cultural compilation is a *consensus reality. Consensus reality* is humanity's imperfect representation of *ultimate reality.* Because humans participate only imperfectly in the *consciousness system* that operates the biosphere, human comprehension of reality is limited to *consensus reality.* It is not humanly possible to comprehend all of reality. In fact, no individual human can even come close to internalizing the entire *consensus reality* of his or her own culture. There are *multiple consensus realities.* Each culture (and each subculture, for that matter) has its own *consensus reality.* No *consensus* captures all of *reality.*

In this essay, I describe *traditional* views about *reality* as understood in Western civilization so that we can compare those traditional views to what I have written about *faith, consciousness*, and *consensus reality.* This essay focuses on foundations laid by Plato and Aristotle. If you have already read the preceding essays, you will know that I am concerned about the looming loss of faith in Plato's *unseen essences* in the Western world that is focused on *physicalism.* The modern scientific world has moved to a modified *Aristotelian point of view.* However, I believe that in the big picture, the *ultimate implications*, if not the *actual expressed views*, of Plato and Aristotle can and must be reconciled. As I reviewed my understanding of their theories, I found that although I am deeply intrigued by Plato's theory of *essences*, I also agree with much of Aristotle's position. But it seems to me that Plato was pointing to some very powerful possibilities that continue to be very important. I believe that we must discern the broad direction in which Plato's thoughts were headed, and see if we can arrive at his destination, even if the map that he provided was only a preliminary sketch.

Aristotle was not a *modern physical scientist*, and Plato was not a modern *scientist of the mind*, and neither had the advantage of the additional *consensus reality* that has accumulated since their time. But we need to carefully maintain the trees that have grown from the sprouts that they planted. To enjoy the fruit, we must prune, graft, fertilize, and cultivate! The theories of Plato and Aristotle that emerged in the *Axial Age* are still very important parts of our Western heritage. Plato and Aristotle were important players in the *Axial Age* that led intellectually to the modern Western world. Their theories provide the foundations for the way we think. But we are now dealing with a colossal building, not just the *foundations*. To mix metaphors, we are dealing with the flowing stream, not just the *fountainhead*. We are into a new *electronic axial age* and must build new understanding, although that understanding arises from the *fountainhead* and rests on *foundations* laid in an earlier age.

PLATO AND ARISTOTLE

Plato used *dialogues* to present his ideas. His dialogues included conversations with his teacher, Socrates, and other speakers, usually a group. Many of Plato's own views are embedded in the dialogues, often revealed in the comments of the participants. That approach sometimes makes it difficult to be sure what Plato himself believed. Aristotle was Plato's student and became the tutor of *Alexander the Great*. Plato and Aristotle did not agree about the nature of *ultimate reality*, but together, their views are the fountainheads of Western philosophy, and have had significant influence in shaping Western views about reality. They are part of the fabric of Western culture. *Plato's thinking* found its way into the philosophical foundations of *Christianity*. *Aristotle's thinking* became the most respected philosophy in *Islam*, and ultimately became the basis for *scientific empiricism*.

The difference between Plato's theory and Aristotle's theory centers on their differing views about *universals*. Let me explain about universals. If I say the word *horse*, you know the type of animal that I am talking about. We are all familiar with the concept of *horse*. Plato held that *ideal concepts* are what is *actually real*, and that they exist *separate and apart* from any particular (physical) example. Separate and apart from any particular horse, there is the perfect *concept* of a horse, and only that concept is *real*, according to Plato. Aristotle said, no, *horsiness* is not what is real. He explained that after humans see enough horses, they know what horses have in common. The commonality is the *universal*. The *universal* can be given a *name*, and recognizing horses as horses promotes knowledge and communication. The *category* of *horse* is the universal, and we can assign it a *name*. Aristotle denied the existence of Plato's perfect horse that exists only as a concept.

Both Plato and Aristotle believed that they were dealing directly with what I am calling *ultimate reality*. They agreed that *knowledge* of that reality is derived from *universals*, but they strongly differed about the nature of *universals*. They differed about not only the *description* of *ultimate reality* but also the nature of *knowledge* of *ultimate reality*. So, both Plato and Aristotle agreed that universals *exist* and are important, especially for *development of knowledge*, but as we will see, they approached the *identification of universals* from very opposite directions. Let's look at their differing approaches.

PLATO

Plato held that *nonphysical essences—concepts*—and *ideas*—are what is real. The *forms* or *nonphysical essences* are *universals* that exist in a *purely transcendent realm* independently of their "come and go" replicas in the physical world. According to Plato, human minds *innately* connect with this *ultimate transcendent reality*. He contended that the *physical objects* that appear to human senses and disintegrate are only *representations* or imperfect copies of the real. The *real* consists of *forms* or *ideals* that are *permanent*, not the transient *physical objects* that we encounter with our senses. So, the objects that are *observed* in the *physical world* are not what is real, according to Plato. In his famous *cave allegory*, easily found on the internet by searching the words *cave allegory*, the physical objects that we observe are, by analogy, only shadows on the wall of his illustrative cave. The real, *nonphysical forms* that are real produce the shadows that we see on the wall. Plato's forms, or *nonphysical essences*, are *transcendent* and *metaphysical*. Plato's *forms* are similar to, and may be, what I have called *nonphysical essences* in this series of essays. Plato believed in *reincarnation*. He believed that humans *recall* the *forms*, or *nonphysical essences*, from previous existence.[54] In this regard, Plato's theory bears at least some resemblance to certain facets of Buddhism and Hinduism. So, for Plato, *learning* occurs through *introspection*, not *observation*. The mind identifies the forms that are real *internally*, within the mind, not through sensory examination of the world that is external to the individual. The external world is only a shadow, or appearance, of what is real. The *ideal*—the universal—is never *immanent* (immediately present) in the *external world*. It is *transcendent*.

ARISTOTLE

Aristotle offered an understanding of *universals* that was quite different from that of his teacher, Plato. Aristotle did not deny the existence of *forms* or *ideas* but contended they are *immanent* in *physical objects*. They always and only exist in *particular* physical examples. For Aristotle, *universals* either exist *within* the physical material composing the world or are imposed on existing material by artisans. He did not believe that universals exist *independently of matter*. (This position laid the foundation for modern *physicalism*.) Universals are not independent *substances*, according to Aristotle. Therefore, *observation* of the external world, not *introspection* of the contents of the mind, is the key to learning, according to Aristotle. Humans learn by looking, listening, smelling, tasting, and feeling. The *forms* of universals are present in the physical *matter*. Humans *sense* the *forms* that exist in matter with their *senses*. Some objects, such as horses, have attributes in common. The common characteristics can be categorized, and the *category* can be given a *name*. Aristotle's approach leads to the conclusion that *abstractions—universals*—are *identified* in human knowledge when humans *name* the categories or objects that share common characteristics. But the name is not the universal. Aristotle's theory is somewhat similar to my description of the *process of abstraction* in other essays. For Aristotle, the thing that is abstracted *contains* the *universals*, but for Aristotle, the *abstractions* are not what is real. The physical material and imbedded forms are what is real. His approach differs from that of Plato in that the abstractions of the *universals never exist as independent entities*, separate and apart from physical existence, in his theory. Aristotle may have been the first to articulate the *concept* of *abstraction*, and Plato may have never encountered Aristotle's *concept* of *abstraction*.

But let's review what I have said about *abstraction* in other essays. The *process* of abstraction, as I have described it in earlier essays, is that multiple human minds identify an object when they encounter its corresponding *nonphysical essence*, which the *senses* present to their minds as a *phenomenon*. The collective human minds assign a *word* that represents that phenomenon that presents the object to their minds. The word that names the phenomenon is an *abstraction of the object*. According to Aristotle, words are just *names* for the objects and forms that they represent. They are not the universals The imbedded forms or common characteristics are the *universals*. Humans identify the universals and give them a name. I agree with Aristotle that the *process of abstraction* makes humans aware of *essences* of objects as *universals*, but agree with Plato as well that there is something *more to the essences* that present the phenomena to the mind than is recognized by Aristotle, and that *nonphysical essences* exist independently of matter. The *nonphysical essences* that present the *physical objects* to the human mind as *phenomena* are something *different* from or in addition to the physical objects that they present. The *impression*, or *appearance*, or the *phenomenon*, is not the object itself, but the *essence of the object*. And even though *sense data* makes its way by means of *physical* processes to present the *nonphysical essence* within the *physical brain*, the *impression—appearance—phenomenon* that presents it to the mind and transforms it in the mind is *not physical*, but a *real nonphysical essence*—a *phenomenon*—whose role is to present it to the mind.

ANALYZING THE DIFFERENCES

The theories of both Plato and Aristotle have stood the test of time and have entered, *still unreconciled*, into modern thought processes. Let's look at their differences in light of what I have explained in earlier essays about *language*, *abstractions*, and *consensus reality*. Plato and Aristotle were necessarily examining reality within the *consensus reality* that existed in Greece in their time. They were doing so with the *words* and *meanings* that had been made possible by their *linguistic* and *symbol recognition participation in consciousness*. I do not believe that either of them conceptualized or recognized the existence and important role of the *entirety of the collection of abstractions* that I am calling *consensus reality* as such. And even if they had recognized its role, the concepts of the *biosphere, evolution, vital force, linguistic participation in consciousness*, atomic theory, physics, including quantum physics, and many others that are available to us now were not part of their *consensus reality*. Nevertheless, *abstractions* in ancient Greece, as now, existed in the *consensus reality* of Greek *society* at that time. Their *consensus reality* had arisen as a result of development of their *language* and their *symbol recognition participation in consciousness*, to the extent that *language* and *participation in consciousness* had developed up to that point in time. Plato and Aristotle differed not just about the *nature* of *ultimate reality* but more particularly about *knowledge* of *ultimate reality*.

Although the *process of abstraction* had been at work all the way back to the time when *linguistic participation in consciousness* first enabled humans to develop language, the *concept of abstraction* had apparently not developed until it was described by Aristotle. As indicated previously, Aristotle may have been the first to articulate a *theory of abstraction* and Plato may not have even encountered Aristotle's theory of abstraction. In his work *De Anima*, Aristotle described *abstraction* as a part of his *theory of knowledge*. But his focus was on *ontology* and *epistemology: knowledge and learning.* His theory ultimately led to the development of the philosophy called *nominalism*, based on the assignment of *names* to concepts, and identification of those names with what he had described as universals. But his *theory of abstraction* did not identify *conceptual thinking* to be the result of the development of language maintained by a group. He did not talk about any concept of the *collected body of knowledge* built by and stored in language, that I have called *consensus reality*.

As best I can tell, the Russian Psychologist Lev Vygotsky was the first to fully articulate the connection between *language* and the development of *concepts*, and even he did not talk about the concept that I have identified as *consensus reality*, the entirety of knowledge collected in language. I do not know of any attempt in either philosophy or psychology to develop or describe the concept of *the total collection of human knowledge* that can be communicated and passed on to succeeding generations that I have called *consensus reality*.[55] It seems to me that it is a very important concept because of its functions that I have described in these essays. Plato's theory about *forms*, or *ideals*, was definitely not articulated as a *theory of abstraction*, even though *abstractions* may have been the actual phenomena that he was dealing with and describing as *forms* or *essences* or *eidos*.

I suggest that an understanding of what I have described as *consensus reality*, which is the sum total of human knowledge expressed in a language at a given time in a given culture, sheds new light on the theories of both Plato and Aristotle. I suggest that *universals* as described by both Plato and Aristotle were *abstractions* arising from and related to the *language* that existed in the Greek *consensus reality* of their time.

Plato would *not* have admitted this to be the case and would have insisted that his *forms* were *eidos* that exist in their own realm. But the connection between that cloudy realm and individual human minds is not clear, and that is a problem for his theory. He thought that somehow human minds have *innate* access to the forms that exist in the *nonphysical* realm that he theorized. But he did not explain *how* the mind connects to that realm. For Plato, knowledge of universals is just in the human mind *as a given* and can be found there. The human mind somehow is connected to his *realm* of *universals*. I believe that Plato's *unseen realm* can be identified, at least in part, with the *consensus reality* maintained by his society. Of course, that alone would not fully explain the role of his *essences* and their operation in the human *mind*. But that unexplained connection in Plato's theory, if *consensus reality* is substituted for his *unseen realm*, would foreshadow the role that I assign to *consciousness* itself. I contend that consciousness came with the original package of creation, and that sentient beings only participate in it. Human *participation in consciousness*, as I have theorized it, gleaned the *essences*, the mental apparitions that Plato called *forms*, from the *biosphere*, captured them in *language*, and posited them in *consensus reality*.

Aristotle would have also disagreed with my suggestion. He would *not* have admitted that human minds utilize *nonphysical essences* that have an actual existence separate from *physical reality* that play a part in the creation of *abstractions*. Aristotle's theory of *abstraction* was a theory of *knowledge* that did not take into account the actual role of language and accumulation of knowledge in *society* that I have described as *consensus reality*. He did not believe that such *knowledge* exists independently of *physical reality*. His theory recognized that *individual minds* abstract *physical reality*, but he did not believe that the *abstractions* exist separate and apart from *physical reality*. And he did not adequately explain how the similar forms that individuals see in physical objects are dealt with as *universals* in a physical *human mind*. The conversion of *perception* to *knowledge that can be shared* is a very big, very important, very mysterious occurrence. *Therein lies the perennial epistemological and ontological gap.* To explain that *conversion*, Aristotle would have had to explain how consciousness works in the human mind, and neither he nor we can do that.

Although Plato and Aristotle both thought they were describing *ultimate reality*, they, like we, and all humanity of all times, were expressing their thoughts in their language, and were limited to the *consensus reality* available to them. They were necessarily dealing with their *consensus reality* and the *abstractions* that it contained. The theories of Plato and Aristotle about universals, although quite different, were both deeply and necessarily rooted in the existence of language. They had no way of analyzing *ultimate reality* from a detached viewpoint that preceded, exceeded, or transcended linguistic and symbol recognition participation in consciousness.

The development of the Greek language, like development of every other language, was made possible by *linguistic participation in consciousness* and involved the *process of abstraction*. *Language*, as I have shown, is the storage place for *abstractions*. Language was a prerequisite for *consensus reality*. As I have mentioned repeatedly in these essays, *words* are *abstractions* that represent *physical objects* and *nonphysical essences*. Language with its words and *abstractions* developed long before the time of Plato and

Aristotle. In their time, the *Axial Age* was occurring. *Symbol recognition participation in consciousness*—a *new form of abstraction*—had begun to operate, and to record and translate into writing the *consensus reality* previously contained only in *oral traditions.* The *process of abstraction* had been in operation for a very long time when Plato and Aristotle articulated their theories—long enough for their inquisitive minds to begin to inquire into the *process of abstraction.* In effect, that is what both Plato and Aristotle were doing with their divergent theories of *universals. Universals* certainly appear to be *abstractions.* Aristotle described the *process of abstraction* but dismissed the possible existence of abstractions as *independent essences* that are real. Plato recognized that the *essences* that we identify as *abstractions* actually exist and theorized that only they are real. But he did not recognize the existence of what I call *consensus reality,* or that the abstractions that he identified as essences exist in *consensus reality*—the *ongoing knowledge of the group.* Even more importantly, he did not admit that the *physical objects* represented by the *abstraction* even exist as part of *reality.*

In their differences concerning universals, which I believe are actually abstractions, Plato and Aristotle looked at the abstraction of the process of abstraction from opposite directions. Plato focused on the abstractions—the ideas—themselves, but thought that he was describing ideal forms that exist in a separate realm. They do, indeed, exist in a somewhat separate realm: consensus reality. Aristotle focused on physical reality that could be abstracted as a word, and denied that abstractions are nonphysical essences that exist independently of physical objects. Plato contended that his universals exist in the minds of individuals, although, as Vygotsky has taught us, they are there because they have been internalized from the surrounding culture. But they do, in fact, reflect the reality that humans encounter in the biosphere, insofar as humans can understand the biosphere. Consistently with Plato's belief, the nonphysical essences that are abstracted from the biosphere by humans, assigned names, and placed into consensus reality, are a bit more permanent than the objects that they represent. In formulating his theory, Plato focused to some extent on geometric forms, such as triangles, that the mind can seemingly intuit, independently of the external world, and that was part of his basis for thinking that the forms, or ideas are innate.

The universals that Aristotle described exist in an *external world*, embedded in physical matter that individuals can *observe*. The *physicality* on which he focused appears, at first blush, to be *objective*. But that is a problem for his universals. That approach ignores the problem of how the universals present themselves to the human mind—which I suggest is accomplished by their *nonphysical essences*, their *phenomena* that present them to the human mind through the senses. *Universals*, even in his theory, have to be something ultimately dealt with *by the human mind.*

Universals are necessarily dealt with by *human minds* in the theories of both Plato and Aristotle. This fact raises the unanswered question of the relationship between *consciousness* (in which the mind, at best, participates) and the *human body* and the external world for both theories. Our top thinkers still don't understand that relationship today, and it is safe to assume that Plato and Aristotle did not understand it any better than they do. That unresolved mystery prevents any unquestionably accurate description of exactly what goes on in the *process of abstraction*. Plato would say that his *innate ideas* enable individuals to *identify* the external objects that were mere shadows on the wall of his cave. Once identified, groups of individuals would *give it a name*. I don't believe that Plato thought that the *name itself—the actual word assigned to the universal*—came from his lofty realm of forms or ideas. Aristotle said that *individuals* observe the commonalty of traits in external reality and that *they* then create a *word* to represent the objects that exhibit the common trait (such as *horse*), and that the word is what the mind deals with. *The explanations provided by both Plato and Aristotle require the operation of consciousness, whatever it is.* No description of

Aristotle's concept of *universals* removes his universals from the operation of consciousness and the human mind.

Aristotle's theory enjoyed a bit of a practical advantage that Plato's does not have. We can *observe* the external world that Aristotle said is real, but not the *subjective internal* world, the world of the mind, that Plato said is real. We can see the *similarities* that exist among objects in the Aristotle's external *physical world*, but we can't see Plato's *innate ideas,* or any other kind of *idea* for that matter, not even today with MRIs. The only thing we can *sense* with our sense organs about *abstractions* is the noise of spoken words, or the sight of written words in *symbolic representation*, that require actions by the individual to *externalize* the abstractions. We can't actually *see* into the mind to see how it deals with either Aristotle's words that represent the universals or with Plato's *eide.*

But Aristotle's practical advantage does not resolve the consciousness issue, although it seems to have beguiled philosophical thought. Here's Aristotle's "advantage": it is easy to "see" how *observed* similarities can "cause" the "*identification*" of concepts to represent objects (Aristotle), but not so easy to "see" how invisible *essences—phenomena—*bring about the "identification" in *individual consciousness*, which is internal to individuals (Plato). Philosophy says there is a *chorismos—*an *ontological gap—*between Plato's world of *forms* and how the forms become thoughts in the human mind. That "gap" actually lies in the unexplained relationship between the *physical body* and the existence of *consciousness*. Plato approached that gap from the *mental side*, and Aristotle from the *physical*! That is what gave Aristotle the practical advantage described above. But actually, they both stopped at the same gap. It is a *significant gap—*it is the *fault line* between their magnificent theories, and is the source of what philosophers call the "hard problem." But the gap between *body and mind* for Aristotle is exactly the same as the gap between *mind and body* for Plato. The fact that Plato might have *believed* that the mind and body exist *dualistically* and Aristotle *believed* that the mind is *embedded in the physical body* does not solve the mystery or eliminate the gap, even though it makes it easier to slough over what philosophers call the "hard" problem! Aristotle did not explain the operation of the human senses and human mind. Neither Plato nor Aristotle explained consciousness. Until the *mystery of consciousness* is resolved, which does not appear to be imminent, the *ontological gap will remain* in place for both theories. That gap persists today, and bridging that gap is a major assignment for our new *axial age*.

The primordial, persistent belief that consciousness originates and resides in *individuals* makes the *process of abstraction* almost impossible to really explain. *Abstraction* is difficult to comprehend if we bypass *consensus reality*, and assume that every *individual* deals directly with *ultimate reality* and obtains knowledge directly from that source, and creates *abstractions* from the raw data of the biosphere rather than *internalizing* the *abstractions* from the surrounding human society and from its storehouse of *consensus reality*. Plato claimed that individuals deal directly with reality that is not physical. He is partly right, but he left out the important *role of the group* that created *consensus reality* and *language*, and he denied the existence of the *physical*.

Although *consensus reality* described in these essays explains certain *facets* of the *process of abstraction*, there are parts of the process that take place within the unexplained mystery of *individual consciousness*. But after a sufficient number of individual minds enter the mysterious realm of *nonphysical essences* and assign a *word* to represent a particular phenomenon or essence as an *abstraction*, the route into the foggy realm is charted and the results are posited in *consensus reality*. After that, other individuals can follow the charted route into the realm of *nonphysical essences* by using the words and concepts maintained by the cultural group to gain access to, and make use of, the *abstraction* or *concept* represented by the word. Plato intuited the *reality* of the *concept* thus created, called it *eidos*, and thought it to be *more durable* than horses and tables and other material things that come and go. But because the connection to the element of the *abstraction* that exists in *consciousness* necessarily occurs within and through *individuals,* it can never be *seen* and therefore will always escape the efforts of *empiricism.* But once identified, *abstractions* actually live for an indefinitely long period of time in the consciousness of the *group,* in the *consensus reality* shared by that group, and that creates the impression of *durability* that beguiled Plato. That is probably why he identified abstractions as *eidos.* And in *reality,* the *essence* or *phenomenon* that is converted into a *human word* is much more durable than the physical thing or category that it represents. Most abstractions are here when individuals are born, and survive their deaths. That, and the fact that the physical objects that they represent disintegrate, is probably why Plato thought that essences—his *eide*—were more durable than the imperfect physical examples that exist in the biosphere.

It was not necessary in ancient Greece, and is not necessary now, that we fully *understand* the *process of abstraction* in order to use it. According to Wikipedia, https://en.wikipedia.org/wiki/Abstraction "Thinking in abstractions is considered by anthropologists, archaeologists, and sociologists to be one of the key traits in modern human behaviour, which is believed to have developed between 50,000 and 100,000 years ago. Its development is likely to have been closely connected with the development of human language, which (whether spoken or written) appears to both involve and facilitate abstract thinking." Wikipedia is right! But understanding that *abstractions* and *conceptual thinking* are closely related to *language* does not explain *how* the mind does it.

Plato focused on the *mental nature* of reality that individual humans *experience* with their minds. He focused on the independent reality of what we now identify as the *abstraction* that *we* know to be created by *linguistic participation in consciousness.* He stopped short of recognizing the *collective* or *social nature* of the mental processes that were necessarily involved in creating the abstractions. He could not have seen that the only way that individuals could experience the world that he was describing was by *internalizing abstractions* from what I call *consensus reality* that had been established through the *linguistic participation in consciousness* of the cultural group that cooperatively brought his *essences* into his language. He missed the fact that as a practical matter, *abstractions* are necessarily collected and maintained in the *collective mind* of the cultural group, where *words* and *language* exist. *That* is why the concept of the horse is *more durable* than any living example of the creature itself. Instead of the collective *group mind*, he attributed his *unseen reality* of what we identify as an *abstraction* directly to a *realm of universals*. I am not suggesting that his realm of universals does not exist at all. *Nonphysical essences* exist independently of physical objects even before they are recognized, and they move into *consensus reality* and are available to *individual consciousness* only after they are recognized. And we certainly don't know where *nonphysical essences* that are *not related* to *physical objects* maintain themselves! They don't seem to have any relationship to *time* and *space*. But they are available to human minds. The essences are there in the biosphere to be recognized by humanity. But our grasp (and Plato's grasp) of the mysterious realm in which purely *nonphysical essences* exist is still very inexact.

Aristotle believed in an observable *external physical reality*. He believed that *universals* inhere in substance, or matter, and never exist independently of physical matter. He believed that individuals sense and deal with that external reality *individually*, and that they can discern the forms that inhere in matter and share their findings with each other. He described the *process of abstraction*, but he explained it as a *theory of knowledge* and did not explain how the process discovers *meaning* and converts *perception* to *knowledge*. And he did not explain how *consciousness* makes these things happen. He recognized the existence of the *soul* but did not explain how the *soul* operates. These things that Aristotle did not explain constitute *the chorismos* in *his theory*. A chorismos is, as explained earlier, an *unexplained gap*. The gap in Aristotle's theory is between *sensing* and *thinking*, just as the chorismos in Plato's theory is between *thinking* and *sensing*. The gap is the same gap. Something in Aristotle's process of observation of an object would have to *mentally* identify a *universal* and recognize its meaning, but he does not explain that mental process. I have suggested that multiple individuals must discern essences, create words and share their impressions of similarities using language and the mental processes that support language, and all of that too involves consciousness. He did not and we cannot explain *how perception occurs*, nor *how perception is converted to communicable knowledge*. Perhaps the *soul* does it, and Aristotle said that, but he did not explain how soul does it. It does not explain the *operations of consciousness* in the *creation of knowledge*. When reduced to these operating principles, his theory does not seem to be far removed from Plato's theory that nonphysical essences have an independent existence separate from physical objects. It is difficult to see how his theory could work without the actual existence of *abstractions*. Aristotle implicitly recognized that some role is played by human society in the recognition of forms and giving them names, but he did not fully develop the vital role that the group plays in creating *abstractions* and making them available for individuals to internalize for abstract thinking. But Plato did not recognize the role of the group at all.

As I have shown, the role of the group in creating and maintaining abstractions is indispensable. The group *verifies* Aristotelian observations of physical objects, and somehow, *participating in consciousness through individuals* creates abstractions that have *meaning*. The group creates *language* and *vocabulary* with which it describes and shares the results of observations. But mental operations are necessarily involved. The group shares and maintains the *collective* perception of reality in what I have identified as *consensus reality*. Aristotle denied the existence of any realm of *essences* in which human *participation in consciousness* connects with the *phenomena* of *physical objects* and *nonphysical essences,* which give rise to *ideas within the human mind.* Perhaps it would be fair to say that Aristotle did not appear to recognize the existence of any *ultimate reality beyond* what I have described as *consensus reality,* but he did not recognize *consensus reality* as such. Aristotelian philosophy did not provide a complete and accurate description of the *role that consciousness plays* in recognizing *universals.*

I suggest that the *mysterious realm of consciousness itself,* in which humans are merely imperfect participants, is the *unseen realm* of *eide* that Plato included in his theory of universals. In my theory of *consciousness as a system,* the biosphere itself includes *essences* that are not yet included in *consensus reality.* Some of them represent *physical objects* but there are also *nonphysical essences* that are available to the human mind, including the *social constructs* that I have described, that do *not* represent any physical object. I am not suggesting that Plato himself had a fully developed *concept of consciousness,* but his recognition of the importance of *unseen essences* seems to anticipate the *role* of *consciousness* that I believe we can now understand a little better, although we can't explain what it is or how it happens.

PLATO, ARISTOTLE, AND THE GRAPH

Now let's look at the differences between the views of Plato and Aristotle in light of the graph that I introduced in *essay six,* in which I analyzed the theory of *consensus reality.*

Plato's theory of reality recognizes only the *nonphysical* above the horizontal line. He believed that the *nonphysical essence* or *form* of an object is what is *real.* Every particular object found in the world is a mere copy or shadow of the real. The *mind's eye,* not the *physical eye,* connects with reality. All of reality is *nonphysical.* Therefore, for Plato, only the *top side* of the graph exists. Everything on the bottom side is just *shadows.*

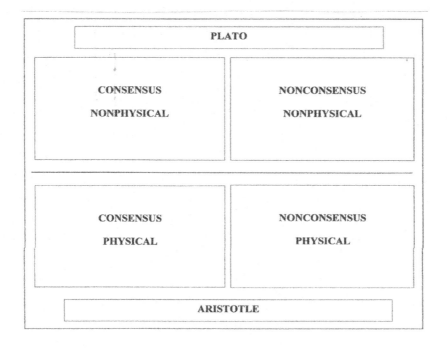

On the contrary, Aristotle argued that the *physical world*, and *forms* embedded in it, are *all* that is real. So, in Aristotle's theory, consciousness exists in the physical human body, and the bottom half of the graph represents *all* that is real. Humans *sense* physical objects and the *forms* or *ideas* that exist in those objects. *Ideas* or *forms* are *implicit* in the physical and do not exist independently of the physical. Humans infer the *forms* or *ideas* and give them names. For Aristotle, because he says that the *nonphysical* does not exist *separate and apart* from the physical, apparently neither the upper left quadrant nor the upper right quadrant exists at all. Although he recognized that humans somehow observe similarities and imbedded forms in the physical, that he recognizes as *universals*, and create *abstractions*, these play no part in his theory of what is *real*. The *universals*, according to Aristotle, are implicit the *physical* and he says the *physical* is *all* that is *real*.

The important point made by the graph is that the difference between *consensus reality and non-consensus reality* is not the same as the difference between *physical and nonphysical*. The vertical line that divides the left from the right side of the graph represents the difference between *consensus reality* and *non-consensus reality*. But for Aristotle, *reality* is *all below* the horizontal line that divides the top half of the graph from the bottom half. The *non-consensus physical* is the only *unknown* in his theory. What humans don't know yet is on the right side of the bottom half of the graph. In Aristotle's theory, there is no *reality* beyond physical existence, so there is apparently no upper half of the graph! This means that there is no place at all in his theory for any aspect of reality that is both *nonphysical* and *non-consensus*.

The horizontal line represents the difference between *physical* and *nonphysical*. For Plato, the *material world* below the line is a mere shadow of reality. All of reality is above the horizontal line. Plato's failure to recognize the importance of *physical reality* is a serious error. Humanity could never have learned what it knows about chemistry, physics, and all physical science using his *introspective* approach alone. Knowledge of the existence of these things does not exist in the mind independently of *physical reality*. The combined laws of conservation of mass and energy that are now known might have allayed some of Plato's concern about the lack of *duration* of objects composed of matter. We now know that the combined total of matter and energy appears to be very durable, but those concepts were not available to Plato. But back to the graph, for Plato, the upper right quadrant is there. His theory leaves room for *nonphysical concepts* about which humans do not know.

THE INFLUENCE OF PLATO AND ARISTOTLE

Platonism deeply affected the development of *Christian faith* in its early stages.[56] Under St. Paul's influence, and the writings of the Patristic Fathers of the Church, and especially St. Augustine, *the tenets of Western Christianity developed within a Platonic worldview*. Aristotelianism, on the other hand, had a profound impact on the *Islamic faith*. Although not embedded in the Koran, as Platonism is embedded in the Bible, *Aristotelianism* became important in the *Islamic* belief system. Aristotle's pupil, *Alexander the Great* had conquered the entire area in which *Islam* developed, and brought Hellenization to that area nine hundred years before Islam emerged. Hellenization was a strong cultural influence and it persisted in the area. That key development occurred during the period of time that Karl Jaspers has now identified as the *Axial Age*. The Greek thinking that Alexander brought to the area included the philosophy of his tutor, Aristotle. Aristotle's thinking likely permeated the culture in the geographic area in which Islam developed, just as the thinking of Plato permeated Greek/European culture. So, the Islamic faith arose and developed within an *Aristotelian worldview*. Plato's philosophy reappeared in Europe in the Middle Ages and was called *realism* or *essentialism*. St. Thomas Aquinas introduced Aristotelian thinking into Christianity in the thirteenth century, and Aristotle's philosophy appeared in Europe during the high Middle Ages and was called *nominalism*. The two were in sharp contrast, and were sharply debated.

Once we grasp Plato's concept of what is real, we can recognize his viewpoint in familiar Biblical passages, such as "And God said, let there be light, and there was light."[57] "In the beginning was the word, and the word was with God, and the word was God, and without him was not anything made that was made."[58] "Faith is the substance of things hoped for, the essence of things not seen."[59] "Now we see through a glass darkly, then face to face."[60] In these quotes, *reality* exists in the *idea*. *Essence precedes existence*. The very idea of an otherworldly *heaven* seems similar to the Platonic realm of perfect essences. The Platonic view of reality as reflected in these passages permeates the New Testament. St. Paul, a Jewish Pharisee from Tarsus, Greece, wrote much of the New Testament. His writing reflects the Platonic worldview. His missionary work was largely responsible for delivering Christianity to gentiles in *Europe* and into *Western culture*. So, Christianity arrived in Europe in a Platonic package, and that worldview deeply affected European thought processes. Regardless of theoretical differences, Jesus and Plato seem to have arrived in Europe in the same package of thoughts.

Both Plato and Aristotle exerted considerable influence throughout the continuation of the Roman Empire in Europe. Plato started his *Academy* in 385 BC. Roman Emperor Justinian closed it in 529 AD. The *Academy* taught some form of Plato's theory throughout the nine-centuries that it was in existence. However, the teaching of Plato's theory spread well beyond the teaching at his *Academy* in Athens. Plotinus, who lived from about 204 until 270 AD, founded *Neoplatonism*. Plotinus taught and wrote in *Rome*. Neoplatonism continued promoting a Platonic view of reality. Plotinus and Neoplatonism influenced St. Augustine, who was the leading philosopher of the fourth and fifth centuries. Throughout this extended time, the powerful Platonic *worldview* permeated the area in which *Western* Christianity was developing. Platonism provided the philosophical *incubator* for Western Christian thought and was a major shaping influence in development of the Western worldview that found its way into the modern era.

When the Western Roman Empire collapsed, and as the Dark Ages settled in, the teachings of both Plato and Aristotle faded in Europe. However, writings of early church fathers like *Clement* and *Origen* preserved Platonism in the Western Church. Platonism was embedded in the Bible, and church leaders, who were influential community leaders, read the Bible. But no one systematically *taught* the philosophy of *"pagan"* philosophers like Plato and Aristotle to any widespread audience in Europe. And Aristotle was not nearly as closely associated with early Christianity as was Plato, so little or nothing systemically preserved Aristotelianism in *European* culture during the Dark Ages.

Aristotle taught his theories about reality at the *Lyceum* in Athens. He started the Lyceum in 335–334 BC. Sulla, a Roman general, destroyed it in 86 BC. The first Ptolemy was one of Alexander's generals, and the Ptolemies succeeded Alexander's rule in Egypt after Alexander had conquered that entire area and died. The Ptolemies started a strong school of Aristotelianism in *Alexandria*, that involved the *Great Museum*. Some of Aristotle's library from Athens found its way into the Great Museum in Alexandria. The school at Alexandria was a powerful intellectual influence in North Africa and preserved and spread the influence of Aristotelianism. In about 600 AD, Islam originated in the Arabian Peninsula. It spread from the Arabian Peninsula into and through North Africa, including Egypt, where Aristotelianism was strong. All of this may help explain how Aristotelianism found its way into Islam. Islam spread across North Africa all the way into Spain. It also spread into the Middle East that had been controlled by the Seleucids, an empire founded by Seleucus, another of Alexander's generals. After Islam arrived in that area, it absorbed the Greek influence, particularly Aristotelian philosophy. During the early Middle Ages, Islam actively promoted development of knowledge of Greek Philosophy, but near the end of the Middle Ages the leaders of Islam put an end to that effort, and the scientific work that it had engendered.

ST. AUGUSTINE

Saint Augustine was the greatest philosopher and theologian in the declining Roman Empire, just before Europe plunged into the Dark Ages. He was born and spent most of his life in North Africa, where he rose to the rank of bishop in the Roman Catholic Church. This was before Islam came to dominate that area. He read the Neoplatonic Philosophy of Porphyry and Plotinus, and Neoplatonism influenced his own philosophy. His own writings included *The City of God* (early fifth century) and *Confessions* (397 AD). His work was the most widely read philosophy in Europe during the ensuing Dark Ages, and his influence helped make Plato's philosophy the leading philosophy in the West during the Middle Ages. The *essences* that Plato thought to be *ultimate reality* were quite consistent with the beliefs of Christianity and formed the basis for the medieval philosophy called *realism*, or *essentialism*.

ST. THOMAS AQUINAS

There was a renewal of interest in Plato and Aristotle in Western culture during the reign of *Charlemagne*, which began in 800 AD. But European scholars had limited access to the works of Plato and Aristotle at that time. It was not until the *thirteenth century* that the revival of strong interest in the philosophies of Plato and Aristotle really occurred in Europe. There was an appreciable continuation of the Platonic worldview from the early church, and Platonism was embedded in the Bible. Because of these factors, Plato's theories were more widely known and deeply embedded in Western thinking and the Church during the Dark Ages than were the views of Aristotle. The New Testament itself helped preserve the Platonic mindset. Philosophy applies the name *realism* to the *Platonic* theory of *universals* that arose in the high Middle Ages. Realism followed the Platonic concept that the *real* exists in *nonphysical eidos*, or *forms*.

In the intellectual ferment that produced universities in the thirteenth century, Aristotle was discovered by European scholars. There were translations from writings of *Averroes*, a Muslim Aristotelian philosopher in Moorish Spain, as well as from the original Greek. Some of Averroes' interpretations of Aristotle were not considered compatible with Christian doctrine. Aquinas, the leading Christian theologian, took the lead in disputing non-Christian aspects of Averroism but he also incorporated much of Aristotle's philosophy into his own theology. He introduced Aristotelian philosophy into Christianity and Western philosophy, but that did not eliminate the existing Platonic influence.

The medieval European philosophy called *nominalism* resulted from the Aristotelian influence that Aquinas introduced. The root word for *nominalism* is the same as the root word for *name*. Nominalists argued that *universals* were only *names* applied to objects and ideas. Like Aristotle, they argued that only the *physical* is real. They opposed *realism's* concept of *universals* that exist independently of *physical matter*. From the thirteenth century forward, Aristotelian philosophy has played a significant role, not only in the Christianity of Western culture, but in the *perception of reality* maintained in Western culture. Its insistence on the reality of external physical objects and acquisition of knowledge by observation provided the basis for *empirical science*. The great nominalist William of Ockham, whose incisive thinking came to be known as "Ockham's Razor," showed that many tedious concepts of Platonic *realism* added nothing to the best understanding of reality. In today's world, dominated by science, the Aristotelian emphasis on the *physical* has eclipsed the Platonic emphasis on the reality of *unseen essences* that was the philosophical underpinning of early Christianity and the basis for medieval *realism* in Europe.

DESCARTES AND DUALISM

We know that there is a *physical world*. We can see, hear, touch, taste, and feel it. We participate in it. Science specializes in detecting and describing it. We also know that humans have minds and *participate in consciousness*. *Individual consciousness*, although seemingly *mental*, and inside individual humans, also seems to connect with the world on the outside of individuals. But the connection between the *internal mental* and *external physical* has proven very difficult to understand. The resulting dichotomy, *internal v. external*, has tantalized Western philosophy from its beginnings. As we have seen, Plato argued that the *idea*—the *mental*—is what is real, while Aristotle argued that the external world, the *physical* is real. Plato thought humans connected to reality *internally*, through the *mental*. Aristotle thought humans connected to reality *externally*, through the *physical* world experienced by the senses. Platonic thinking entered early

Christianity and persisted. Aquinas writings about Aristotle, including the controversy about Averroism, attracted a lot of attention in the thirteenth century in Europe, in a mindset already permeated by Platonism, and the combination laid the foundation for *modern empirical science*. At about the time Islam was putting an end to the science that had been introduced in its realms by the Aristotelian influence, Aristotelian influence with its emphasis on physical reality was growing in the West. With the protestant reformation that occurred near the close of the Middle Ages, the power to the Christian Church to curtail philosophies that challenged its dogmas was somewhat diminished, and the stage was set for the evolution of science in Europe.

While Aristotelian influence was finding its way into the West, another important element of *participation in consciousness* was also arriving in the West via the Arabic influence. Although Westerners credited *Arabic numerals* to Arabian mathematicians, *Arabic numerals* actually originated in *India*. The recognition of *zero* as an *integer*, which was a critically important advance in mathematics, came from that source. Thus, Western humanity developed the capacity for full *mathematical participation in consciousness* in a form that would support modern science and technology during the high Middle Ages in the same time frame that Aristotelianism was finding its way into Europe. The theories of Pythagoras and other early mathematicians had influenced Plato, and Plato's theories are much more "mathematical" than those of Aristotle, who was more into biology. Although *mathematics* is not considered to be *Platonic*, its *essences* are compatible with and likely influenced Plato's belief in an *unseen* world of *essences*. *Mathematical participation in consciousness*, including the critically important Indian contributions, was a prerequisite for modern science and technology. And Platonism was still strong in the West.

The philosophical foundations of science in the theories of Plato and Aristotle and *mathematical participation in consciousness* enabled Galileo to carve out a "measurable" role for science and culminated in the thinking of *Descartes*. Before Descartes, Galileo had laid the foundation for modern science by pushing aside the *subjective* and *nonphysical* part of reality that could not be dealt with by science and creating a concept of science that dealt only with the *material world* that can be dealt with using mathematics and physical measurements.[61]

Early in the age of reason, Descartes said, *"I think, and therefore I am."* According to Descartes, an individual human is a *mind* with a body. Plato would have agreed with that assessment. And like Plato, Descartes dichotomized *mind* and *matter*. However, unlike Plato, Descartes recognized *both* the *mental* and the *physical*, but not as a united, *monistic* system of reality. He placed *consciousness* in the *individual mind*. He held that only *representations of the physical* exist there. That side of his dualism may be somewhat *Platonic*, but Plato had actually denied the existence of the *physical*. For Descartes, the mind exists independently of physical matter. Descartes did not deny existence of the physical. The reality of the physical world, as envisioned by Descartes, is more *Aristotelian*. It is an *external reality* that individual minds deal with, by creating and using *representations*. Descartes argued that the physical *appears to the senses* and advanced a complicated argument that concluded that the mind can rely on the evidence presented by the senses and thereby know that the physical exists. When reality is viewed as Descartes saw it, *dualism is unavoidable*. It expresses itself as the *observer* and the *observed*, the *subject* and the *object, subjective* and the *objective*, and *mind* and *matter,* and *mental* and *physical*. Descartes thoughts exercised tremendous influence in the ensuing Enlightenment philosophy in Europe. Immanuel Kant argued that *external reality* is composed of *"things in themselves,"* while the mind deals internally with *mere representations* of the *"things in themselves."* In the present discussion, we are tracing the transmission of the philosophies of *Plato and Aristotle* into the modern world. I will return to the problem of dualism and offer an explanation and solution in the *ninth essay* in this series, after dealing extensively with the nature of consciousness itself in the *eighth essay*.

THE GREEK LEGACY

The Greek metaphysics of Plato and Aristotle have dominated the thought patterns of Western civilization. They occupy the opposite poles of a very persistent dualism. It is difficult to escape their way of thinking, especially after *Descartes* refined their views and articulated his formidable *dualistic* approach to reality. We vacillate between Plato or Aristotle in deciding what is real. Aristotle dominates in *science*. Plato is still present in *theology, as well as some forms of phenomenology, and some theories of psychology*. Plato and Aristotle have not been reconciled in today's prevailing mindset with its opposing thoughts about *physicalism* and *consciousness*. It is difficult to see and understand that *both Plato and Aristotle were at least partly, but only partly, right*. Their viewpoints that arose during *Jaspers' Axial Age*, when philosophy itself was arising, shaped the very minds with which we Westerners think. Both became a part of the structure of Western faith. They had a powerful influence on what we believe about ourselves and the universe, but they differ significantly, and it is almost as if Western culture has a split personality. That split personality set the stage for the modern debate about *physicalism*, in which physicalists seek to eliminate dualism by totally discounting the existence of anything *nonphysical* and contend that the *physical human brain produces consciousness* that only exists in *individual minds*. That approach totally negates Platonic thinking. But there is a better way to reconcile the differences that I will explain in the *eighth essay*.

The revival and reunion of Platonism and Aristotelianism in the thirteenth century under Aquinas had remarkable results. Plato had believed that one can find truth and reality by searching the mind, inwardly. The truth lies within. The soul can access it. He did not believe that observation of the external world played a necessary role in humanity's search for truth and reality. But Aristotle, whose thinking had not been significantly present in the West during the Dark Ages, had insisted that to learn what is real, *observation* of the world is necessary. By incorporating the physical, *empirical* aspects of Aristotle into Western philosophy, Aquinas established a philosophical basis for development of *empirical science*. But Aquinas' thinking actually superimposed Aristotle's *empiricism onto the existing European Platonic mindset*. When this philosophical base also incorporated fully developed *mathematical participation in consciousness*, partly imported from India via Arabia, the stage was set for the development of *empirical science* in Western culture. Of course, Aquinas was not a scientist when he incorporated Aristotle's view into the mainstream of Christian faith, and his effort was not intended to establish science. *His* interest in Aristotle included not only the *physical, empirical* aspects of Aristotle's philosophy that gave rise to science but also Aristotle's concepts of *causation*, particularly the *prime and end causes: God*, for which science has not found a place.

Although Aquinas' work provided the philosophical foundation for science, the Church quickly opposed the *work product of* science that seemingly contradicted the biblical descriptions of the cosmos, Biblical myths of origin and Church dogma. However, the development of science, despite much Church opposition, increasingly shaped the mindset of the modern Western world from that point in time forward. It did so because *science works*. It produces powerful results. But while modern science accepts Aristotle's *empiricism*, it largely rejects or ignores parts of his theories that deal with *causation*, such as his *prime cause* and *end cause*. Christianity had been nurtured in the *incubator of Platonism*. Aquinas removed it from the incubator, equipped it with *Aristotle's empiricism*, and placed it on the road to its *end or final causes*. Science embraced *empiricism*, but did not incorporate *God as the prime mover and final or end cause* into its system of thinking. Those elements just did not seem to be necessary in order for science to work.

Empirical science has produced *useful* results. The successes of empirical science brought significant changes in what Western culture believes about *reality*. It moved Westerners away from faith based solely in the Platonic worldview of the reality of the *unseen* that had supported Christianity up to that time. It moved them to a worldview in the Aristotelian tradition that better supports *empirical science*. That change has created a *chasm* between *religions*—particularly the Christian *faith*, on the one hand—and the growing worldview that supports *science* on the other. Empirical science involves *observation*. It embraces *materialism* and *physicalism*. Its success has produced widespread belief that science is *the only way* to establish *truth*. Without the *empiricism* advocated by Aristotle, science could not have been successful. The modern world would not exist but for the *success* of science, and everyone knows that. Faith in God just seems to be based on nostalgia. But there is more to be said about *reality* from Plato's point of view.

Platonism, that recognizes *unseen essences*, actually played a crucial role in the development of science, as did the related *mathematical participation in consciousness*. *Mathematical participation in consciousness* is more akin to Platonism than it is to Aristotelianism. It deals in *unseen essences*. In this series of essays about faith and consciousness, I am describing a possible worldview that recognizes the continuing importance of *nonphysical essences*, and that includes the offspring of both the *Platonic eide, or forms*, and the *nonphysical* concepts of *mathematical theory*, along with the *physical*. As stated previously, Aristotelianism was *superimposed* on the existing *Platonic worldview* in the West. Platonic *nonphysical essences* combined with mathematics to provide the *theories* and *hypotheses* that were, and remain, crucial to the development of science. Science cannot function without them.

But there are important reasons to reconnect to Plato's line of thought that extend beyond the role that Platonic theory played in the development of science. The *unseen reality* that Plato's philosophy was seeking to describe is an important part of *ultimate reality* that we now tend to ignore. Plato's views play an indispensable role in *faith* itself. They play an important role in the indispensable *social systems* and *institutions* described in the *fifth essay* in this series. For instance, the indispensable roles of *morality* and *law* are dependent on truths that *physicalism* and *science* cannot prove and support. They play an essential role in the *institutionalization* of *social structures* that is absolutely necessary for human existence. We probably need to re-envision the social sciences of *psychology* and *sociology* and realize the *limitations of empiricism* with regard to them and bring them to focus on the nonphysical. *Religion* also depends on a continuation of Plato's vision. Plato's theory was a very important forerunner of important elements of the most *accurate view of reality* that is available to humanity. We now need to fully develop those aspects of reality that Platonism suggested. We need to apply the same vigor to Plato's *unseen elements of reality* that science has applied the Aristotelian physicalism.

Plato's philosophy pointed toward a critical part of the operation of *consciousness*—the *nonphysical* part of reality. In the *eighth essay* in this series, I continue this analysis by exploring the *system of consciousness* in the biosphere in depth. I will examine what we can know about consciousness, but frankly admit that parts of consciousness are, and are likely to remain, very mysterious. But *consciousness* is the key to all human endeavor. *Collective human consciousness* produces *consensus reality* which is, at best, only a shadow of the *ultimate environment*. The *essences*, or *phenomena*, provide the link that connects sentient beings to the physical biosphere. By recognizing the roles of *nonphysical essences* and *consciousness* in reality, we can re-envision the viewpoint of Plato and see how it anticipates the role of *consciousness as a system*.

A FLICKER OF PLATO IN PHENOMENALISM

During the twentieth century, especially the first half, there was a renewed interest in further development of philosophy of Plato. Edmund Husserl, Martin Heidegger, Maurice Merleau-Ponty, Jean-Paul Sartre, and others actually tried to provide a foundation for a philosophy by discussing the *essences*—the *phenomena*—that present themselves to the human mind. *Husserl*, a German of Jewish descent, was the leading voice in the *phenomenology* effort during the period leading up to World War II. His efforts were disrupted by the advent of Nazism. Phenomenology was a deliberate study of *consciousness*, and Husserl clearly based his efforts on the work of Plato, as he explicitly stated in one of his main works, *Ideas*. Although the phenomenology effort had an impact, it is my impression that the flicker of interest in Plato evidenced by the effort was overshadowed by the onrush of *physicalism* in science and philosophy, and the effect of World War II in Germany and the world. A branch of philosophy called *philosophy of mind* seems to be an Anglo-American counterpart of *phenomenology*. But the *philosophy of mind* tradition has come to be dominated by the debate about *physicalism*, and the *physicalists* have been more vocal up until now.

THE BEST OF BOTH

The accomplishments of Plato, Aristotle, and all the other Greek philosophers, who did not have the benefit of all of the scientific and other knowledge that has now accumulated, are truly remarkable. They provide a strong example for the progress that modern minds can make in the realm of faith, by moving beyond a mindset that is totally dominated by science. Modern society has its *consensus reality. Consensus reality* embraces both Plato and Aristotle and has not reconciled their differences. *Consensus reality* itself does not require reconciliation of the two. It can maintain conflicting theories. But there is a need for reconciliation of the two worldviews. Otherwise, Platonism may just disappear, and the loss will be tragic. We have Plato's *thesis*, Aristotle's *antithesis,* and now we need *synthesis*. Descartes did not provide that synthesis. Our understanding of the theories of reality that both Plato and Aristotle were struggling with need to evolve to a new level as we live into our new, *electronic axial age*.

Aristotelian observation has produced a huge mass of information about *physical reality*. Society has fitted the data into *concepts* and has stored the information in *consensus reality*. But that magnificent accomplishment does not contradict the Platonic belief that *essences have independent existence*. Adequate faith will embrace and complete the development of both the Platonic and the Aristotelian approaches to reality. The physical objects discovered by observation were there all along. New physical objects, including those that have been created by human imagination, have evolved. *Nonphysical essences* that exist independently of physical objects, including but not limited to *concepts* of *physical objects*, were also there all along. And in an evolving biosphere, it is possible that entirely new concepts will evolve. In the realm of faith, there is *unlimited room* for expanding the power of *human intellect* to deal with *unseen essences*. There are, quite likely, an inexhaustible number of *unused nonphysical essences* that are potential ideas. Humanity has not tapped into these powerful possibilities, except somewhat accidentally, because the powerful, limiting existing mindset, inspired by the success of science and technology, has strapped Western intellect into a straitjacket of *physicalism*.

Comprehensive *empiricism* is totally consistent with the *existence of nonphysical essences* that *explain* the products of observation as well as nonphysical essences that exist independently of physical matter. Human use of *nonphysical essences*, converted into words and narratives, supply *meaning* for human existence. Humans capture *biospheric essences* in *words and language,* and can share them in groups through *speech*. Individuals struggle to wrestle meaning from the words. That is precisely what gives rise to what humans know *as meaning, concepts, thoughts, and knowledge.* Thought itself seems to arise from the struggle of individuals to discern *meaning* for words and narratives internalized from *consensus reality* that represent concepts that arose from essences that humanity detected in the biosphere by perception. Although that does not explain the *existence* of consciousness, it adds to our understanding of human *participation in consciousness.*

One task of the *noosphere* is and has always been to match *Platonic ideals* with *Aristotelian observations* of physical objects and their behavior. The human mind participates in the process of matching ideals and observations. It takes in sensory perceptions and processes them. But it adds something from a *mysterious realm* that, based on traditional understanding of the word *physical,* is *not physical* and cannot be explained by *processes of sensory perception alone.* Group interaction in language completes the process. The possibilities for developing the power of the *nonphysical* is not limited to *abstraction* of *physical reality.* We presently cannot even imagine the vast expanse of the realm of the *nonphysical* that is available to consciousness, and undeveloped.

As mentioned earlier, Aristotle was among the first to describe the concept of *abstraction.* But he may not have realized the full extent of the role that language plays in abstraction, and *that cultural* groups are necessarily involved in the process *of abstraction.* He probably did not realize the extent to which the group *process of abstraction* generates the *concepts* and *knowledge* that individuals use in abstract thinking, as Vygotsky figured out. He did not admit that the *abstractions*—the *essences*—exist and are real, just as the physical objects exist and are real. He did not address the possibility that the knowledge portion—the *meaning* of the abstraction—is *Platonic,* and is, as Plato believed, the *essence of reality.* But *essences, and abstractions* are just as real and just as important—maybe more important—than the physical objects of the biosphere. That part of reality has been silently operating in the background of all scientific progress and is in dire need of *further intentional development.* It is my dream that this book is a start.

8) THE SYSTEM THAT IS CONSCIOUSNESS

THIS ESSAY WILL DESCRIBE CONSCIOUSNESS as the *system that operates the biosphere*, the culmination of a theme I have been developing in the seven preceding essays. That theme began in the *introduction* with a detailed description of *faith—what humans really believe*—and the role that *faith* and *participation in consciousness* plays in enabling humanity to cope in the biosphere. Without consciousness, there obviously could be no faith. Faith is belief, and consciousness is the only way belief can happen. The production of *language* by collective humanity empowered individuals to think *abstractly* and to assemble *consensus reality*. Language and abstract thinking were the keys to cultural evolution and human *participation in consciousness*, from that point forward. Faith and consciousness empowered humans collectively and individually to cope with the biosphere. The biosphere itself would not exist without consciousness.

Consciousness is *not* something that *evolved* in *human brains*, but something that *existed from the beginning*. It did not result *from* evolution;

it *caused* evolution! The human brain evolved to *utilize consciousness* in the biosphere. In a sense, the biosphere itself is *"conscious."* Consciousness in the biosphere *operates as a system* and has numerous elements. It involves the entirety of the biosphere in its operation. It is not likely a *single essence*, although there may be some *field* or *particle(s)* that play essential roles in the causation of consciousness. I am not saying that the *only* function of consciousness is to *operate the biosphere* or that it only exists in and is *limited to* the biosphere, but the important role of consciousness in the biosphere is a function that we can examine *abductively* and *comprehend*, without exploring its farther reaches. Consciousness likely has a much broader scope of operation. Its causal factors may permeate the universe.

A SUMMARY OF IDEAS FROM PREVIOUS ESSAYS

The first seven essays in this series are building blocks for the theory described in this essay, so I believe that a review will be helpful at this point. Those seven essays have already described much about how consciousness operates the biosphere.

1) The *introductory essay* described the ideas that are presented in this series of essays. In it, I suggested that consciousness did not evolve in humans and other sentient animals in the biosphere; humans *participate in consciousness*, along with all other sentient beings. And I also suggested that *language* plays a critical role in human *participation in consciousness*.

(2) In the *first essay*, I asserted that the biosphere is the *environment* in which human faith develops and pointed out that the whole human enterprise is part of the biosphere. *Consciousness* plays a crucial role in that environment, in which individual human beings are only temporary *participants*. I described *linguistic participation in consciousness* and the role that it plays in creating concepts for individual abstract thinking. *Collective human faith* builds what I called *consensus reality* by collecting the concepts

built by language and passing them from person to person, group to group, and generation to generation. *Consensus reality* and the knowledge it contains is maintained and transmitted by cultural groups.

(3) I described the *stages* of individual development of faith and the *sources* of that faith in the *second essay*. Faith is knowledge. The *primary sources* of knowledge for humans are found in the social/cultural environment in the biosphere. Individuals acting alone would not be able to examine the entire biosphere and extract from it all the knowledge that humanity needs for survival, but cultures—*groups of people*—can glean information *from the biosphere* and maintain it in the *consensus reality* of the culture. Consciousness enables that process.

(4) The *third essay* described the role of faith in *human motivation*: individuals do what they do to get what they need. What they need is supplied by the biosphere, including human society in the biosphere. Consciousness plays a crucial role. Individuals *internalize* and *differentiate themselves from* their social and physical environment in order to cope with their environments.

(5) In the *fourth essay*, I showed that *individual participation in consciousness* establishes *personal identity*. Establishment of individual identity continues the discussion of how individuals *differentiate* themselves from the biosphere to satisfy needs. Once differentiation occurs, *individual consciousness* collects the *personal story* that provides identity.

(6) In the *fifth essay*, I described the role of *collective faith* in the operation of the *social systems*, including religion, morality, law, and economics, as well as education, politics, and government. *Social systems* arise naturally as humans interact with other humans to satisfy needs. Some occur automatically as the result of interaction of individuals with each other, but as the systems become more complex, some of the systems require intentional planning. *Institutionalization* evolved, and that enabled *faith* to posit

social systems and to construct the *social entities* that the systems need as *"things"* external to individuals that serve human needs. Evolution of the ability to read and write provided a basis for a second explosive expansion of *participation in consciousness* and gave rise to the *institutionalization* of effective, widespread *social systems*. Humanity has used its *faith systems* to *institutionalize* the immense *social structure* that is required for the support of humanity in the biosphere. Society *institutionalizes systems* and *entities* and the essences of those systems and entities are *abstracted* into *language* and *consensus reality*, and individuals *internalize* them as part of reality.

The role that *faith* plays in human activity that arises from *human participation in consciousness*, both individual and collective, was the focal point for the discussions contained in the introduction and the first five essays just described. Then, in the next two essays, I developed and explored *philosophical implications* of the ideas that I had described in the first five essays.

(7) In the *sixth essay*, I discussed in detail how *individual and collective participation in consciousness* establishes *consensus reality*, the sum total of knowledge maintained and handed down from generation to generation by human cultures. Of course, human faith and consciousness can achieve only a partial understanding of *ultimate reality*. *Consensus reality* is the storehouse for the abstractions that humans have created for communication and for abstract thinking. *Consensus reality* is not *ultimate reality*, and different cultures develop differing *consensus realities*, and that results in multiple *consensus realities*, whose differences are significant.

(8) I used the *seventh essay* to describe traditional approaches to reality that were introduced by Plato and Aristotle during the *Axial Age*, and discussed how the concepts of faith and *consensus reality* relate to those traditional theories of reality. I introduced the abiding problem of *dualism* that exists in Western civilization that arises from differences between the theories that Plato and Aristotle advanced, and was specifically adopted by Descartes as part of his theory.

These seven essays have thoroughly demonstrated the important role that elements of reality that are *not physical* play in *human social existence* in the *biosphere*. Building on the ideas described in the first seven essays, I am now ready to describe *the system that is consciousness* that operates the biosphere.

THE THESIS OF THIS ESSAY

As indicated above, the contention presented in this essay is that consciousness is not a single essence but a system that operates the biosphere. The core of the *consciousness system* is the *awareness* that empowers *perception* of the physical biosphere. But both *perception* and *conceptualization* play important roles in *human participation in consciousness*. The *consciousness system* empowers sentient animals, with various sensory capacities, to engage the biosphere in their efforts to survive. *Participation in consciousness* plays an important role in the mobility of animals and their ability to decide what action to take next. All their decisions are made in the moving slice of time identified as *now*, which all animals in the biosphere share in common. But the *consciousness system* that operates the biosphere includes much more than the *core of awareness*. Awareness is just one function within a holistic system of *conscious life* in the biosphere.

All of the biosphere participates in the *consciousness system*. Every element of the biosphere *presents itself* to sentient beings to the extent necessary to support the life of sentient beings. The living parts of the biosphere other than sentient beings bear evidence of the inherent existence of consciousness in the biosphere in ways that are obvious. For example, plant life *pursues* solar energy. Upward mobility of matter into higher forms of life is a part of the how the biosphere works. Plants appear in the conscious awareness of sentient beings. They are selectively consumed. Some of the physical matter of the plants selected for consumption becomes a part of the animal that consumes it, and contributes to growth or tissue replacement.

Consciousness guides the animal's selection of plants to be consumed. The biosphere itself is a living system, and consciousness plays an indispensable role in the entirety of its operation.

Consciousness did not *evolve* in sentient beings. Sentient beings evolved the *capacity to participate in consciousness*. Consciousness was present or available in the biosphere from the beginning. Everything that exists has a *nonphysical essence—a phenomenon*—that presents it to every-thing else that exists. The *nonphysical essences* play crucial roles in con-sciousness and are a pivotal part of *the system that is consciousness*. Senses enable sentient beings to deal with the essences in the *consciousness system*.

Essences played a critical role in the *evolution* of the *human capacity to participate in consciousness*. By developing the *capacity for language*, humans developed a unique way to deal with *essences*. Speech creates *oral sounds* to represent *essences* found in the biosphere. Language operates by using *symbols*. Groups create *symbols* in the form of *words* and *language*. Language created concepts and enabled humans to *store knowledge* about the biosphere in *consensus reality*. *Internalization* of the *language* of the cultural group by individuals empowers *individual abstract thinking* and individual use of the knowledge stored in *consensus reality*. The development of language and its oral symbolism eventually led to writing—*symbol recog-nition participation in consciousness*—and the capacity of collective human-ity to store knowledge *outside* individual minds. That development was the essence of Karl Jaspers' *Axial Age* that saw an explosion in the creation of faith dependent *social systems* and *social institutions* that *participate in consciousness*. Now human *participation in consciousness* has moved to an even higher level—*electronic participation in consciousness*. Humanity is into a new *axial age*, and its implications are portentous.

Full development of the meaning of this terse description of the *bio-spheric consciousness system* will require detailed explanation, and that is the purpose of this essay.

ASSUMPTIONS TO OVERCOME

Many philosophers and scientists who deal with consciousness make the following the assumptions that I believe are unsound, and I will try to refute them in this essay:

(1) Somehow consciousness *evolved* in humans and other animals.

(2) The *human brain* and analogous physical organs in other sentient beings *produce consciousness.*

(3) There is a *physical basis* for consciousness; that is, consciousness is *physical* or results from physical processes in the brain.

(4) Consciousness only occurs in, and does not extend beyond, *individual organisms.*

In the preface to his book *The Mystery of Consciousness* (1997), philosopher John R. Searle contends, "We will understand consciousness when we understand in detail how the brain does it." If the four assumptions listed above were correct, then Searle probably would be right. Those unwarranted assumptions seem to reduce the problem of understanding consciousness to figuring out *how physical brains produce consciousness.* But I suggest that we don't know what consciousness is and should not assume that individual physical brains produce it.

The assumptions that there is a *physical* basis for consciousness, and that it is a function of the *physical brain,* are widespread, but far from universal. I will deal with the *physicality* argument in the course of this essay. Ample evidence supports the proposal that the human brain *participates* in consciousness, but there is no reason to conclude that the human brain *produces* consciousness. Any evidence that the brain *produces* consciousness also supports the conclusion that it *participates* in consciousness. Human *participation in consciousness* in the biosphere expanded dramatically after the development of language. *No evolutionary change* in the *physical human brain* explains that *huge expansion of consciousness.* This fact, together with other *functional* ways in which consciousness operates in many parts of the biosphere, points to the much more credible theory that humans *participate in consciousness* and that it did not evolve.

The assumption that human consciousness *evolved* in the human species seems to be *universal.* Everyone assumes that consciousness evolved. They assume that it evolved *in the brain.* They assume that it is *produced by the brain.* I have not seen where anyone has actually questioned the assumption that human consciousness evolved in the brain of the human species. Practically no one seems to have considered the possibility that consciousness is something that just exists in the biosphere, or even the universe, and that humans evolved the capacity to participate in it, as I am contending in these essays, unless Russellian monism is interpreted to endorse that position.[62]

The assumption that consciousness is produced by *individual* brains, and does not occur anywhere else, is not so much *stated* by writers as *implicit* in what they write. That is obviously what the writers think. This assumption probably follows from the assumption that human consciousness *evolved in the brain.* Each person has only one brain (unless you consider the left and right sides separate brains), so the assumption that consciousness is produced by and only occurs in *individuals* is implicit in the assumption that consciousness evolved in the brain. In the background of these assumptions is a powerful ideology. *Individualism* is a very powerful *ideology* in Western thought, and the idea that consciousness is *a shared reality* is therefore *counterintuitive* for Western thinkers.

For all of these reasons, most philosophers identify *consciousness* with the *conscious experience* of *individual* human beings. If, as I suggest, consciousness exists as a part of reality, and plays an important role in the *operation of the biosphere*, and is *not produced by the brain*, the untenable *illusion of individualism* disappears. And it must. The biosphere and evolution deal in species, not individuals.

THE MYSTERY OF CONSCIOUSNESS

No one has explained consciousness. Although Daniel C. Dennett purported to explain consciousness in his book, *Consciousness Explained* (1991), leading thinkers continue to agree that **consciousness is a mystery**. Ironically, Douglas Hofstadter, who had co-authored *The Mind's I* (1990) with Dennett, included the following telling sentence in a short quote that is included among the usual laudatory comments at the beginning of Dennett's book: "Daniel Dennett's book *Consciousness Explained* is a masterful tapestry of deep insights into this **eternal riddle**." (Emphasis added.) Like Dennett, Hofstadter was subtle and skillful with words! John R. Searle titled one of his books *The **Mystery** of Consciousness* (1997). (Emphasis added.) David J. Chalmers begins his book *The Conscious Mind* (1996) with the sentence, "Conscious experience is at once the most familiar thing in the world and the most **mysterious**." (Emphasis added) Colin McGinn titled his book about consciousness *The **Mysterious** Flame* (1999). (Emphasis added) McGinn argues that the human mind cannot penetrate the mystery of the existence of consciousness, and I agree. Human ability to **participate in consciousness** did not evolve for the purpose of **explaining** consciousness; it evolved to assist human survival in the biosphere.

In the course of human mental development, **consciousness** enabled **humanity** to **embrace** the concepts of **time, space, matter, energy**, and **motion** that structure and help define **physical reality**. **Faith** enabled humanity to store those concepts in **consensus reality**. Ironically, scientists and philosophers **now look for the explanation of consciousness within the structure of reality that consciousness itself revealed to humans.** How can concepts that consciousness itself revealed to human understanding explain the consciousness that did the revealing? Efforts to **use consciousness** to capture the **essence of consciousness** is a bit like an eye trying to see itself.

Philosophers earnestly want to solve the *mystery of consciousness*. They want to find the very *essence* of *individual awareness*, and to limit *consciousness* to that *essence*. For instance, Searle believes that a *conscious state* is an important part of consciousness, if not its *irreducible essence*. McGinn describes consciousness as the *mysterious flame*, and sought the *essence* of that flame. Thomas Nagel wrote the classic and influential analogy, "What it is like to be a bat." He suggests that the *essence* of consciousness is described by *what it is like to be a particular thing*. David Chalmers agrees with Nagel's assessment of consciousness as *what it is like to be something*. All of these approaches focus on some *limited aspect* having to do with *awareness* as the *essence of individual consciousness*. The capacity for awareness is perhaps the most mysterious part of consciousness, but it is not all there is to consciousness.

It is clear that *no essence of consciousness has been identified*. There is no agreement about the exact nature of consciousness. David Chalmers contends that consciousness is *not physical*, but John Searle contends that consciousness is *physical*. He believes that it is produced by the *physical brain*. McGinn admits that the question of *physicality* is open. Nagel contends that consciousness is *not physical*. I will deal more fully with the *physicality question* later in this essay but mention these points only to describe the lack of any agreement about what consciousness is and the lack of any explanation for its existence.

Colin McGinn called for *radically new theories* about *consciousness*, and I am offering one. I cannot explain consciousness, but there are some facts that I can suggest about the *operations* of consciousness that shed light on its *nature*. Many of these operations don't seem to be taken into account in any existing theory that I have seen. I arrived at these facts by looking at the development of human *participation in consciousness* in the large framework of the *biosphere* and *evolution,* and in light of the fact that everything human is totally involved in the *biosphere*. I assert that consciousness was included in the original package that produced the biosphere—it came with creation. This contention is consistent with the thoughts expressed by Philip Goff in his recent book, *Galileo's Error*. As a matter of fact, many of the views that I am expressing are consistent with those of Goff, including the possibility of some form of panpsychism. *Awareness* within the biosphere—the universe—is an essential part of the operations of the biosphere. I now realize that I arrived at my conclusions in these matters using a process the philosopher Charles Sanders Peirce called *abductive reasoning*. I looked at the entire body of facts, and am providing the simplest explanation for them. That appears to be the process that *Charles Darwin* used in formulating the *theory of evolution*, and that Vladmir Vernadsky used in formulating the theory of the biosphere. The solution posed is *plausible*, although my arguments cannot fully validate them. *Abductive reasoning* is probably the only viable approach to what I will call *big picture* theories. It seems to run counter to a trend of modern scholarship to focus narrowly on specific topics and to try to apply very tight logic to that narrow topic.

CONSCIOUSNESS AND LIFE IN THE BIOSPHERE

The energy for life in the biosphere is provided by the sun, as Vernadsky indicated. Plants and animals *move* to capture and participate in the sun's energy and the stored energy that it has provided. *Mobility* is associated more closely with *animals* than with *plants*. Interestingly, practically all motion that occurs on earth can be traced to energy supplied directly or indirectly by the sun. Consciousness is very beneficial to life that *moves*. It creates the possibility of *intentional activity*. Intentional *movement* is usually more beneficial for survival than movement that is not directed by *intentionality*. Evolving animal life developed the *ability to move*. The capacity to *participate directly in consciousness* made the ability to move more beneficial to sentient organisms. The evolution of the capability for these two functions—*motion* and *conscious awareness*—are probably closely related, and probably relate to energy provided by the sun. Consciousness enables individuals to make choices. I will not digress here to develop the importance and reality of the ability of sentient beings, including humans, to choose what they will do, but in *essay ten* in this series, I will discuss *freewill*.

All consciousness that we know about is associated with *life* that evolved in the *biosphere.* That fact suggests that there is a strong connection between *consciousness* and *life,* and places consciousness *in,* but does not necessarily *limit it to,* the biosphere. It exists, and the biosphere uses it in its operations, but that certainly does not limit it to the biosphere. A rich variety of *participation in consciousness* exists in the biosphere. The life forms that exist in the biosphere are *interdependent and symbiotic.* None exists in isolation from all others. Both the *existence of life* itself and the existence of consciousness are *mysteries.* Nothing compels us to think that *life is* a prerequisite for *consciousness* or that *consciousness* does not exist *independently of life.* But consciousness may have been, and probably was, a prerequisite for *animal* life as we know it. Life had to evolve to a certain *functional* point in order to "become *conscious*"; that is, to *directly* and *intentionally participate* in the *consciousness system.* Evolution of the *ability to move* would have invited the evolution of the *ability to participate in consciousness.* I will discuss the topic of *functionality* later in this essay. The availability and *functional advantages* offered by consciousness in the biosphere likely induced the *evolution of animals.* Increasing levels of human participation in the *consciousness system* continue to evolve. *Electronic participation in consciousness* is the most important recent example.

As I indicated in the description of the *faith environment,* in the *first essay,* humans do not actually know of conscious life anywhere in the universe other than in the earth's biosphere. If humans ever discover such extraterrestrial consciousness, it is likely to be associated with *life in a larger system,* similar to the earth's *biosphere.* While individual organisms might *participate in consciousness,* as they do here on earth, consciousness will be a causative factor in the evolution of the life, and not the other way around. *Evolution of life* is likely to involve *evolution of species*. Individuals can't just pop up. A system is required. And if the evolution of life was a bit *improbable*, how likely was the *evolution of consciousness* in which all sentient beings participate systematically and synchronistically but independently? I submit that the development of such a system was far more likely if consciousness simply exists, and all life evolved in the biosphere to use it.

The ancient Greek Philosopher Heraclitus said that the only thing constant is change. The flux of existence described by Heraclitus led Plato to believe that the *real* consists of enduring, *nonphysical essences*, not the constantly changing, disintegrating physical world. Plato reasoned that the *essences* are permanent and that temporary physical manifestations of objects that pass in and out of being are not what is real. Consistently with Plato's thoughts, *consciousness* that maintains knowledge is, in fact, *much more durable* than individual life. At a minimum, consciousness operates and is perpetuated, both genetically and culturally within groups—species, if you wish—that continually populate the earth's biosphere, in spite of the death of individuals. Consciousness has existed in an unbroken chain at least throughout the history of civilization, and clearly has roots in the mythology that preceded history.

Here is a question to ponder. If humanity wipes itself out and another species that *participates in consciousness* eventually evolves the capacity for language, what concepts will emerge? Time, space, matter, energy, and motion? What about Pi? What colors will be included in the rainbow? Will the they identify an A note with 440 vibrations per second? If you think that the new participants in consciousness will come to *any* of the same conclusions that humans did, then you are well on your way to believing that consciousness is not just a product of the brain but is part of a system that includes *nonphysical essences* in the biosphere, and involves *interaction* with the biosphere. Consciousness is not mere awareness. At a minimum it is a *system* in which *something* has all the *functional equipment* to be aware of *something*, and the *somethings* and all of the *equipment* are parts of the system.

Groups, not just individuals, participate in consciousness. Very effective group participation in consciousness began with the appearance of linguistic participation in consciousness. Linguistic participation in consciousness empowered group participation in consciousness and is one of the important reasons that human participation in consciousness is so powerful. As Plato contended, nonphysical essences are much more durable than most physical objects. Linguistic participation in consciousness enabled humans to assign words to nonphysical essences associated with physical objects. The consensus reality that humans maintain contains concepts that are more durable than the evanescent physical world. But the nonphysical essences— the phenomena—that exist in the biosphere and can present themselves to human minds, including those that can present physical objects to the minds of sentient beings are even more durable! They exist independently of the human mind and its symbols, but have the ability to activate abstractions and concepts in humans that they can express with their oral and written symbols. And they don't seem to be confined by any relationship to time and space.

I am asserting that consciousness is intimately involved in the *life in the biosphere*. *Granted, awareness* is the meaning *traditionally* assigned to the word *consciousness*. Be assured, I am not asserting that *all life* is *conscious* in the sense of *awareness*. Plant life may not be *aware* of anything. Nevertheless, even plant life—indeed the entire biosphere—behaves rather intelligently! The biosphere seems to know what it is doing! Plants respond in many "intelligent" ways to the sun. Sunflower blooms follow the sun throughout the day. Trees develop canopies that maximize exposure to the sun, and vegetation competes for exposure to the sun. Indoor plants stretch toward windows in search of the sun. Although plants do not have *individual consciousness* like humans, there is a *purposefulness* in their actions and movement that *resembles intelligence* in the operation of the *ecosystems* and plant life of the biosphere.

Plant life *presents itself* to *sentient organisms* very effectively in the *consciousness system*, making itself available for consumption and use, as if Bergson's *vital force* is pushing it to a higher level of participation in conscious life. As I have pointed out, everything in the biosphere, which includes everything at or near the crust of the earth, is either alive or has the potential to become a part of a living being and to participate in life—*life that has awareness.* Vitamin B that develops in an edible plant can become part of a human brain and *participate* in the *thinking* process by presenting itself to a hungry thinker. Indeed, everything in the biosphere appears to *aspire to* conscious life, and everything in the biosphere seems to push toward *participation in consciousness* at a higher level! The constant supply of energy by the sun and the biosphere's response to it dispel the notion that evolution of life to increasingly higher levels violates the third law of thermodynamics. The upward movement to higher levels is energized by the sun. But nevertheless, evolution to increasing *levels of complexity* is *mysterious* because of the impression that *entropy* usually reduces *complexity*. Plants are a part of the biospheric process, converting inert, lifeless matter into living matter and then presenting themselves to animal life for possible further upward movement toward *participation in consciousness*.

Even more fundamentally and directly, plants produce oxygen, on which animals depend! Animals make choices and move about to satisfy their needs. Altogether, these facts confirm the majestic, mysterious suspicion that the entire biosphere is systemically involved in living processes that involve *consciousness*, and that culminate in human *participation in consciousness*. Although we cannot identify an *essence* of either *consciousness* or *life,* we know that *life* exists in conscious physical organisms in the biosphere. And we know that life itself involves complex systems. And, as stated previously, we do not actually know of any instance anywhere in which either life or consciousness exists separate and apart from our own biosphere.

One of the arguments of *physicalists* is that only something physical can cause a physical thing to move. Therefore, they argue, *consciousness must be physical*. Later in this essay, and again in the *ninth essay* in this series, I will discuss the *physicality argument*. But the fact that all the consciousness that we know about is *associated with life* suggests the interesting possibility that *nonphysical consciousness* produces thought that *can* in fact cause movement *in living organisms*.[63] That is certainly what it looks like. In the biosphere, the capacity for functions essential for life is transmitted from generation to generation by genes. Genes contain the patterns that produce the structures required to replicate life—very complex structures. No doubt, genes transmit the human *capacity to participate in consciousness*. Somehow, the *structures that genes produce* have the capability of producing motion in response to the stimulation of knowledge acquired through consciousness. The ability to do so is involved in the *essence of life* itself for the human species. That suggestion certainly seems to be supported by empiricism.

Inorganic matter does not have a complex structure comparable to the structural plan transmitted through genes and does not have the capability of acquiring and *interacting* with *biospheric consciousness* in the same way. But the ability of *life* to interact with consciousness goes to the very essence of the biosphere itself. So, while we do not know what consciousness is, we know that it *produces thoughts* in living humans. And it certainly appears to have induced the evolution of genetically transmitted structures that can respond to those thoughts to cause *intentional actions*. Subatomic particles like the Higgs boson that can cause other subatomic particles either to have mass or not have mass, but we just don't know, and I'll wait on science to solve that problem.

THROWING LIGHT ON CONSCIOUSNESS

Throughout these essays, I have cautiously avoided expression of any opinion about the *root cause* of the consciousness that humans experience. I have maintained that consciousness is an *unexplained mystery*. I have contended that consciousness is not *physical*, within the meaning that is currently assigned to the word *physical*, but have suggested that in this *new axial age*, the distinction between what is *physical* and what is *not physical* will *blur*, as we learn more about *subatomic particles*. Please note that I have not contended that *no substance or particle* is involved in the *root causes of consciousness*. I don't know what causes consciousness but suspect that *some particle* or field, like the *Higgs field*, may be involved. But I don't believe that what I am describing as the *consciousness system* is totally *physical* in any traditional meaning of the word *physical*, although I contend that the entire *physical* biosphere is included in the *system that is consciousness*. It will not be surprising if quantum physics figures out that there is *reality* that includes consciousness that is not subject to the limitations of *time*, *space matter* and *energy*, all of which seem to be related to the *physical* and *motion*. In this brief section of this essay, I will point out some things that I think may be important in the continuing investigation about the *root causes* of consciousness.

Some of the things that I have mentioned in the course of these essays may have important implications. In the very *first essay*, I pointed out the connection of *life* and *consciousness* to the *biosphere*, and mentioned the role that the *sun* plays and has played in the biosphere and the evolution of life. Life evolved in the biosphere, but I contend that *consciousness did not evolve*: sentient beings evolved the *capacity* to *participate in consciousness*. If consciousness was produced by evolution, it occurred at least at the level of the biosphere, and all the elements necessary for it were present in the biosphere from the outset. In the immediately preceding section of this essay, I again pointed out the close connection of *life and consciousness*. I pointed out the appearance of *intelligence* in the way that *life in the biosphere* responds to the *energy coming from the sun*. Later in this essay, I will point out the fact that humans tend to be *awake and conscious* during the *daylight hours*, and sleep at night, when the sun is not shining. Elsewhere in these essays, I have discussed the fact that *sight* is the *sense* that is most often associated with *consciousness*, and the role that *light* plays in *sight*. Of course, the *physicalists* argue that to cause *motion*, consciousness would have to be *physical*. Earlier in this essay, I stated, "Interestingly, practically all *motion* that occurs on earth can be traced to energy supplied directly or indirectly by the sun." In short, there is significant *correlation* between *consciousness* and *sunlight*. No one would deny that motion requires *energy* or *force*. The question is whether *consciousness* that is *not physical* within the present meaning of that word can *invoke* the necessary energy or force to cause motion.

So, returning to the theme I want to develop in this section, the *sun* and *energy from the sun* played a strong role in the *evolution of life*. The sun plays a strong role directly or indirectly in *all motion* that occurs on earth. The fact that *sentient life moves*, and consciousness appears to direct its motion, plays an important role in the *operation of the biosphere as a system*.

In the preceding section I discussed the *physicalist argument* that only something *physical* can *produce motion* in something else *physical*, and suggested something about *life itself*, transmitted by genes, overcomes this otherwise generally valid point. From time to time in these essays, I have mentioned the recently confirmed *Higgs field*, and *Higgs boson*, and the fact that Higgs boson interacts with other subatomic particles, and the interaction determines whether or not the *other particle* has mass. Needless to say, all of that is above the head of this retired judge who is in his eightieth year, and whose last course in physics was in 1963!

However, it is my understanding that the *Higgs boson* is produced by the *Higgs field* that permeates the universe, and that the *photon*, the bearer or essence of *light*, is a *massless gauge boson*. Apparently, its interaction with the *Higgs boson* results or resulted in its *lack of mass*. *Quarks*, on the other hand, apparently because of their interaction with the *Higgs boson*, have *mass*. Philip Goff and Sam Coleman think maybe *quark*s are involved in consciousness. I understand that *everything* that has mass, such as *protons* and *neutrons*, so far as is presently known, consists of *quarks*. I think that *Higgs bosons* are also involved in the *origin of force*. If the *Higgs field* that produces *Higgs bosons*, is present throughout the cosmos, I suppose that it permeates *human brains* and the organic bodies of *all sentient beings*. I don't know whether the interaction of Higgs bosons with other particles is an *ongoing occurrence*. But I have seen a suggestion on the internet that *"biophotons"*—photons produced by life—have been discovered in the *human brain*. *Photons* themselves are obviously forms of *energy*, and *carry force*. Sunflower blooms respond to sunlight, and "follow the sun" throughout the daylight hours. Apparently, something about massless sunlight can *cause motion*!

I am suggesting that *photons* or *sunlight* have something to do with the *root causes of consciousness*. Sunlight is known to produce physiological results in the human body that impact on *mental operations*. The human body produces *vitamin D* and *serotonin* in response to sunlight, both of which have impact on *mental* and *emotional health*. Prolonged absence of light can produce *depression* in humans. So, there is baseline evidence of the involvement of *sunlight* in *matters mental*, and there is, no doubt, a lot more that I don't know about.

Of course, life and consciousness go on in the absence of light. I don't know how long they would go on in a total absence of light, but at least on a temporary basis they continue to exist. In the *biosphere*, in which evolution of life was induced by sunlight, that does not seem to even raise a question. Sunlight is responsible for the production of all food in the biosphere. Everything that humans eat is produced, directly or indirectly by the influence of sunlight. *Photosynthesis* utilizes *sunshine* and *stores energy*. The energy of the sun is stored in food. If sunlight is involved in the **root causes of consciousness**, whatever it is could be stored in the food we eat. The sun was even shining on the dinosaurs and primordial forests that produced the fossil fuel that we use to move about in vehicles.

There are numerous articles on the internet suggesting that **photons** or **light** may be involved in **consciousness**. Some even suggest that the **photon** itself is somehow **conscious**, or has the quality of consciousness. I doubt that. If photons or quarks are involved, I suspect that in the complex structures transmitted by genes, they play a role in the **participation in consciousness** by sentient beings.

In these paragraphs, I've suggested some big picture things (or should I say "little picture things?") that I really don't know enough about to describe with any authority, but they seemed too important to ignore. I believe that there may be something here that is involved in the **root causes** of con**sciousness**, and that can explain how **consciousness causes motion**! Human **participation in consciousness** appears to have evolved for the purpose of allowing intentional motion in the biosphere, and most motion, including human motion, can be traced back **directly** or **indirectly** to the **energy of the sun**. And the **empirical evidence** certainly suggests that **consciousness can cause motion**. But are light or photons involved immediately in the cause of human motion and the cause of consciousness? These ideas seem to me to be consistent with **Russellian monism**. They may be consistent with the works of Philosophers Galen Strawson, Philip Goff, and others. I submit that there is a connection between **consciousness** and **sunlight**, and that there is something here worthy of scientific research!

Research must look at the **role of consciousness** in the **biosphere**, not just in the **human brain**. The brain **participates in consciousness**, so that is one of the places to look. But the mysterious synchrony of **consciousness** in the eternally moving instant of **now** in the biosphere is a clue that **the entire biosphere is participating**, and the investigation needs to include the **entire** *system* that is required for the operation of consciousness. This section of this essay needs to be read in the context of the entirety of these essays. Even if *particles that emanate from the sun* were involved in the evolution of the *capacity to participate in consciousness*, consciousness is still a *nonphysical mystery* that *operates as a system* in the biosphere!

MORE ABOUT THE CONSCIOUSNESS SYSTEM

When we look at how *evolution* has *used* consciousness in the *biosphere,* consciousness certainly appears to be *more than* just the *essence of individual awareness* or anything that evolved in the human brain. Consciousness *permeates the biosphere* and humans participate in it. Consciousness is the biosphere's way of making itself known to its sentient organisms. It enables sentient organisms in the biosphere to *intentionally engage* in survival activities. It enables them to make choices. The biosphere's *presentation of itself to its sentient organisms* is an essential function of *consciousness. Perception* involves more than an activity of the perceiving sentient being: the *objects* of perception are also involved, as I will discuss in detail later in this essay. The *objects of perception* that present themselves in the consciousness of sentient beings are likely what induced the evolution of the capacity in sentient organisms to *participate in consciousness.* That function is very valuable to the sentient being. But even though that function is quite obvious, philosophers have had little or nothing to say about this *biospheric, evolutionary function* of consciousness because they are tied to the belief that consciousness exists only in the *physical bodies* of individual organisms. Consciousness may be associated with the *physical, but not that way*!

It is important to see the *systematic function* that consciousness plays in the totality of the biosphere. The physical elements of the biosphere— indeed of the entire known universe—*participate* in the *consciousness system.* They *present* themselves to *sentient organisms* in the biosphere. As indicated above, that is the purpose for which *human capacity* to *participate in consciousness evolved.* Consciousness enables humans and other sentient organisms to function in the biosphere. It enables them to do things that promote their survival. The *senses* use *light, sound,* and other *media* to collect data from the biosphere. All of these media are parts of the biosphere's *consciousness system.* The *biosphere* empowers human senses to use the *media* available in the biosphere to collect the *essences* of things that exist in the biosphere (and universe) and present them to the human mind.

In the branch of philosophy known as *phenomenology,* the *essences* that the senses collect and present to the human mind are called *phenomena.* Here is a fundamental point: the *consciousness system includes the essences of physical objects that present themselves to sentient organisms* in the biosphere, which we will discuss in detail later in this essay. It includes the *physical objects.* The *consciousness system* includes the *media* through which presentation occurs as well. All are parts of a *system of presentation* of the *essences of the objects in the biosphere* to the *minds of sentient beings* in the biosphere. The *consciousness system* includes *concepts* created in *speech and language* and *internalized* by individuals. The individual's *participation in consciousness* involves simultaneous access to *perception externally* and *concepts internally.*

Of course, the *consciousness system* includes the *individual consciousness* of individual organisms, including humans. *Individual consciousness* in humans includes *internal awareness,* such as *pain that an individual experiences.* If I break my arm, it is *my* broken arm that hurts, and I have to deal with that problem as I encounter the biosphere. The brain processes the *sensation of pain* coming from within my physical body, the same as it processes the *visual perceptions* of the external world. It senses where the pain is; it lets me know where I hurt. That is useful information. My doctors can use the information that I report about the pain. Of course, the brain can make mistakes about the sensations from inside of an individual, just as it makes mistakes about external perceptions. But the *sensing,* inside or

264

outside, is *part of individual participation in the consciousness system* or *individual consciousness* and enables the individual organism to cope in the biosphere. So, the *consciousness system* includes the *sensory* and *mental* processes of human beings.

But consciousness adds a *mysterious quality* to mental analyses. The *consciousness system* presents *physical objects* and *nonphysical essences* to human minds as *phenomena*. Consciousness converts *sensory data* presented as *phenomena* into *understanding, insight, meaning, and/or experience*. No one knows exactly how that happens. This is a mystery about consciousness that no one has fully explained. That unexplained *gap* is the chasm between the theories of Plato and Aristotle that neither of them could span. It is a mistake to try to *limit* consciousness either to that mysterious capability of converting *phenomena* into *thought* or to the *mystery of awareness* itself. Consciousness is not limited to the mysterious *essence of awareness*. And it is not limited to the conversion of *nonphysical essences* into *knowledge*. The system includes both *biospheric essences* and the *knowledge* that they conjure up. To try to reduce consciousness to some imaginary essence of awareness is a form of reductionism and leaves out important parts of the *holistic consciousness system* that operates the *biosphere*.

I have suggested in these essays that *thoughts, meaning*, and *knowledge* actually originate in the use of *language* and *human efforts for meaningful communication* using *language*. Of course, the physical capacity that supports those efforts is transmitted physically through genes. But the ability to use language is *internalized* into *individuals* from the *surrounding group* and its *language*. Many of the concepts that individuals use in thinking originate in language. So, let's review the origin of human thought. Human groups struggle to detect *essences* in the *biosphere* and to assign words to them, and to then communicate meaningfully about the objects and essences represented by words that the group has created. The struggle of individuals to assign meaning to the symbols used in speech and writing to communicate those essences *may invoke the mental ability that converts perception to thought.* For example, there is a word for *tree.* Someone uses the word *tree* to tell me something. In my learning, internalizing process, I learned to produce the thought or maybe even an image of a tree in my mind that responds to the spoken or written word. *Thoughts are apparently produced by the struggle for meaning.* The ability to *share meaning* enables society to function, and enables individuals to think! The meaning of concepts lies in the human interpretation of things that exist in the biosphere itself, and it takes a group of humans, using speech and language, to develop it in the first instance. That effort to deal with the biosphere *abstractly,* using abstractions maintained by the group, that conjures up images—thoughts—in *individual consciousness* may explain *abstract thinking.* As Vygotsky taught us, internalized language is the basis for the *higher mental processes.* But understanding the human effort that converts *nonphysical essences,* including *nonphysical essences of physical objects,* into *thoughts* still does not explain *how the mind does any of that.* And none of those facts explain the part of consciousness that is *perception,* that only occurs in the instant of *now.* So, consciousness remains a mystery.

The human *capacity* for *participating in consciousness* is transmitted by *DNA.* The **DNA** contains the blueprint for the *physical structures* that functionally enable humans to *participate in consciousness.* But the *consciousness system* requires *much more* than a DNA blueprint. Consciousness enables the *biosphere* itself to function systematically. The biosphere could not function without consciousness. Physical elements of the biosphere that are external to humans play important roles in the *consciousness system.* That is not a claim that *everything* thinks and has mystical intelligence. But it is a claim that *consciousness empowers thought.* It is not a claim that the *physical* does not exist, as Plato contended, nor is it the *immaterialism* proposed by Bishop Berkeley. And it is not a claim that the *mental* is *all* that exists, as contended by Plato. It is a claim that the *physical is very real, very* *physical, and exists within and as part of the biospheric consciousness system.* In that system, the physical biosphere presents itself to sentient beings. The physical is *very real* and plays a vital role in reality. It is a claim that *all abstractions* and other mental operations are *included in the consciousness system.* Abstractions are very real—they exist—and are integral parts of the *consciousness system* that operates the biosphere. And as we have seen, it takes a *group* to fully create *abstractions* and *concepts.* But the group does not create the biospheric *nonphysical essences* that *give rise to* the *abstractions* and *concepts.*

All individual humans participate in one and the same *consciousness system,* just as they participate in the same *physical biosphere.* They can't participate in one without participating in the other. The *consciousness system* is not *"part"* of the biosphere: it necessarily embraces and includes the entire biosphere. It embraces all that humans can know. The *phenomena* associated with *physical objects* in the biosphere present themselves, in various ways, to all sentient beings. The physical objects *appear* in consciousness to *sentient organisms* as *phenomena.* Butterflies detect the zinnias and roses that I raise in my garden. They are *conscious* of them. They may not process that *information* the same way that I do, but they know what they need to know to participate in the biosphere.

That brings us to a very important point. The *physical world* is the reassuring *common denominator* in the *system that is consciousness:* humans and all other sentient organisms in the biosphere experience the same *physical world,* each in its own way. If two sentient beings are at the same place at the same time, their mutual *participation in consciousness* enables them to experience the same *physical environment,* although their imperfect senses may present it to them in markedly different ways. The mosquito knows that I am there and sucks my blood! If you and I are together, the same environment appears to your *individual consciousness* and mine at the same time. It might *look, sound, smell, feel, and taste* a bit different to you than to me because we experience it from different vantage points and because of differences in the way our senses work, but there is enough commonalty in our separate experiences to confirm that we are dealing with the same physical reality. We both experience *essences* of the *same objects*, and that enables us to *create words* to represent the reality we are experiencing. Our combined consciousnesses of an object is *more comprehensive* that our *individual consciousness*. We are experiencing the commonly shared environment within *the same consciousness system*. All humans participate in the same physical world *within the same consciousness system* that includes all the *essences* of the *physical world*, as well as all essences of things that are not physical.

And the ever-present *NOW* in which we exist together is one important aspect of how the *consciousness system* operates the biosphere. We are all in the same biosphere, conscious of it, and conscious of each other as parts of it at precisely the same time. All parts of the biosphere *participate in consciousness* in their own way. The functions of the biosphere support life, and consciousness is central to its functions. The same *objects* appear both in your participating consciousness and mine, *at the same time*. They appear to us simultaneously precisely because *consciousness is shared* in an *eternal now*.

The consciousness that sentient beings share includes the entire *physical biosphere*. Group *objectivity* that empowers *empiricism,* and is the basis for science, would not work if sentient beings did not all share it. All scientists work with the same *physical facts*. They derive them from *empiricism* that uses *direct perception*. The fact that we share perceptions of *physical objects* that appear in shared consciousness strengthens our faith that the object exists. The fact that *consciousness* is *shared* is evidenced by the fact that it is *available to multiple observers,* and not peculiar to an individual. If an object is not *in* consciousness, we have no knowledge of it at all. If only one individual becomes "aware" of an unusual object, there may be suspicion that it doesn't exist. If other people become aware of it, the probability of its physical existence is strengthened. If other people cannot become aware of it, the probability of its existence is weakened. The observer's *subjective consciousness* may have been mistaken.

The facts described in the preceding paragraph show why the *objectivity of a group* is more accurate than the totally subjective observations made by an individual. The observations of individuals are always subjective, never objective. *Individual participation in consciousness* is completely *subjective*. *Individual consciousness* is always internal to the individual, so individuals are always *on the inside looking out*. Individuals *participate in consciousness*, but the extent of their participation is limited by their *individual capacity* for participation. They always operate subjectively, from the perspective of their limited individual *participation in consciousness*. So, individuals are prone to make mistakes in their observations. Scientists work hard to take advantage of the greater objectivity of observations that can be shared and confirmed by multiple individuals. But unfortunately, even the objectivity of groups of people is nowhere near perfect.

The physical biosphere is included, to the extent needed for survival, in the *mental* operations of *sentient beings*. If the *physical* were not included in the *mental*, we would have no way to know about the physical. But the physical world is *real*. All sentient beings share the physical world, so its existence is confirmed by the consciousness that all sentient beings share. The *physical* is unquestionably included in the *mental*. But while all that is physical is a part of the *mental* and consciousness, not everything that is *mental* is *physical*.

Not all *physical objects* can think, but every *object*, whether mental or physical, exists in and is part of the *consciousness system*. Otherwise, we would not know about it. Humans must *use* their imperfect *individual participation in consciousness*, whatever it is, to *think*. *Consciousness* empowers *thinking*. If individuals were *fully* conscious (i.e., had access to the entirety of consciousness), they would not need to think, look, listen, or talk, etc. They would *know*. Learning would not be necessary. We know about *physical objects* because they *present themselves in the biosphere.* That *presentation* is a function of the *consciousness system.* That is how the *biosphere functions* and the presentation function is absolutely essential to the *biosphere.* Of course, individuals don't know *everything* about all physical objects just because the objects exist in consciousness, but individuals don't have to know everything in order to survive.

What I am suggesting concerning the *consciousness system* that operates the biosphere is not exactly *panpsychism,* although there are similarities. Certainly, *panpsychism* and *universal consciousness* are not new ideas. They formed the basis for ancient religions and philosophies,[64] and are still facets of some Eastern religions. Western science, with its extremely successful focus on the *physical,* has pushed these ancient theories, along with Plato's *nonphysical essences* completely into the background of *Western* faith. However, the mystery of consciousness naggingly retains the possibility that Plato and the religions that believe in panpsychism were at least partly correct. I believe that without rejecting the theories of Plato and Aristotle, the theory I am presenting moves beyond them, just as chemistry moved beyond the theories of Leucippus and Democritus. And although the theory I am advancing is similar to *panpsychism,* it moves beyond panpsychism as described in the ancient religions. Philip Goff makes the same, or a similar, suggestion about consciousness and panpsychism.[65]Sam Coleman argues for a variation called panprotopsychism, that may actually be even closer to the theory I am suggesting.

The *consciousness system* even embraces things that humans, and life itself, may *not* be *aware* of at a given time. I can't be sure, but don't believe that objects that present themselves to sentient beings change their properties of presentation just because there is no sentient being close enough to sense them. Objects that glow can glow when there is no one to see. When objects are presenting themselves, and no sentient being experiencing the presentation, the part of the biospheric *consciousness system* that does the presentation is working! The "information" that humans *could have seen* and possibly interpreted is available. And there is information in books, and other storage places, readily available to humanity that no one in the world is thinking about. But the *information* is real, although it is not currently active in any individual brain. The *Rosetta Stone* was there before anyone found it; it contained *knowledge*. So were the Dead Sea Scrolls that also contained knowledge. The knowledge that the Rosetta Stone and Dead Sea Scrolls contained was not in anyone's mind until they were discovered, but the knowledge was there to be uncovered. Long ago, symbolism empowered *externalization of knowledge* and enabled it to maintain its existence, independently of any existing human brain. These facts lead to another important point. *Essences* exist that can become human *concepts* upon their discovery, although presently unknown. All these things are parts of the *consciousness system*. They exist as *latent knowledge*, although just as unknown as the Rosetta Stone and Dead Sea Scrolls before they were discovered.

The *consciousness system* that I am describing embraces the current understanding of both *consciousness* and the *unconscious*. The unconscious part that the system embraces is *potential consciousness* or *pre-consciousness*. The fact that the word *unconscious* already exists and has been put into use in psychology as a seeming opposite of *conscious* is a bit unfortunate. *Latent consciousness* would have captured the reality that it represents much more accurately. The system that consciousness operates excludes only the *nonexistent*, and even the nonexistent exists as a *nonphysical abstraction*—the word *nothing!* In *mathematical participation in consciousness*, it is represented by **zero**. Many, perhaps most, aspects of the *consciousness system* and reality have *no physical aspect*, in the way that *physicality* and its properties are presently understood.

THE BIOSPHERE PRESENTS ITSELF TO SENTIENT ORGANISMS

I have indicated that in the **consciousness system**, the biosphere **"presents"** itself to sentient organisms. That is probably a little difficult to comprehend. Let me explain more fully how the biosphere, in the absence of better terminology, "presents itself" to sentient beings. John R. Searle makes an important point: "Where basic perceptual features are concerned there is a **backward road** from the **perceptual feature** to the type of **perceptual experience**. The **object causes** the conscious experience of the observer." (Emphasis added.) Let's focus on that **backward road** and the idea that the object **causes** the conscious experience of the observer.

Phenomenologist Hannah Arendt noted the almost universal tendency to **display**.[66] Animals do it. Plants do it. Even inanimate objects do it. The **causal display** of physical objects by presentation of **phenomena** to sentient beings is an integral part of the operation of the **consciousness system**. The idea of objects **presenting** themselves is not new; it traces back through phenomenologists Heidegger and Husserl to Brentano. But to begin the explanation about how objects in the biosphere **present** themselves to the human mind, I will use the **backward road** described by Searle, that leads from the **object** to the **observer**. Understanding that backward road is absolutely necessary for understanding the **consciousness system that operates the biosphere**. Without the backward road—if objects did not present themselves to observers—perceptual consciousness would be useless.

The **process of abstraction** that I described in earlier essays could not have occurred without the backward road. The backward road enables the **physical object** to project itself into the human mind (and into the focus of other sentient beings) by presenting its **essence** as a **phenomenon** for the mind. For groups of humans, that process makes possible the **abstraction** of the object. Only if the **essence** presents itself to **multiple** human minds can cultural groups assign a *word* or *name* that represents the object or essence. So, the backward road is essential for the development of *language* and *concepts*. But the *consciousness system* uses the *backward road* in an even more fundamental way, and fundamental operations of the biosphere itself would not work without it! If there were no backward road, whereby the environment presents itself to sentient beings, food would not present itself to hungry animals, so animals could not find food. And by the way, humans utilize the backward road to present themselves to each other.

The biosphere is equipped with and supports what humans have identified as *light waves*, *sound waves*, *radio wavelengths*, and *a variety of waves that produce heat*. The biosphere produces what humans have identified as *odors*. Its fruits and meats are *tasty*. Gravity holds the biosphere in place and helps to organize it. All these naturally occurring *media* are utilized by *individual consciousness*. Through them, even inanimate objects like rocks and clouds are enabled to *causally present* themselves to *sentient organisms*, using Searle's *backward road*. The *light, sounds, odors, tastes*, and *surfaces* that empower the senses of sentient organisms to *see, hear, smell, taste*, and *feel physical objects* are all parts of *the consciousness system*. Every tangible object projects an *intangible essence*, transmitted by these media to sentient beings, through which consciousness operates. Then the *essence* presents itself by way of the *human senses* to the human mind.

So, the biosphere *displays itself.* The *consciousness system* is an *integrated system* that includes both *the observers and what they observe,* and the operations of the biosphere depend on both the observers and the observed. Both the observer and the observed are parts of a *holistic system*. In the biosphere, *animals* evolved as *observers*, and were able to survive, because the *useful objects* of the biosphere were kind enough to present themselves to the *sentient organisms*. The sentient organisms were totally dependent on the biosphere's display and bounty.

To try to extract from this gigantic holistic, operational system an *essence of individual awareness* that is **consciousness**, separate and apart from the systematically interacting processes that I have been describing, is a mistake. The *biosphere* is a *system* that is alive, and *consciousness* is its essence. It contains many living objects. No life on earth exists independently of the biosphere. Environment is a requirement for all life. *Consciousness* operates the system by which the biosphere is aware of itself, which enables the components of the biosphere to interact with each other. The sentient *organisms* are just *participants*. They die; the *biosphere, consciousness, consensus reality*, and *species* live on.

Any "*essence of individual awareness*," separate and apart from the biosphere's display, would be useless. The objects on display are not "*things in themselves*" separate and apart from the *consciousness system*, as philosophers like Kant, and even Descartes, vainly imagined. The *objects* are a part of the *interacting system* that is the biosphere, as are the *observers*. Consciousness connects the *observers* and the *observed* and enables them to interact intentionally and symbiotically. More specifically, *nonphysical essences* connect *observers* and the *observed*. Perhaps an identification of nonphysical essence as whatever it is that connects physical objects with the minds of sentient beings will be useful. Elsewhere, I have suggested that there are different categories of *nonphysical essences*. The *nonphysical essences* that represent *physical objects* may *differ in kind* from nonphysical essences that represent *social constructs*, or *numbers* or *geometric forms*, or *time* and *space*, or *nothing*—the absence of anything—or other possible categories. The *consciousness system* includes all the participating components: *plants, brains, nerves, senses, media, physical objects, nonphysical essences of every category, phenomena*, and *organisms*, and probably other things that I can't even think about and am not listing here!

ESSENCES, LANGUAGE, AND PHYSICALISM

In the preceding section, I suggested that the biosphere *presents* itself to sentient organisms. I used John R. Searle's *metaphor* of the *"backward road."* That "road" was obviously totally *metaphoric*: there is no "road" from objects to eyes, but the metaphor conveys a powerful truth. Now deeper nonmetaphorical analysis is required. The metaphor is helpful, because words fall short in the attempt to describe this *operation of consciousness*. Objects of the biosphere *do nothing* to "present" themselves. They simply *appear*. But notice that even the word *"appear"* seems to indicate *action*. Objects aren't doing anything! The English language is poorly equipped to accurately describe what happens in *conscious perception*. The language has *nouns and verbs*, and in our mental operations, we recognize *subjects and objects* that correspond to *nouns* and *verbs*. We use the *nouns and verbs* to represent *subjects and objects and actions*. The *subject* usually acts on the *object* and the *verb* indicates the *action*. The English language that is available in nouns and verbs to represent subjects, objects, and action do a poor job of describing what happens in an event of *conscious perception*. Both the *subject and object* are nouns, and play important roles in the *event of conscious perception*. That event (or is it a process?) is hard to capture with *active* verbs. Nothing is doing anything in the precise event of *conscious perception* itself *until* the *perception* itself actually *occurs*. Teachers of writing teach that the *active voice* is more powerful writing than the *passive voice*. The writing is more powerful if the subject acts through the verb! But neither the active voice nor the passive voice captures what is going on between the objects in the biosphere and sentient beings in an event of perception! The words *consciousness, awareness*, and *perception* share a nuance of meaning that does not lend itself to expression through any verb. In a strange way, the *nonphysical essence* (another noun) is what is *"going on"* between the *objects* and the *sentient beings*! It is somehow involved in the *meaning* shared by *consciousness, awareness* and *perception*. As I suggested in the preceding section, the *nonphysical essence* is the "thing" that connects the *observer* with the *physical object.*

The individual organism *"sees* or *perceives."* But it sees or perceives things it wasn't looking for. The object *"appears* or *presents."* But those verbs, connected to nouns, too strongly imply action. No statement that can be made using these elements of speech accurately describes the *conscious perception event* independently of the other elements. *The seeing and appearing and presenting are a single event!* They all involve the illusive *nonphysical essence.* Perhaps we should coin a word *appearsee* to try to capture the largely passive *single event of perception.* Or even generate a verb from the noun *essence.* The observer might *"essence"* the object, or vice versa! But the nonphysical essence is something *real* and it *"essences"* both the *observer* and the *observed.* My whole point here is that *perception* involves *seeing, appearing,* and *presenting, and* constitutes a *single event* in which the *phenomenon* becomes active in the mind. It is the starting point for the *activity of the mind.* And we have no language structure that adequately captures and conveys the *unitary* event. Perhaps that is because we just don't fully understand the identity and role of the *nonphysical essence* of the *object.* Although the *sentient being* may have been *"looking,"* there is no conscious perceptual event until the object *"appears."* Although the object may have been *"presenting,"* there was no conscious perceptual event until the observer *"sees."* In short, there was no conscious *perceptual event* until all the components converged. In that *instant of perception,* the *nonphysical essence* connects the *sentient being* and the *observed object.* The *nonphysical essence* is the way consciousness operates in the biosphere. The perceptual event is a function of the conscious biosphere!

The *object* is associated with its *essence.* The essence of the object is *sensed* by the sentient being. In the perception event, the sentient being *becomes aware* of the object. The *essence connects* or *unites* the *sentient being* and the *object* in a *unitary event.* Nothing *physical* "moves" from the object to the mind of the sentient being. Sure, light is involved, but it is available in every direction, and nothing is "moving." And remember that I have suggested a connection between light itself and consciousness. Nothing moves at all in the split second of *now* when perception occurs. Even if someone argues that *photons*, or quanta, of light are moving, I don't believe that affects the point I am making. Moving in what direction? It just means that the *nonphysical essence* is occupying light from the object to the observer. That, too, is just part of the *consciousness system*. Perhaps, as I suggested, the object *"essences"* the observer, without doing anything. But now let me suggest that the *essence presents* the *object* to the *observer*. The *consciousness system* that operates the biosphere really seems to be the cause of the event of perception.

The sliver of time that we call *now* whose importance I mentioned earlier plays a major role in perception. Perception always and only occurs *now*. In fact, that moving sliver that we call *now* is the *only* time that anything can ever happen. These observations about the *unity of perception*: *appear-see-present, essence connects,* apply to all aspects of perception: sight, sound, taste, smell, touch, and proprioception.

If the sentient being is a *human* and *"recognizes"* the object, it means that the *essence* has triggered pre-existing, *language-dependent knowledge*, and a thought occurs. For that to happen, the language and meaning must have already been internalized from a cultural group by the individual observer. Memory is involved. "Hey, that was a shooting star!" But a knowledgeable friend might reply, "No, a meteor burned on entering the earth's atmosphere." The words of the first speaker have triggered pre-existing, *language-dependent* knowledge in the friend. *Consciousness and thought* includes both the *perception* and the ensuing *language-dependent* interpretation of the perception.

The *transformation* of an *essence* into a *thought* does not make either the *essence* or the *thought physical*. I don't gain weight by looking at a cake.

I don't wear a face mask in a Zoom meeting during COVID-19 pandemic times. It would be very difficult to say exactly where and how an *essence* becomes a *concept* or *thought*. That is the great gap between Plato's world of essences and Aristotle's physical world. It would be fair to say that phenomena NEVER become enduring thoughts in the absence of a mediating group that shares and maintains the phenomena, and create words and concepts, and find meaning. But somehow it happens. I hope that this discussion lends understanding to the *role of language* in *abstract thinking*.

But let me take the explanation about the fact that thoughts and concepts are *not physical* a step further. As you read this essay, hopefully it will transfer *thoughts* from my mind to yours. But when you read them, *nothing physical* will move from me to you. If you "get it," you are not taking anything *physical* from me. The *physical*, as the physicalists explain it, has *mass* and occupies space. But you will be no heavier and I no lighter because of your reading this! Transfer of weight (mass) is not how *consciousness* works. That is not how *essences that are operative in consciousness* work. Nothing physical is transferred when I write and you read. But the *nonphysical thought* is transferred.

Society depends on participation in *linguistic, symbol recognition and electronic participation in consciousness* to share *meaning*. *Consciousness* supplies and enables the transmission of meaning. It uses weightless *concepts* (and images) maintained by the group for transmission of knowledge. All those concepts originated as *essences* in the biosphere that had no weight. The *essences* were assigned words, and that gave rise to *language*. Words and language have no weight. Humanity commuted the *language* into *knowledge* that has no weight. That is how humanity arrives at *understanding and meaning*, as best it can, and *deals with reality*. *Meaning* and *understanding* are group things as well as individual things and are not physical.

Communication requires consciousness. *Physical objects* in the biosphere play the roles in consciousness that I have described, by *presenting themselves*—by appearing as *essences*. But even if *physical* objects present essences to the mind, using *physical media*, the consciousness that I am describing cannot be totally *physical*, even if *parts* of the physical play roles in the *consciousness system*. The *brain* and *sense organs* are physical. But *information and thoughts* are parts of consciousness, and they are not physical within the meaning of any current usage of the word *physical*, as we have just shown. You will not experience the *information* that I transfer to you by my writing as something *physical*. Thoughts that are transferred from my mind to yours are not physical. That is obvious. The *essences* that arise in the biosphere and present themselves to human minds are not physical.

The computer in front of you or the paper in your hand is *physical*, but the *information* they present to your mind is not physical. While I am writing, the essay is part of *my conceptual thinking*, and while you are reading, or listening, my ideas become parts of *your conceptual thinking*. But nothing physical is being transferred. The concepts that are transferred are *essences* represented by *words* that represent *nonphysical ideas*. *Physical objects* are capable of conjuring up *phenomena* for the mind by the *essences* that present them. *Conceptual thinking*, as we know and experience it, was made possible by *linguistic, symbol recognition* and *mathematical participation in consciousness* and is an important part of the *consciousness system*. Those things are *not physical*, to the extent that they are part of shared knowledge.

This discussion of *thoughts vs. physicalism* brings up the problem of *dualism*, which I will discuss in depth in the next essay, the *ninth essay* in this series. Searle, Honderich, and most other philosophers *want* to reject *dualism* and find a *monistic* approach. After all, *knowledge* and *physical objects* have to be parts of the same reality. They don't exist in divided reality. There are not two realities. So, dualism is almost unimaginable. The aggravating problem of *dualism* and the desire to eliminate it is probably one of the major factors that lead philosophers to adopt *physicalism*. They try to eliminate dualism by resorting to pure *physicalism* and contending that mind and thought are physical. But that is particularly problematic insofar as thoughts, essences, and concepts are concerned, as I have just demonstrated. The theory I am describing solves the problem of dualism, but further discussion of dualism will add nothing to the description of *consciousness as a system* in the current essay. Dualism deserves its own discussion, so I will defer a detailed discussion of how the theory of *consciousness as a system* eliminates dualism to the next essay, the *ninth essay* in this series.

CONSCIOUSNESS: THE ROLE OF THE SENSES

I have suggested that *consciousness as a system* causes the biosphere to make its constituent parts available to sentient beings. We now need to examine in greater detail the *role of the senses* of the sentient beings in the *system that is consciousness*. It is the *senses* that receive and transmit the *biospheric presentation* of objects and essences to the human brain. The *senses* are integral parts of *the consciousness system* that enable *individual organisms* to cope with the environment in which they evolved. In the absence of organs of perception, the brain would be useless. Imagine a detached brain floating around in the biosphere! Philosophers have actually fantasized detached brains in a vat in their effort to identify *physical brains* as the source of consciousness! They point out that the cranial vault can be conceptualized as a vat.

But living brains are not in vats. They are parts of living *bodies*, and individual bodies are parts of living organisms, and living organisms are parts of social *groups* of humans that exist in *environments* in the *biosphere*. Along with the *senses*, the *entire human organism*, and the *environment, including the individual's social groups*, the *brain* is part of the system that enables individuals to *participate in consciousness*. The brain is the most powerful component in the constellation of human physical structures that provide the human capacity to *participate in consciousness*. The senses and the brain work together to enable *individuals to participate in consciousness* in order to engage the environment. If a sentient organism can *sense* something, it can eat it, hit it, hide from it, chase it, run from it, or do whatever seems necessary or appropriate! Each of the senses makes a powerful contribution to human *participation in consciousness*. I agree with Ted Honderich[67] and John R. Searle[68] that *sensory perception* is *actual participation* in reality.

Sight is what we usually think about first when we talk about *perception*. Both Honderich and Searle talked about *sight*. The participation by means of *sight* is definitely a part of consciousness. *But all of the senses* are important parts of consciousness. For instance, hearing receives the speech and language, that enables the internalization of concepts. As I have indicated, the senses gather data, using their particular power, and feed that data to the brain, where it is processed to produce the *conscious experience of the individual*. The integration of the work of the senses by *individual consciousness* allows the individual living organism to *directly participate* in its *environment*.

The sentient organism's effective participation in the environment requires the *entire participatory process*, utilizing all the senses and all elements of the *consciousness system*. It is a mistake to try to reduce *consciousness* to *perception* or the resulting *mental product*. All of the senses are involved and play important roles in the total human *participation in consciousness*. Individual humans participate *directly* in their *physical environment—the biosphere*—using their *senses*. They use the *essences* of the biosphere in their quest for survival. When dealing directly with the biosphere itself, individuals are not using an *internal* world of *representations*, as Kant and other philosophers argued. They use the senses to interact directly within and as part of the biosphere. The food and many other things that satisfy *human needs* are found outside the individual. The individual uses the *senses* to find and deal with them very directly. Of course, information stored as *abstractions* and *concepts* are used in the *interpretation* of the *nonphysical essences* of the biosphere.

LANGUAGE, CONCEPTUAL THINKING AND PERCEPTION

Consciousness is a system that empowers humans and other sentient beings to cope with their environments. But for humans, the most important part of the *biosphere* is the *human cultural* environment and the essences and meanings that the cultural group has collected in *language* and *consensus reality*. I am returning now to the discussion about how language was involved in the cultural evolution of individual *conceptual thinking*. *Conceptualization* is just as important as *perception* for *participation in consciousness*.

It is well known that the *eyes* create an *actual image* that the brain processes. The *retinal images* are upside down and inverted, but the brain fixes that. If special lenses are used to invert the images presented to the retina, after a few weeks, the brain will fix that too! Perhaps the discovery of the existence of *retinal images* suggested the mistaken belief that *all* human mental impressions, including sensory perception, create some kind of internal *representation* with which the individual mind deals internally, but that was not accurate. The internal process is *presentation* by the senses, not *representation* through symbols within the mind, so far as perception of the physical environment is concerned. Let me be quick to say that *representations* play a vital and necessary role in the complex processes of *group participation in consciousness*, but *representations* are not a part of the *individual's* "internal" mental process for interacting directly with the physical environment. Individuals use representations in the form of words and language for *communication* with other humans and for *interpreting* their environment and *thinking* abstractly, but *not* for *directly perceiving* the environment. Perception is direct.

Representations *are* an important part of the process by which individuals deal with *other individuals*. Other *individuals* are a part of the individual's social environment. Representations also play an active part in *individual participation in consciousness* as a part of the *abstractions maintained by the group and installed into the individual* for use in what Vygotsky called "higher mental functions." And, as mentioned above, the retained representations enable the individual to interpret the biosphere. If I see a horse or a tree, I know that it is a *horse* or *tree*, not because of *perception*, but because I have *internalized* those *concepts*. The individual also uses representations for *conceptual thinking*. And for an individual to participate in the consciousness of a group, there must be representations—*words*, or *abstractions*—that transmit thoughts from one individual to another. *Linguistic, symbol recognition, mathematical, and electronic participation in consciousness* enable groups to *participate in consciousness* and deal with *concepts*. But the fact that individuals use representations to *work with other individuals* does not alter the fact that seeing, hearing, tasting, feeling, and smelling is direct *participation in the biosphere. It is direct participation in the biosphere that involves and includes the perceived objects.* When the individual is participating directly in the environment *without* any involvement of any group, the brain assimilates the data that the *senses* gather, and the individual uses the product to guide the individual's operations in the environment, and *representations* play no role in the actual *direct perception.*

But *conceptualization* is very important. Even on a solo hike on a lonely mountain trail, most of the *perceptions* of a modern educated human will be "seen" in light of *concepts* that have been *internalized* from the individual's *cultural group*. All the rocks, trees, and even the bears can only be *identified* by *internalized concepts*. They are *perceived* in light of the understanding provided by those stored mental impressions. An educated person who has never seen an actual bear will immediately recognize a bear, despite the fact that a woman, (who is well known in philosophical discussions), who had only experienced a black-and-white environment might not recognize the color red the first time she sees it, even if she has learned all there is to know conceptually about color while in the black and white environment![69] The color red is a qualia. Qualia are experienced perceptually, and must be experienced perceptually before they can be conceptualized. A bear is not a *qualia*! *Qualia* can only be experienced in *perception*. The word *red* can convey the *concept of red* only if the parties to the conversation have experienced the red qualia. Most of what *perception* deals with is *probably qualia*, but the conscious processes become *dominated* by the *stored concepts*, and interpretation of the qualia. That makes the entire conscious process, involving perception, and its interpretation by stored concepts very useful in using perception to deal with the environment.

At the *group* level, *representations* are absolutely essential for participation in *linguistic, symbol recognition and electronic participation in consciousness*. The *group* shares and participates in consciousness collectively by means of *representations*. *Words* are *representations*. They represent *nonphysical essences,* and indirectly, they also represent *physical objects* whose essences are represented by the words. Written words represent spoken words that represent objects and ideas. Words are applied by groups of humans to represent the *phenomena*—the essences that the biosphere presents to human minds. *Concepts* and *ideas—abstractions—*are fundamental to *conceptual thinking*, which is a tremendously important function of *consciousness* in the modern world.

The group installs *language* and *mathematical knowledge* into children, and the children learn to intentionally use the linguistic abstractions for *conceptual thinking*. Children *internalize* the language and culture that surrounds them. Can you imagine my excitement when I discovered that the great Russian psychologist Vygotsky had described this process in detail, after I had been working on similar ideas for over twenty-five years, almost totally isolated from academia except for its books! My background is in law, and I had realized that law was faith dependent and based on collective thought. That led me to examine the role of *language* and consciousness. I had almost completed the writing of these essays by the time I found the writings of Vygotsky. It was very exciting to find strong academic support for the idea that *internalized language* is the basis for *abstract thinking*. Please think about the paradigm shift involved in this understanding of *abstract thinking*. The common notion is that children "learn to talk." For most people, thinking is just something that happens as a child grows older. The popular notion of learning to talk is not usually associated at all with learning to think! But even though the conversion of *phenomena* to *thought* remains a mystery, at least we can now understand that *internalization* of the *language* of the surrounding cultural group provides the entire basis for *abstract thinking* that Vygotsky called "higher mental functions."

Concepts and abstractions result from *language* and are created and maintained as *group functions.* Without language, and groups, there would be no *concepts* and *abstractions* as such. Individuals use *concepts* and *abstractions* internalized from language in *individual* mental operations. As mentioned earlier, if I see a "big green tree," I just see something and have to find the descriptive concepts in my internalized *consensus reality*, the linguistic storehouse of knowledge.

Abstract thinking, empowered by language, took human *participation in consciousness* to a new and different level. The *power of abstract individual thinking*, if it existed at all prior to the development of language, was greatly enhanced by the development and use of language. In the modern world, consciousness includes an astronomical number of abstractions. *Individual consciousness* is not what it was 100,000 years ago; it has evolved. The evolution was *cultural evolution*—the expansion of knowledge maintained by the cultural group. But the expansion also necessarily developed concurrently within *individuals* as they internalized the expanding language.

Language has *evolved* tremendously since it first appeared. It had to evolve to contain the growing body of knowledge that was collecting in *consensus reality. Symbol recognition participation in consciousness* and *electronic participation in consciousness* greatly enhanced the growth rate of both *language* and *consensus reality.* Human *participation in consciousness—participation in abstract thinking*—has increased commensurately.

Perceptual consciousness is a wonderful thing. It promoted evolution. It plays a pivotal role in Honderich's theory of *actual consciousness*. In the modern world, perceptual consciousness remains extremely important for many fundamental processes of life. We should not text while driving; we need to watch the road. However, *abstractions* and *conceptual thinking* engage the human mind today to a much greater degree than does *direct perception*. The conscious human mind is, in large measure, a vast storehouse of *abstracted information* that the individual has internalized from the group. That information provides a very useful interpretation of the biosphere, which becomes the basis for the individual's decisions about actions. Cultural groups are even larger storehouses of information. With the advent of *electronic participation in consciousness*, groups collected information *electronically* into storehouses that are even more vast than all the reservoirs of written language. Those abstractions, not direct perception, are the main things that human consciousness deals with in the twenty-first century.

Direct perception plays a much *smaller* role in the useful function of consciousness in the modern world than does *conceptual thinking*. *Conceptual thinking* need not involve *direct perception* at all. Given the strong Western ideology of *individualism*, it is ironic that without a *cultural group*, there would be little meaningful use of concepts by *individuals*. If Descartes and Kant had *not* been surrounded by parents, peers, and teachers, they would have never learned to *talk*. And without the concepts represented by the *words* that they learned from their cultural groups, they could not have participated in *conceptual thinking*. And they could not have said the things that they said and written the things they wrote for *group* consumption and recollection.

CONSCIOUSNESS AND EVOLUTION

Evolution empowered animals to *participate in consciousness.* Unique sense organs evolved in the various species, all directed to the *biosphere* that they share. All senses of all species of animals participate in the same biosphere and the same biospheric consciousness. Animals in the biosphere are *aware* of the *awareness* of other animals. But each species *participates in consciousness* in its own unique way. A very unique way of *participating in consciousness* in the biosphere evolved within humans. As I have said repeatedly, *consciousness itself did not evolve.* It was there along. It probably was a major factor in *causing evolution* to happen.

Active consciousness itself, for humans, roughly corresponds to day-light, when we are usually awake. Nonhuman species evolved differently and they *participate in consciousness* and the biosphere differently. Some organisms have eyes that actually equip them for night vision. Bats are even equipped with sonar that does not depend on light and sight at all. That is what it is like to be a bat! Rattlesnakes "see" with infrared or other waves outside the spectrum of so-called light that the human eyes use. Butterflies have all kinds of sensory receptors, including ultraviolet sensors, that differ greatly from those of humans, but as I pointed out earlier, they are able to find the zinnias that I planted. But humans evolved a unique capacity to deal with *essences* that the *biosphere presents.*

The unique capacity of humans to deal with essences that enabled humans to use *linguistic participation in consciousness* is the distinctive feature of human *participation in consciousness.* Consciousness *in humans* includes capacity to work with *nonphysical essences* including those that match the world of *physical matter.* Other animals don't have that capacity, at least not to the same extent as humans. And without *nonphysical essences,* the *physical objects* of the *biosphere* could not present themselves to *human minds* as *phenomena.* Nonphysical essences *existed* and were *available* in the biosphere. Humans *evolved* the capacity to use the *nonphysical essences* of *physical objects*, as well as *nonphysical essences* that are not related to physical objects, and to convert them to language.

All life, including animal life, evolved in the physical biosphere with its essences. Evolution strengthened the ability of all species of animal life to participate in their environments. *Consciousness* that was built into the biosphere played a critical role in that process. Evolution found the *resources available* in the environment to promote the survival of animals. Species evolved in response to differing environments, conditions, and genetic accidents. Different species evolved *different sense organs* to *participate in consciousness*. In humans, *eyes* evolved to utilize *light, ears* to utilize *sound waves, touch* to *sense physical contact*, the *olfactory system* to *detect odors, taste* to sense the properties of *food*, and *proprioception* to sense *body position* in the earth's *gravitational field*. The brain evolved to *process* the *sensory data* that the organism gathers from the environment, via the senses. *Brains and nervous systems evolved to participate in consciousness.*

The light, sound, odors, tastes, positions and surfaces that can be sensed are all integral parts of the *biospheric system used by humans in their individual participation in consciousness. Physical objects* that present themselves to sentient beings are integral parts of the *consciousness system* that operates the biosphere. After receiving sensory data, the brain sends messages, via nerves, to direct the body's responses to that data. *Sensing* and *reacting* are means of *survival.* The "external" world of *physical objects* and the "internal" mental world of *nonphysical essences* that the biosphere presents as *phenomena* are parts of the *consciousness system* that operates the biosphere. The evolution of human *sensory organs* promoted survival. The brain is ultimate *sensory organ*. It evolved to *participate in consciousness* by integrating sensory data.

Life always exists in a *particular environment* and depends on that environment. Contact between *life* and its *environment* guided the course of evolution. *Giraffes* evolved *long necks* to graze on *leaves* high above the ground and humans evolved *big brains* to deal with *essences* and *concepts*. Species retained biological changes that promoted survival. Evolution empowered *animal* life to participate directly in the *consciousness system*. Consciousness *promoted* the ability of *animal life* to deal with its environment. Consciousness *supported survival*. Evolution empowered *humans* to *utilize consciousness* to deal with *nonphysical essences*, and *concepts*, just as it empowered giraffes to eat leaves high on a tree. Colin McGinn argued that consciousness supports *survival needs* and suggested that because it evolved for that purpose, it is not equipped to examine itself.[70] He is right. Conscious animals *sense* the surrounding environment. Consciousness is a practical tool for survival.

Human *participation in consciousness* has expanded in response to the expanding needs of the expanding human population. *Linguistic participation in consciousness* (expanded by *symbol recognition* and *mathematical* and *electronic participation in consciousness*) greatly enhanced the aid that primary consciousness had provided and carried it to a different level. *Linguistic participation in consciousness* empowered language, and language enabled groups of humans to operate systems that perform tasks necessary for survival more effectively than individuals could perform acting alone. In fact, individuals acting alone simply could not have accomplished many of these tasks; cooperative group effort was an absolute prerequisite. Individuals would not need to build interstate highways, or cities or bridges but social groups that include individuals need them. Groups need a lot of structure, both social and physical, that an individual trying to survive alone in the biosphere would not need. But Individuals can function better as members of a social group. Society institutionalizes the social structures and entities that are necessary to support the population of humans now living in the biosphere. Over the ages, hunting, fishing, farming, construction work, teaching, providing medical care, computer technology, and all other human endeavors have been rendered much easier with the help of *linguistic participation in consciousness* and language. Human brains grasping for greater *participation in consciousness* would not have evolved if the essences that become concepts had not been present in the biosphere any more than the giraffe's long necks would have evolved had there been no high leaves. The concepts and essences are crucial elements for human *participation in consciousness.*

The *developmental processes* of life shed light on the evolution of the capacity for *participation in consciousness.* Children are not born with fully developed ability to *participate in consciousness.* Their *participation in consciousness* develops in stages and is evidenced in the stages of faith development that I described in the *second essay* dealing with stages and sources of faith. With the deterioration that results from aging, *participation in consciousness* declines. Biological *participation in consciousness* appears to end with death. The developmental process that gradually empowers children to *participate in consciousness* at increasing levels is consistent with the idea that evolution gradually developed the power in humanity itself to *participate in consciousness* in the biosphere.

The process of individual development likely begins with *qualia.* Philosophers use the word *qualia* to describe certain types of *conscious experience.* The word *qualia* is derived from the same root as *quality.* Qualia are the *direct, subjective experiences* of the conscious organism. Wikipedia Qualia - Wikipedia states, "Examples of qualia include the pain of a headache, the taste of wine, or the perceived redness of an evening sky." Individual human *participation in consciousness* may have begun with *qualia.* Newborn babies likely experience pure *qualia.* The development of mental processes starts there. Human evolution gradually expanded that participation. I suspect that *perception,* in and of itself, primarily experiences *qualia* throughout a lifetime. Interpretation by *internalized conceptualization* gradually dominates the operations of perception, so that we "see" things that we recognize because of *internalized concepts!* The *stages of human faith development* and growing *participation in consciousness* in individuals likely recapitulates the evolution of *participation in consciousness* by humanity. That individual development results from physical maturation, increasing social development, and increasing participation in *concept formation* by the *internalization of language.* As I have repeatedly mentioned, the greatest expansion of *participation in consciousness* came with the development of language by groups and *internalization* by individuals. Accordingly, a child's greatest step in *participation in consciousness* is learning to talk. The development of *conceptualization* provides meaning to the *qualia,* and directs the *focus of attention* of *perception* to the things that *individual consciousness needs* to see.

FUNCTIONALISM

It was necessary for the human physical apparatus—the human body—to evolve to a certain level of *functionality* to be able to *participate in consciousness.* Bats, rattlesnakes, and butterflies have remarkable sensory equipment that humans do not have, but they do not have the ability for *linguistic participation in consciousness* that has evolved in humans. Their evolution produced other functional biological equipment to *participate in consciousness* so that they cope with the biosphere in their own ways. Even primate mammals that are closely related to humans do not have nearly the capacity that humans have for using oral and written signs to convey meaning. I have described the role of the *senses* in consciousness. The *functional level of the human physical apparatus,* including the senses and the *human brain,* plays an important role in human *participation in consciousness.*

The *physical apparatus* that supports human *participation in consciousness* must replicate itself in each succeeding generation of individuals. The *functional apparatus* that enables *participation in consciousness* is *transmitted by genes.* Humans evolved to a *functional level* that enabled them to *participate in consciousness* sufficiently to *develop language*. Language enabled *human groups* to *participate in consciousness* at a *more proficient level* than other animals.

Human *groups*, with their capacity for developing language, operate in consciousness at a higher functional level than *individuals. Functionality* of the *apparatus, organism*, or *group* determines the *level of participation in consciousness*. In a delightful book,[71] *The Mind's I*, Douglas Hofstadter and Daniel Dennett included a clever description of the intelligence exercised by an *anthill* that they named *Aunt Hillary*. The anthill has a form of *consciousness*, in which the individual ants *do not participate. Aunt Hillary—* the colony—participates in the consciousness. *Aunt Hillary* uses individual ants to accomplish tasks for the colony that the individual ants don't know about, even though they are carrying out the activity. The primary intended analogy of *Aunt Hillary* seemed to be the functioning of the *human brain*. Individual brain cells do not have to be "conscious" for the animal with the brain to enjoy conscious experience. However, the powerful *analogy* of *Aunt Hillary* can also apply to *humans functioning as groups* as Hofstadter recognizes in commentary on the story. Language, with the strong role that it plays in human consciousness, is a social function. That fact is strong evidence that consciousness is not simply manufactured by individual human brains. *Language* is created and maintained by human social groups, largely outside the brains of individual members of the groups. But *abstract thinking* results from *internalization* of language.

The *functional* components transmitted by human *genes* empower *participation in consciousness* by *individual* humans, and through individuals, by social *groups of humans. Linguistic participation in consciousness* is not merely an *individual* human brain thing, although capacity for it is transmitted for the benefit of the group through the genes of individuals. The genes of individuals are also the genes of their social groups. It is important to remember that genes are maintained and perpetuated by *breeding groups*, not by *individuals*. Individuals do not just appear by magic; they are products of the species: the group.

Groups participate in consciousness. Robert Pirsig points to the functioning intelligence of a city like New York City.[72] Organized groups have a greater functional capacity for participation in consciousness than do the individuals who make up the group. The individuals do not necessarily know exactly what the group is doing, even though they are playing a role in the effort and know what actions they are taking. They don't necessarily foresee the product of their effort. A sewer worker in New York City does not have to understand the social importance of his or her work. He or she just has to know how to do it. Other New Yorkers do other things and don't have to know how to do sewer work! That is how human *social systems participate in consciousness* and exert intelligence that exceeds the intelligence of the participating individuals. Perhaps a better illustration is the way human intelligence is aggregated in the functions of *markets*, such as stock markets. Markets make decisions about *market value* that are controlled by no individual. The existence of consciousness at a *higher level of social organization* supports the idea that *consciousness* exists *independently* of the *physical* organization of *individual* human brains. Consciousness is not just a *brain* thing. The only prerequisite for *participation in consciousness* is that the organism, group, or computer be *functionally capable* of participation. *Consciousness* is in the *biosphere* and available for sentient beings to use, like air, water, sunshine, matter, and energy. And it is also available for anything else that has the *functional capacity* to use it. Because consciousness functions in the biosphere as a *system* and there are separate components of that system, it is possible for a computer, for instance, to participate in the *system that is consciousness* for a particular function. If the sentient life on earth is wiped out and the earth remains, new conscious life is likely to evolve over eons of time, because consciousness will be available, and will induce evolution of conscious life.

The growth of the *use* of consciousness since the development of language has been dramatic. Indeed, the growth of the *use* of consciousness in the past thousand years, or even the past hundred years, has been fantastic. *That growth did not occur because of escalated evolution of the human brain.* There may have been a little evolution of the brain but not nearly enough to account for the explosion of human *participation in consciousness.* The fantastic growth in human *participation in consciousness* occurred because of the *evolution of group functions—cultural evolution.* It results from increased *cultural* or *social participation in consciousness.* The growth of *language, mathematics, science,* and *technology—*all *group functions—*is the basis for the growth of cultural functions. The fact that groups continue developing useful *abstractions* is both the cause and the effect of the tremendous expansion of human *participation in consciousness.* The *functionality of social groups* has evolved to *participate in consciousness* much more fully and completely than an individual roaming around in the biosphere could ever have accomplished alone. Although human brains are involved in all these human activities, the growth of the use of consciousness is not just in *physical, individual brains!*

The *functionality* for group *participation in consciousness* has been greatly enhanced by the ability of social groups of humans to use *technology.* As pointed out earlier, the use of computers and electronic means of communication is an *enhancement of human consciousness.* It *is electronic participation in consciousness.* Among scholars, there is debate about whether computers and robots can *"become conscious."* That question is seen from a very different angle, and sounds a little strange, once we understand that humans *just participate in consciousness* and consciousness is something that is available in the biosphere. Computers expanded human *participation in consciousness.* Computers are functionally capable of performing certain tasks much more efficiently, faster, and more accurately than most human brains. That efficiency provided by *electronic participation in consciousness* promotes human survival. Computers and robots are *functional* devices created by *conscious humans* to promote human survival in the biosphere. Philosophers are tantalized by the possibility that computers are, or possibly can *become, conscious*. That fascination arises in part from the mistaken assumption that consciousness is an *individual human brain thing* rather than a *biospheric* thing. If, as I contend, consciousness is *not* merely a product of individual human brains, but something that human brains *participate* in, and that operates the *system* that is the biosphere, the role of computers and electronic communication becomes obvious. They are *extensions* of *human participation in consciousness. Electronic participation in consciousness expands* the ability of human *senses and brains* to *participate in consciousness.* There are no computers roaming around in the biosphere that no human knows or has known about! They were not discovered in the Galapagos Islands, having evolved there as an exotic specimen in isolation from the rest of the biosphere! The devices make human *participation in consciousness* more effective. They expand the *functionality* of human senses and human group processes, and the expanded ability is more for *collective* social purposes than for individuals. The computers *are* participating in the *system that is consciousness.*

But technology *also* expands the functionality of *individual consciousness*. My glasses let me see more clearly. My hearing aids may help a little! These tools expand my personal ability to *participate in consciousness.* Computers are much more complex, but the principle is the same. Understanding that *technology* simply expands human *participation in consciousness* explains how electronic devices are able to seemingly *participate in consciousness. They are in fact participating in consciousness.* They have become parts of the *biospheric consciousness system.* The ability of humanity to *expand* its *functional* capacity for *participation in consciousness* shows that consciousness is not merely a product of the *human brain* that evolved in individuals. The expansion is primarily at the group and cultural level. If there were no social groups, would an individual need a computer? Although individual brains are involved in the use of consciousness, *consciousness is much bigger*!

The real difference between *humans* and *computers* is not *consciousness*; it is *life*. I have repeatedly emphasized the connection between consciousness and life. Humans *evolved* in the biosphere and are *alive* and participate in consciousness. Computers aren't alive and didn't evolve in the same way that life evolved. They are human artifacts. They "evolved" *in human thinking* as part of *cultural evolution*. They are machines that are *subject* to the laws of physics, including the *law of entropy*: they progress to lower, not higher, states. They don't participate in utilizing solar energy the same way living organisms do, unless that is what they are programmed by humans to do. When their functionality improves, it is because of active human thought, perhaps enhanced by electronic capabilities. *Cause-and-effect*, not *intentionality* and *end cause*, governs the operations of machines. The activity of *humans*, not the activity of the *computers*, is attracted by *purpose*, although computers can be *programmed* to make choices. If GPS starts making the actual decision about where my car will go, instead of giving me information for my decisions, it will be no good for me! Of course, stopping a car to prevent an accident is a wonderful function. And I expect that we will soon have cars with apps that can be programmed for an entire journey. But we will still decide where we want to go. But computers have no *motivation* separate and apart from installed *human motivation*. Consciousness and evolution are associated with *life* in the biosphere, and computers simply improve the *functionality* of human consciousness and decision making. But with all that said, consciousness is present in the biosphere and nothing prevents computer participation other than the limitations of functionality. And finally, the lawyer in me forces me to say that computers are not likely ever to have legal rights—at least I have never heard of such a proposal.

CONCLUSION

In this essay, I have described the *biospheric system that is consciousness*. Admittedly, I have not unraveled the *mystery of consciousness* itself, but I believe that I have provided a better insight into the role that consciousness plays *in the biosphere* and have shown that consciousness is not something that evolved in the *physical brain*. In the next two essays I will discuss *implications* that arise from the theory that *consciousness is a system*. First, I will dispose of *dualism*, and then I will discuss *free will and determinism* and I will complete the refutation of physicalism. Those two essays will provide strong additional support for the theory advanced in the current essay. In *essay eleven*, the final short essay in this series, I will identify some *ultimate mysteries*.

9) DUALISM AND DIRECT REALISM

IMPORTANT IMPLICATIONS ARISE FROM THE theory that *consciousness is a system* and is not merely a product of evolution in sentient beings. In the present essay, I will show how the theory of consciousness as a *biospheric system* eliminates the messy dualism that has plagued the philosophy of the Western world since the time of Plato and Aristotle. First, I will describe the *problem of dualism*. Then I will explain the important concept of *semblance*. And finally, I will review the important role of *direct realism* and complete the refutation of *physicalism*. The present essay provides strong additional support for the theory that consciousness is the operating system of the biosphere and that sentient beings simply *participate in consciousness*.

MIND AND BODY

In the *seventh essay* in this series that dealt with traditional theories of reality, I introduced the *problem of dualism*, and promised to return to it for further discussion. Descartes is often blamed for planting the notion of dualism into the Western conception of reality. Actually, Descartes' dualistic concepts of mind and body (or material) were deeply embedded in Western philosophy, at least back to the time of Plato and Aristotle. But Descartes famously said, "I think, and therefore I am." He suggested that individuals have (or are) subjective minds that are distinct from the matter that composes their bodies, so he is often blamed with the philosophically messy idea of dualism.

Descartes' articulation of the relationship of mind and body involves a very false impression that *I* am a *mind* (mental) and that I have a *body* (physical). In his theory of reality, the body is basically a machine that the mind operates. That conceptualization is not very tidy. And despite his famous quote, the statement that he made does not accurately describe the way we experience our own existence. Drawing on Nagel's suggestion that *consciousness* may be captured by "what it's like to be a bat," Descartes statement does not describe what it is like to be a human being. Humans experience conscious life in the biosphere surrounded by other humans, and that is what being human is like. Descartes dualistic approach is *not* how it feels.

In an effort to escape Descartes' messy dualism, *physicalists* contend that somehow the *material* that is the body *produces consciousness*, but so far, have not succeeded in describing how that happens. The "hard question" for physicalists is "How can the physical body produce thoughts," as well as "How does physical matter that is human become aware of anything?" The *function* of *individual brains* is the focal point for the arguments of the *physicalists* who try to eliminate the problem of dualism with the contention that the *nonphysical* just doesn't exist. They apparently believe that science will ultimately explain the physical electronics, etc. of the brain sufficiently to provide an adequate explanation of matter being aware of its surroundings and producing thought.

The *mind/body* problem is a subset of the larger mystery of the relationship between *physical matter* and *consciousness*. Our *individual consciousness* constructs an *image of the world* that we use in our mental operations. The *problem* presented by *dualism* is figuring out just how that internal *image* of the world relates to the *world* that exists *externally* to us.

Dualism suggests that there are two worlds: the *internal subjective world* and the *external physical world*. After first disposing of *dualism*, I will discuss *direct realism* in the second part of this essay, and that will help to explain the relationship of consciousness to physical matter. Human minds engage the biosphere directly in order to survive in it.

My argument that consciousness necessarily *embraces* the *physical* resolves the problem of dualism in a sense, but how it solves that problem requires a detailed explanation. Obviously, the physical exists *within* consciousness. Although there is much about *the physical* that we don't know and can't explain, everything that we do know about it obviously exists in consciousness. There may be *limits* to human *knowledge,* and there may be *depths* of *being, physical* and *nonphysical*, that human *participation in consciousness* cannot penetrate. But this we know: *matter exists in consciousness*. We know that, because otherwise, we would not be aware of physical matter. But the mere fact that *all* humans *know* about *physical matter*, which makes it clear that physical matter is contained in human *consciousness*, is the only starting point for solving the problem of dualism. There are other things about dualism that we can understand in order to discredit it, so let's examine it in more depth.

If consciousness is real (and it certainly is—Descartes had that right) then, as stated above, the physical is included in it. And if it weren't, we wouldn't even know about it. So, there is no dualism. Matter exists in consciousness. *Existence* and *knowledge of existence* are two parts of a single reality. But still there is a nagging impression that there may be a world *internal to individuals* and a world of *external reality* outside of individuals. To resolve the problem of dualism, we must carefully examine *how the impression of dualism* arises. First let's agree that *dualism* is a *mental* impression. It is a *concept* that exists in our minds. It is a *nonphysical concept*. Like Wednesday and Thursday, that we discussed in the *sixth essay*, you can't look out the window and see dualism. All you see when you look out the window is the *physical biosphere!* You have to look inside yourself for the *other component* of what we call dualism. And then we have to create a *concept* that deals with the *two components.* And it is important to remember that concepts are created by groups. The problem of *dualism* arises in the implausible notion that there are as many *systems of consciousness* as there are *sentient beings,* each with its own consciousness. That doesn't seem very likely, does it? It seems pretty obvious, as we have shown in the previous essay, that that is not the way it is. As we have ploddingly shown, individual sentient beings simply *participate in consciousness.* The *system that is consciousness* is *one system* with many participants. The dualism problem arises from the mistaken assumptions that (1) consciousness only exists in individuals and (2) even more unlikely, it exists separately in each individual. A *participatory role in consciousness* for individual sentient beings makes a lot more sense. I have now described the problem of dualism theoretically and explained why it doesn't exist, but the explanation still probably *feels* very theoretical. That is because we all *experience consciousness* and the *biosphere* separately and *individually.* So, I will describe how the false impression of dualism arose, and that will help dispel it.

DIRECT PERCEPTION AND SEMBLANCE

In earlier essays, I described *direct perception* and the role that it plays in consciousness. Direct perception enables sentient beings to participate directly in the biosphere. Direct *participation in the biosphere* is an important part of what consciousness is about. The physical world that we sense is the *real world.* What we experience is the biosphere that produced humans and all other sentient beings. Consciousness enables animals to engage the biosphere and decide what to do to survive in it. Human ability to sense the physical world and cope with it and survive in it is the most obvious and important role that consciousness plays in the biosphere. Ted Honderich seems to regard that capability as the essence of consciousness, even though he continues to mistakenly believe that each of us has our own version of consciousness.[73]

But *direct perception* from the limited perspective of *individual consciousness* sometimes encounters a significant problem called *semblance*. Not everything that presents itself to *individual consciousness* in direct perception is what it appears to be. The sun *appears* to "rise" and "set." But, although the *appearance* of the rising and setting sun is *directly perceived*, and that is what it *looks like* to *everyone*, the sun does not "rise" and "set"; the earth rotates on its axis. The sun doesn't revolve around the earth. And the sun actually looks much smaller than the earth, from our perspective on the earth's surface, 93,000,000 miles away from it. Such false appearances are called *semblances*. The mind and senses are not playing tricks on us when semblance occurs; the appearance that presents itself to our senses is real, but the appearance is actually deceiving, because of our perspective from our limited *participation in consciousness*. Those false impressions arise because our vantage point from individual *participation in consciousness* is very limited, and evolved to serve our immediate needs. Although *senses* empower *direct perception*, and *participation in the biosphere*, *not every impression* that the senses create as a result of *direct perception* reflects an accurate *concept* of reality. But remember that *groups* create concepts. The *appearances* of a *flat earth* and a *small sun* that *rises* and *sets* are *semblances*. *Semblances* are different from *mirages* or *hallucinations*, in which the mind or senses are in fact playing tricks, and the *thing perceived* is *not* real. The *perception* that produces *semblance* is quite real, but the *impression* that it creates in multiple individual minds that the group then uses to produce a word—a *concept* for *consensus reality*—is *inaccurate*. Semblances are errors of *conceptualization*, not *perception*. Individuals can enjoy the qualia presented by a magnificent sunset without dealing with the conceptualization of the rotating earth!

The capacity for individual participation in consciousness evolved to assist the survival of the individual. Mere participation in consciousness does indeed place individual sentient beings at the center of the part of the biosphere with which he or she must contend, and creates a self-centered vantage point. Perceiving the blazing sun as it actually exists and the earth rotating on its axis would not immediately benefit the survival of little sentient creatures moving around in a very small area of the surface of the earth! Of course, the perception of the sun disappearing below the horizon is totally consistent with the accurate conceptualization that the earth rotates on its axis! If it had not been, humans probably never would have figured it out. So, the perception is not false, but produces a false impression for individual perception, and gives rise to a false meaning in conceptualization, like sunrises, sunsets and a small sun. Now, I will show that dualism is also a semblance.

INDIVIDUAL CONSCIOUSNESS AND DUALISM

Semblances arise from *actual perceptions* but create false impressions that result in *inaccurate conceptualizations*. So, let's analyze the *appearance* of *dualism* against the background of what I described in essays three and four about how *individual consciousness* enables individuals to differentiate themselves from the rest of the biosphere and establish their personal identity. Animal participation in *primary consciousness* began long ago in the earliest stages of evolution. Evolving participation in *primary consciousness* empowered animals to distinguish themselves from the surrounding environment and established them as *observers* of that environment. The power of observation was very important because it allowed individuals to choose their next move. In that functional context in the biosphere, individual humans are *observing* subjects and the *environment* contains the *observed* objects. It is important for individuals to be able to *differentiate* themselves from the *other objects* in the biosphere, for reasons that we discussed in the essays dealing with *human motivation* and how faith establishes *individual identity*.

All individuals—all sentient beings—*always* participate in the biosphere as *subjective observers*. They have to distinguish their own physical being from everything else that exists. *Every* individual always sees reality from a *unique individual* vantage point. From that vantage point, it *always* appears to *every* sentient being that there is an *external reality*. That appearance is an inherent part of the process by which the individual differentiates himself or herself from that environment, establishes individual identity, and copes with the environment. Each individual is an *I* participating in *individual consciousness*. The mental processes of each individual is *totally internal* to that individual. So, it seems to *every human being* as though he or she is *IN HERE,* but *It, (the observed environment) is OUT THERE.* Of course, there *is* an environment that *is* external to every *individual* and their *individual participation in consciousness,* but *it is not external to the consciousness system that operates the biosphere in which the individual is participating.* It is part of and exists within the *biospheric consciousness system.* The biosphere produced the individual observer! Both the individual and the environment are part of the same *biospheric system.* The perception of *inside/outside* is *not inaccurate,* but the *universal* impression that it creates is misleading and leads to incorrect *conceptualization.*

Concepts arise in language, so let's consider the function of language that I have carefully developed in earlier essays. *Dualism* is a *word* in the language. It represents a concept. Individuals use *language* to share their impressions with other human beings. As we have seen, humans create *consensus reality* when they communicate their subjective experiences within the groups of which they are a part. The impression *"I'm in here, and it's out there"* is universal. Individuals share their impressions about *internal/external* with their cultural group. That's the way it looks to everyone. So, they created a *word* that represents that impression. The word in English is *dualism*. The word *dualism* then entered *consensus reality*.

The impression that *my* consciousness is something totally different from *your* consciousness adds to the false impression. But *consciousness* is not mine and yours; we only *participate* in it. Consciousness is the *system that operates the biosphere*. Each of us participates in it individually, but consciousness itself was here when we individuals were born and will be here when we are gone. Compilation of *everyone's individual perception* of an *"external reality"* that is distinct from all *"internal individual realities"* creates the *semblance* of *dualism*. That compilation process produces a lot of *useful* concepts in *consensus reality*, but dualism is not one of them!

The *semblance* of *internal/external* experienced by all individuals is *abstracted* into *consensus reality* as *dualism*. The word *dualism*, and the *meaning* it conveys, found its way into language, just as the words *sunset* and *sunrise* found their way into the language. The words *dualism, sunset* and *sunrise* all accurately describe universal *appearances*, but are merely appearances, and led to inaccurate conceptualizations. *All individuals participate in consciousness* from a totally subjective *individual* viewpoint. They share their mistaken impression of *internal/external* with regard to their environment, and the resulting *consensus reality* contains the erroneous concepts of an *"internal world"* and an *"external world."* Those false impressions were created and maintained just as the erroneous concepts of *flat earth, sunrises, sunsets*, and *small sun* were created and maintained. *Semblances* occur because of the *compilation* of individual impressions that produce a word representing a *mistaken conceptualization*. Once *dualism* became a word and concept, and was included in *consensus reality*, language perpetuated that *semblance* in *individual* conceptual thinking.

With some misgivings, I must admit that the explanation of dualism that I have just provided does not completely depend on my overarching theory that humans just *participate in consciousness*. This explanation of dualism would be accurate, even if each individual has his or her own subjective consciousness. Every *individual* would still be participating in a *single biosphere* that produces every sentient being and in which every sentient being is an *observer*, and everything else (including all other individuals) appears to be *external* to the individual observers! But while perception is always an *individual* thing, *conceptualization* is always a group thing. *Dualism* is a *semblance*, any way you look at it. However, this explanation of *dualism* as *semblance* is very consistent with my larger contention that the individuals all *participate, not only in the same biosphere, but also in the same consciousness*, and that is the much more elegant theory.

THE TWIN SEMBLANCES OF DUALISM AND INDIVIDUALISM

The semblance error of *dualism* is reinforced and complicated by the mistaken assumption that consciousness is something that originates and exists only in *individual brains*. The impression that consciousness is something that originates and exists only in individual brains *is just another semblance*. The *semblance of individualism* arises because the only *participation in consciousness* that subjective *individual consciousness* can confirm is *its own*. That was Descartes' mistake. The semblances of *individualism* and *dualism* are closely related and actually arise from the same mistaken appearance.

Semblance, such as *sunrises*, sunsets, a *small sun* and *flat earth* arise from the relationship between *individual consciousness* and the *external physical* world. By *external world*, I mean the environment that exists *outside of individuals*. Of course, the "external world" includes all other individuals who are external to each individual. *External* semblances (sunrises, sunsets, small sun, and flat earth) present themselves to *individual consciousness* a little differently from the way *dualism and individualism* do. They are external to *ALL individual consciousnesses*. But *individualism* and *dualism* actually arise in large measure *within* the *INTERNAL world* of *individual consciousness*. The misimpression is very *internal* to *individual consciousness. Individualism* and *dualism* arise as the result *of the individual's differentiation* of the *self* from the *environment.*

Both types of semblances—*internal* and *external*—arise within *individual consciousness.* However, the way that internal semblances arise is quite different from the way external semblances arise. The semblances of *individualism* and *dualism* involve the perception of *a difference between self and the external world*, while the appearance of sunsets, flat earth, and small sun are *totally external* and don't involve consciousness of the *self.* Other individuals have similar *perceptions*, but those perceptions are *internal* to the *other* individuals, who are *external* to the *individual perceiver*, and therefore the *perceptions* of those other individuals are *imperceptible* to the *individual perceiver.* The *mental impression* that creates the *internal/external semblance* of *dualism* and *individualism* is *internal* and *subjective* and arises directly from *individual participation* in the *consciousness system* itself, whereas sunsets and the earth are *external* and more *objective.* The *internal/external* appearance that produces *dualism* and *individualism* is mainly *mental*; the *earth's rotation* is *physical.* Because *dualism* and *individualism* arise from *internal* feedback to the mind, it would have been much more difficult for *collective humanity* to figure out that *dualism* and *individualism* are *semblances* than for *collective humanity* to figure out that sunrises, sunsets, small sun and flat earth are *semblances.* The appearance of both *individualism and dualism* were brought about by powerful *internal conscious experience.*

MORE ABOUT DIRECT PERCEPTION

Semblances are the product of *direct perception.* For some thinkers, the existence of *semblances*, in which phenomena are not what they appear to be, raises questions about the reliability of *direct perception.* Some thinkers have used the existence of *semblance* to make arguments that *direct perception* and *direct realism* are not valid. However, *semblance* does not impair the validity of *direct perception*. It merely confirms that *erroneous impressions* arising from observations by *subjective individual consciousnesses* can find their way into *consensus reality*, and that *collective human consciousness,* although superior to *individual consciousness*, is also subjective and imperfect and can make mistakes. Although *semblance* is problematic in that it shows that *direct perception* of physical reality can produce *false impressions*, ultimately *groups*, participating in consciousness at a higher level than the limited subjective participation of individuals, have been effective in weeding out *external* semblance in the quest for reality. Unfortunately, it has been much more difficult for collective humanity to sort out the *internal mental semblances of dualism* and *individualism* than it was to figure out that sunrises and sunsets were caused by the rotation of the earth. If Descartes could have seen from the observation posts of *all individuals*, instead of choosing to doubt whether other individuals existed, he would not have just posited his own existence! It looks like he could have at least acknowledged the existence of his mama and daddy! They taught him to talk! The advantage that we now have is that we now know that language, a group function, is involved in the formation of concepts, and concepts are a necessary part of thinking. If Descartes mama and daddy had not taught him to talk, he would not have had the capacity for conceptual thinking! He wrote as if his mind had just popped up out of nowhere. Other people had to exist for Descartes' thinking to occur. But Descartes' dualism has persisted for a long time despite the existence of many bright minds!

There is no dualism, and consciousness is not created in the individual brain. The consciousness system completely encompasses the dualisms of mind/body, mental/physical, subject/object, and perceiver/perceived. Both sides of each of these expressions of dualism exist within the consciousness system. They are two parts of a single system, both of which are deeply embedded in the operation of the biosphere. Individuals are merely participants.

The *dualism* semblance arises because of the beguiling isolation of *subjective individual human experience*. But it is the *individual* human mind or brain and its limited *participation in consciousness, not consciousness* itself, that is *confined and limited*. If consciousness is *not* understood to be *shared reality*, and one accepts at face value the *appearances* that are produced by and in *individual brains*, it is almost impossible to escape from the erroneous *semblance* of *dualism* and equally difficult to escape the corollary *semblance* of *individualism*. I think that it was the realization that *linguistic participation in consciousness* produces *consensus reality* and abstract thinking that enabled me to realize that *dualism is semblance*.

DESCARTES AND DUALISM

"I think, and therefore I am," said Descartes, a *subjective individual*. The physical Descartes is long since dead. He does not think anymore. But *the important ideas that he thought did not disappear*, and the biosphere and all humanity did not die and disappear when he died. The biosphere, noosphere, collective consciousness, and *consensus reality* are all still here. His thoughts—and the consciousness in which he was merely a *participant*—live on in *consensus reality*. Consciousness and existence are not dependent on Descartes or any other mortal being. Other individuals *are*, and are *thinking*, whether Descartes *thinks* and *is* or not. It is a bit ironic in our world that only trusts the evidence of reality that has been verified by *empirical* science and multiple observers that Descartes' starting point for affirmation of existence was *his own subjective thinking that no one else could see!* His ability to think was just as unobservable to others as theirs was to him! Science generally depends on multiple *observers* for confirmation of its findings.

When Descartes wrote "*I* think, and therefore *I* am," (Emphasis mine.) he placed *himself* at the center of existence and tried to derive everything else that exists from that vantage point. He was operating from and within one of Ted Honderich's *subjective individual worlds*. His perspective arose from the speck of consciousness that was his personal *participation in consciousness* at the time, from which he operated as an observer. And, as Plato had recommended, he was looking inward to confirm the existence of anything! But subjective individuals are not the center of *any* world, except the environment that immediately surrounds them with which they must contend. By placing himself in that position, he implicitly endorsed *individualism*, and as an individual, he explicitly endorsed and articulated the appearance of the *physical/mental* dualism. His *participation in consciousness* allowed him to **think**, but it was his participation in *consensus reality* that had enabled him to think *conceptually* in the first place. His thinking occurred in the *biosphere*. His thinking confirmed that he existed, but from the perspective that I have developed in these essays, his *thinking* confirmed that *language* and *other people* existed. His ability to think conceptually was derived from *internalization of language*, so his thinking proved not only that *he existed*, but that *society exists*. Consciousness was present, and he shared in it. He used words that were contained in the *consensus reality* maintained by his cultural *group* to express his *thoughts*. Culture has preserved his thoughts, so that we are *conscious* of his words and meaning today. His very thoughts still exist in *consensus reality*. The consciousness in which he was participating is still here!

As indicated above, the Cartesian division between *mind* and *matter* mistakenly makes the "*I*" the center of existence. One can only escape that trap by recognizing that consciousness is *not an individual thing* but, at a minimum, a *biospheric* thing. *Mind* and *matter* are components of a single, holistic system. The *consciousness system* embraces and includes both *mental* and *physical*. It includes the *observer* and the *observed*. It includes *objective* and *subjective*. Instead of a *mind* with a *body*, or a *body* with a *mind, humans are integrated physical organisms that evolved in the biosphere and participate in consciousness that is inherent in the biosphere.*

My neighbor and I get electricity from the same utility company to light our homes, and that company also supplies electricity for street lights. That allows both my neighbor and me to see stuff in the street, but it doesn't allow me to see what goes on in the privacy of his home, nor him in mine. Consciousness is the light for everyone in the biosphere, and is both public and private.

THE PHYSICALITY FALLACY

The debate about *physicalism* is closely tied to the problem of dualism. Many scientists and philosophers, probably a majority, believe that the **brain produces consciousness.** They are looking for explanations of consciousness in *physical structures* and *assume* that it is a function of *physical* structures. These scientists and philosophers of the mind identify themselves as *physicalists.* The tremendous success of modern science hinged on the success of *observation.* Science came to be understood, and even defined, as a product of *empiricism*; that is, observation. I am asserting that the *consciousness* that empowers observation is built into the **biosphere as a system**, and that the **human brain evolved capacity to participate** in it. Science is doing very useful work about how the brain works. However, as I argue throughout these essays, any evidence that the human brain **produces** consciousness also supports the conclusion that the brain **participates** in consciousness. Therefore, it is not necessary for me to discuss the **science of the brain**. Science of the brain will never **explain** consciousness, and what it has found and explained is not inconsistent with the theory that I am describing. However, it would be more productive for the science of the brain to focus on **how** the brain **participates in the system that is consciousness** rather than how the brain **produces consciousness.** Perhaps, as I suggested in the **eighth essay**, there is a "substance" or substances that permeate the universe, such as the **Higgs field** with the **Higgs boson**, interacting with **photons** or **other particles**, that is the root cause for consciousness. Science can examine those matters and try to figure out how the human organism participates in *universal consciousness* and the system that it operates as the biosphere!

In the *physical* world, no two objects, regardless of size, can occupy the same space at the same time. But to understand that sentence, the human mind is comprehending the *nonphysical* concepts of *physical, object, space,* and *time,* all in the *same mind* all at the *same time.* So, that law of physics, which is part of the reason for the laws of *cause-and-effect* that operate the *physical* part of the world, obviously does not apply to *nonphysical essences.* Consciousness can maintain multiple essences and choose among them.

When the brain assimilates all the sensory perceptions provided by sense organs so that an *individual* experiences a *conscious state,* the physicalists contend that the brain itself *produces consciousness,* not that it *participates* in a larger system. But the *awareness* of sentient beings deals *directly* with the things that they sense. As I have suggested in earlier essays, sight, hearing, taste, smell, feel, and proprioception *are direct means of participation in consciousness.* They are *parts of the consciousness system.* They use the media available in the biosphere. They deal directly with the physical biosphere. Like other media, *consciousness* is also *present in the biosphere.* It is the biosphere's awareness of itself, a part of the way it works, and was a part of the basis for evolution. How would animals have evolved if there had been no consciousness? What would they have become? The brain *uses* consciousness, like the eyes *use* light. What are the chances that *sight, hearing, smell, taste, touch,* and *proprioception* would have evolved if the *media—the means by which they present* objects to the brain—had not *already existed*? They are all parts of the *system that is consciousness,* and evolved to do their part in the system. There is no greater chance that *brains* would have *evolved* if *consciousness* had not been available in the biosphere than that eyes would have evolved if there had been no light. And as I suggested in the *eighth essay,* maybe it was something about *sunlight itself* that brains evolved to utilize and participate with as the *core element of consciousness.* The *capacity* for *participation in consciousness* evolved, and the *core element of consciousness* and the nonphysical *possibility* of consciousness had to be available and inducing the evolution.

But physicalists would have us believe that *brains* evolved to a very complicated state of functional sophistication to produce consciousness and that the *consciousness* that it engages had no previous existence; consciousness just popped up out of the *physical matter* of the brain. But no other animate capability evolved that way. All other animate capabilities evolved in response to some medium that existed in the biosphere that the organism could *use* to *promote survival* in the biosphere. The senses, and the media that presents the biosphere to them and through them to the mind, are all themselves integral parts of the *consciousness system.* Consciousness is the media for the brain, but the brain is just one part of the *system that is consciousness.*

The brain "interprets" *essences,* when they are presented to the brain as phenomena. *Essences* are important parts of the *consciousness system* and arise *outside* the brain. The essences that humans encounter exist in the biosphere. With evolution of the capacity for *linguistic participation in consciousness,* collective human minds—all part of the biosphere—became involved in transforming the *essences,* the data extracted from the biosphere and presented to the mind by the senses, into language. Individuals then *internalized the language* to generate *thoughts*—identifiable concepts. It all works together. I have mentioned my strong suspicion that language that enables humans to transfer thoughts between humans may explain the actual origin of thought; that the individual *internalizes language* and *struggles to interpret* language to gain *meaning,* and that the *struggle for meaning* gives rise to *thoughts* and produces *concepts* for the individual. But where were those *concepts* before that? Where does knowledge actually exist? And even though *thought* may result from the human struggle to comprehend the meaning of words, that does not explain *why or how* it happens. None of the components of the *consciousness system* have meaning *as consciousness* without the others. Consciousness requires the *entire system* that operates the biosphere with all its components. And *how* it works is an ultimate mystery.

Physicalists contend that *consciousness* arises in *physical matter* as a result of *physical* causes. This position is faithful to the Aristotelian theory that *ideas*, or *forms*, are inherent in matter and do not exist independently of matter. If, as I suggest, Plato's theory of *forms* was a precursor of my theory that *consciousness is the biospheric system* then the *essences* or *forms* that he described play a role in consciousness. If forms or ideas *exist* in matter as Aristotle contended, why not *consciousness itself*? If physicalists *prove* that consciousness exists in matter, *they have also proven that at least some matter is a part of consciousness*, haven't they? Humans are *physical* and have *thoughts*. So, *consciousness* exists in *matter*, but matter also exists in *the system that is consciousness*. That is the only way we can know about it. And the *consciousness system* includes *essences*. That is the more inclusive theory.

I am agreeing with Aristotle in a significant way with regard to the physical world: the *essences* of *physical objects* that present themselves to human senses, and through the senses to the mind, are associated with the *physical objects* and travel Searle's backward road to the mind. And they use *light* and *sound* and *sense organs* to do so. But there are also other *nonphysical essences*, like *mathematical ideas*, and *social constructs*, that exist independently of matter, and present themselves to the human mind as *phenomena*.

Scientific empiricism is biased in favor of *physicalism*. One can observe, measure, and apply mathematics to physical matter. Galileo invented that system for science, and it works. But *physical science* can work effectively only with the physical, so that is where it now looks for *consciousness*. But physical science cannot use its tools to engage the *nonphysical*, so physicalists just deny that the nonphysical exists. Empiricism works! (For matters physical.) Any other approach requires a Platonic approach, and Platonism is somewhat a taboo. Such an approach puts a *ghost in the machine*, to use the common expression. So, physicalists are willing to use totally imaginary space aliens and zombies in serious discussions of consciousness, but not Platonic *essences*. It is easier for them to look for consciousness as a *product* of the *physical brain*.

I had not found where any philosopher has entertained the present argument that consciousness is actually built into the biosphere and empowers the work of brains, until I found Philip Goff's book *Galileo's Error*. But no one has explained how *consciousness* transforms *essences* into *thoughts* in the human mind. This mysterious, unexplainable aspect of consciousness is the *ghost in the machine*. My suggestion that thoughts originate in the mental struggle to understand the meaning of words included in language may be the best suggestion available to explain the *origin of thought*. After all, it is the *internalization of language* that produces *concepts*, and *concepts* are involved in *thought*. But I have shown that *perception* itself requires the entire biospheric *consciousness system* that presents itself and does not just occur in an individual; so, even if we can suggest what gives rise to thought *after perception* occurs, we haven't explained how consciousness *makes perception happen*. And we have not explained *what causes the "struggle for meaning" to successfully produce thoughts* in the mind.

INDIVIDUAL CONSCIOUSNESS AND DIRECT REALISM

I mentioned *direct reality* earlier in this essay. Here's the philosophical debate about *direct reality*. There are philosophers, like Emanuel Kant, who contended that the subjective human mind can only deal *indirectly* and *mentally* with *external* reality. That seems to be Descartes legacy. But there are others, me included, who believe that the *main function of consciousness is to enable sentient beings to deal directly with the biosphere*. My description in this essay of *direct perception* and *semblance* and their role in producing the concept of *dualism* leads naturally to a discussion of *direct realism*, which is an important facet of my theory of *consciousness as a system*. Sentient beings use their senses to deal *directly* with the biosphere. That is what consciousness is about. Human *perception* deals very *directly* with the *external* world, and *individual consciousness* supplies *concepts* and *abstractions* that the individual has *internalized* that provide *meaning* for the things perceived. That is *direct realism*.

As we have seen, *individual consciousness* cannot always separate *reality* from *semblance, mirages, hallucinations,* and *outright mistakes*. That is one reason that the physical sciences are so important. Group effort is more objective. But the fact that individuals have hallucinations or make other errors of perception does not invalidate *direct sensory experience*. After all, sensory perception and thinking are *all* that humans, *including scientists*, have to work with. *Humanity* can only learn and expand knowledge by using the totally *subjective consciousness* of individual minds. Individual misimpressions just mean that we are humans using *subjective* biological human sensory equipment and intuition.

David Hume, a Scottish enlightenment philosopher, suggested that the *double vision* produced by using a finger to push on one eyeball disproves the reality of *direct perception*.[74] Hume was wrong! The eyeball pusher *knows* that what he is seeing is not real, and *knows why*. The double vision happens because humans have *two eyeballs*, and does not suggest that there are *two worlds*, or that the world is distorted, or that the senses are totally untrustworthy. And it certainly does not mean that one-eyed people see more clearly. The eyeball pusher proves the *subjectivity* of *individual consciousness*, not that *direct perception doesn't engage any reality! Direct perception* is always *subject to error and is never all comprehensive*, but it *participates* in reality. A great deal of *direct perception* is *substantially* correct. The whole purpose of *individual consciousness* is to enable sentient beings to operate successfully in the biosphere, and *direct perception* as a whole is trustworthy. If it did not work reasonably well, sentient beings would not survive! The *objectivity* of direct *perception* is increased when *multiple* subjective individual observers see the same things and assemble their knowledge in the group in the form of *consensus reality*. This is precisely what gives validity to the rigorous collective impressions that science has added to *consensus reality*. Hannah Arendt observed this important point: "[O]ur certainty that what we perceive has an existence independent of the act of perceiving, depends entirely on the object's also appearing as such to others and being acknowledged by them."[75]

As I have said several times in this series of essays, *physical reality* is the common denominator of consciousness. That is what assures us that we are all on the same planet, dealing with the same reality. The need—the absolute necessity—for the *objectivity* that science seeks can only arise from the limited, subjective participation of multiple individual scientists in consciousness. Science works because of *collective consciousness* that the world is out there and does not change willy-nilly. And that belief is purely a product of the *faith system* and by inference shows that not only do we share *physical reality*, but *we also share the consciousness* that presents it to us. If physical reality were not enfolded in one *consciousness system*, different observers would get differing results from observation that could not be pieced together although they are looking at the same thing! Fortunately, nature apparently presents the same essences to all sentient beings. All sentient beings share in the power of consciousness provided by the biosphere. All humans experience the same *essences* as *phenomena*, and even though individual *direct perception* is *imperfect*, the *concepts* that arise from the *phenomena* clarify themselves in *collective* experience.

No individual can experience everything, and everything that individuals experience is subject to distortion by mistakes of *subjective perception* and *semblance*. But groups are composed of *individuals*, and *only* those totally *subjective individuals* can perceive and act for the group. There are no disconnected, objective individual observers who are independent of the biosphere and free from error. Observation and communication by *completely subjective individuals* empower group *participation in consciousness* that is usually more accurate than the perceptions of an individual. Multiple observers are dealing with the same *essences* as *phenomena* in the same *consciousness system. Participation in consciousness* from the subjective observation posts occupied by different individuals strengthens the group's hold on the total reality that is unified and held together by physical reality. I see only one side of the dog but you can see the other, and we can talk about it. "Yep, it's a dog alright, but at first, I thought it was a 'possum.'" Our shared observations would not work if we *all* did not *participate in both the same consciousness system and the same physical reality.*

CONCLUDING OBSERVATIONS

If we didn't all *share a consciousness* that includes the same *essences*, we couldn't share our thoughts about physical reality in conversation. *Essences* collected by senses from the biosphere present the same *phenomena* to multiple sentient beings and enable humans to assign *words* and *names* to objects. *Nonphysical essences* like *time, space, nothing*, and *zero* and other *numbers* also present themselves to multiple human minds. *Weightless words* are *nonphysical phenomena* that conjure up the *physical objects* and the *nonphysical essences* they present to sentient beings in the *consciousness system* and give rise to thoughts in the individual mind. And society has *institutionalized* and *abstracted* important *nonphysical social constructs.* Individuals could never have *abstracted* all these things independently of their *human groups*, but groups have *abstracted* them, collected them, and maintained them in *continuing consciousness* that is not dependent on any one individual. Each subjective individual *participates in consciousness* for his or her allotted and limited time in his or her allotted and limited space. All *individual participation* occurs at a particular place and time. It is a quite limited vantage point. The individual dies mortal death. *Individual participation in consciousness* in this world ends. **Consciousness** exists and **continues** despite the biological death of individuals. Consciousness is in the group. Indeed, it is in and beyond all sentient beings; it is in the biosphere and beyond. **Ultimate reality** in which humans participate is reflected, although imperfectly, in **consensus reality**. **Consensus reality**—faith—the operation of consciousness in humans, is the most precious property of humanity. **Consensus reality** is an important part of the **consciousness system**. The **consciousness** that **creates and contains** it has to be even bigger.

There is no **dualism**. Humans are animals that evolved in the biosphere and participate in the **biospheric consciousness system**. Their **participation in consciousness** enables them to cope in the biosphere, and that consciousness is not merely the product of individual brains.

10) CONSCIOUSNESS, CAUSATION, AND FREEWILL

THE THEORY THAT CONSCIOUSNESS IS the *system that operates the bio-sphere* has important implications for theories of *causation* and *freewill*. This essay explores those implications. *Consciousness* is not *physical*, and is not governed by the laws that govern physical matter. Although consciousness *includes* the system that operates the physical parts of reality, it operates on *different principles*. Sentient beings always and only act in the eternally moving instant called *now*. All sentient beings share that *eternal instant*. Consciousness empowers them to decide what to do in that instant. Everything that ever happens occurs in that instant. Sentient beings obviously can do nothing in the past, and they can do nothing in the future. The instant that is *now* keeps moving on, carrying everything that exists with it. Humans and some other animals remember the past and use the remembered information in deciding what to do in that instant called *now*. Although humans use the information that they compile in memory to anticipate and plan for the future, they cannot *do* anything in the future; they have to wait for the *eternal now* to move into the anticipated time. When considered in this way, the *eternal now*, in which conscious beings are able to do things, is almost an alternative view of reality, structuring reality a bit differently from the usual concepts of *time, space, matter, energy*, and *motion* that we use to structure the *physical world*. It is like a platform, with time and the things that are arranged in traditional space and time sliding by it, with motion creating kaleidoscopic changes in the arrangements of physical matter in space. I don't plan to further develop the possibility that existence is merely *constant change* but mention this powerful background for the ideas presented in this essay. The *eternal instant* that is always *now* may be the structure of reality in which consciousness operates that is not totally included in the structure that it has empowered humanity to envision, based on time, space, matter, energy, and motion that works so well for physical reality. Please try to visualize this unique viewpoint to deal with the thoughts that I am about to present. The idea is not at all new: *Heraclitus* began its articulation long ago. He contended that *the only thing constant is change*, and is famous for the saying that you *can't step into the same river twice*.

An important point from the preceding paragraph is that all sentient beings in the biosphere, including humans, share the instant of *now* and only do what they can do and only exercise the power of *perception* as *conscious experience* in that *continuing instant*. The changes that have occurred in what we *conceive* to be the past lay down a history that is the basis for *ontology*. We can *know the things we know*, and rationally believe the things we believe, based only on the mentally recorded and remembered data from the past. Using that data, humans have accumulated a lot of useful information.

But when we examine the past from the vantage point of *now*, there always appear to be *physical causes* for the things that have happened, in the *physical realm*. And as we have discussed earlier, *physicalists* believe that the *physical* is the *only* realm. The laws of *cause-and-effect* reign supreme in the *physical realm*. If the *physicalists* are right, perhaps *cause-and-effect* could enable us to predict everything that will happen. But that certainly does not seem to be the case. We are all familiar with the analogies to *clocks* and *billiard balls*. And in that *cause-and-effect worldview*, the idea that past events may have been working to *fulfill a purpose* is not currently popular, although at times in the past, the concept of *end causes* played a major role in the human *faith* system. For instance, *Aristotle* believed in *end causes*. But, despite the fact that the modern Western world affirms Aristotle's theories about *physicality*, it really doesn't buy into his idea of *end causes*.

We will analyze both *cause-and-effect* and *end causes* in this essay, but actually, those are not the only possible theories of causation. The *theory of evolution* combined with the theory that consciousness is the *system that operates the biosphere* suggests *another possibility* that I will return to later in this essay.

FREEWILL AND DETERMINISM

The suggestion that consciousness enables sentient organisms to *make choices*, evokes the eternal debate about *freewill and determinism*. I have advanced the idea that consciousness is built into the biosphere and enables sentient organisms to cope in the biosphere. Abductive reasoning tells me that is the case. At the most basic level, animals that *participate in consciousness* are able to choose between alternative courses of action. They make *choices*. Humans make plans and take actions to implement those plans. It certainly *feels as if* we have the power to make choices. But if freewill is an illusion, if *physical cause-and-effect* governs everything that happens, and if we do not really have the *power to choose* what we are going to do next, then obviously free choice could not be the purpose for which humans evolved the *capacity* for *participation in consciousness*.

In this essay, I will limit my discussion of the philosophical debate about *freewill and determinism* to the implications associated with my theory that consciousness is built into—indeed is the essence of—the biosphere and not just a product of individual brains. Even at its most basic level, the argument that consciousness was in existence, and was a factor in causing evolution strongly suggests that sentient organisms are endowed with *freewill* and are empowered by consciousness to make *choices*. That certainly *seems* to be the purpose of consciousness, or at least the use to which sentient beings have put it. As I said earlier, when organisms that *participate in consciousness* encounter situations, they can decide whether to run, fight, hide, eat, be friendly, or any number of other courses of action. Consciousness—including information that humans have *internalized* in the form of *concepts* or *abstractions*—certainly appears to be there to assist them in making choices about how to cope with the challenges presented by the biosphere. But there are deeper levels of reasoning to consider that provide even stronger evidence for the existence of *free will* as opposed to *determinism*.

Linguistic participation in consciousness and the ability to *conceptualize* empowered humans to recognize *concepts* such as *time, space, matter, energy, force*, and *motion* that provide a structure for understanding the *physical world*. In the physical world, when we examine what has happened in the past, *laws of cause-and-effect* seem to have operated in the physical world without exception. Things seem to have happened mechanically. Of course, that may be mere *semblance*, but the appearance is quite strong. The structure and events in which we discern the laws of *cause-and-effect* do not explain *consciousness* itself: *consciousness explains the structure*. The vantage point of human *participation in consciousness* that produces the *conceptual structure* for *physical reality* immediately suggests that consciousness is not *contained within* it and, in fact, *contains it*. Therefore, there is no reason to believe that consciousness is governed by the laws of *cause-and-effect* that govern the physical world structured by the concepts that it discovered. The fact that humans, participating in consciousness, can focus on the physical world and observe the facts that give rise to the impression of unerring *cause-and-effect in that world* suggests the possibility that as *participants* in consciousness, *the human vantage point itself is not governed by cause-and-effect.* The individual differentiates the *self* from the rest of the biosphere, and the *physical reality* that humans encounter is merely the rest of the biosphere. Individuals are part of the biosphere, and the consciousness that enables them to differentiate themselves from it also allows them to act as free agents in it. Their *participation in consciousness* enables them to make choices about how to interpret and deal with the structure, objects and essences that the biosphere presents. It enables them to cope in the biosphere. They are making choices as they deal with the reality that consciousness enabled them to construct mentally.

As I pointed out in the *ninth essay* in this series, in the physical world, no two objects, regardless of size, can occupy the same space at the same time, according to one of the laws of physics. But to understand that sentence, the human mind is actually comprehending the *nonphysical concepts* of the *physical, objects, space*, and *time* simultaneously. That law of physics, which is part of the reason for *cause-and-effect* in the physical world, obviously does not apply to *nonphysical essences. Nonphysical essences* actually don't seem to be limited by the structure of time and space. Consciousness maintains numerous *essences* or *abstractions* simultaneously and chooses among them. As consciousness operates the biosphere, *choice seems to be the reason for the existence of consciousness. Purpose,* or *end cause*, or *intentionality* seem to be important operative forms of *causation for consciousness.* As Abraham Maslow taught us, *humans do what they do* to *get what they need.* That certainly implies that you can decide what to do next to get what you need. Needs pull from the future; they don't push from the past. Applied *metaphorically* to consciousness writ large—the *consciousness system* in which humans are mere participants—the way that humans actually use consciousness has *portentous implications.* The world—the

Biosphere itself—could be *working toward an end cause.* I am not making that ascertain, but I am asserting that we can make choices about what we are going to do to fulfill our goals, and I am acknowledging the *possibility* of *end causes* as a *form of causation.* Unlike the physical realm that consciousness contains and explains, in the mysterious world of *consciousness* and *nonphysical essences,* operating always and only in the *eternal now,* the *causation of purpose and end causes is obvious and makes perfect sense.* I can choose between and among all possible actions available to me, and do whatever I want to do, NOW!

Against the background of *evolution,* including both *biological evolution* and *cultural evolution,* even *purpose* and *end causes* do not seem to be all the possibilities, as we will see shortly. Evolution can choose from among *unlimited nonphysical essences,* and bring totally new things into existence. The *consciousness system that operates the biosphere* appears to itself make choices in *biological evolution.* But before getting into that theory, I need to complete the discussion of *purpose* and *end causes.* As I discussed in the *eighth essay,* there are those who say that every *physical action* requires a *physical cause* and that *nonphysical thoughts* alone never cause anything to happen. This is an important part of the argument of *physicalists,* who reason that for the human mind to produce action, something *physical* must take place in the operation of the mind. As I pointed out in *the eighth* essay, that argument simply ignores the mysterious, unexplained role of *life* in the biosphere. Consciousness is *not confined to the individual bodies of sentient organisms.* The consciousness in which humans and other sentient beings participate is *built into the biosphere.* The mental and physical are commingled in *living organisms. The human mind can and does cause human activity,* and that is the nature of the operation of consciousness in the biosphere. That point is essential to life itself. Just as evolution of life to increasingly complex forms seems, in a sense, to defy the physical law of entropy, *life that evolved to participate in consciousness defies the physical law of cause-and-effect.* The biosphere is not a bunch of billiard balls encountering each other, nor is it a clock created and wound up by the creator. It is a *living system*, in which *conscious awareness* is an *operative principle*, empowering *sentient organisms* to *make choices.*

The preceding paragraph provides a good topic for exploration by *brain scientists* and *physicists.* The investigation that I suggested in the *eighth and ninth essays* is needed. Using our present understanding of the *physical* and *nonphysical,* the *Higgs boson* can cause other particles either to have mass or not have mass. Are there *other such particles?* The Higgs boson field *permeates all space.* Can it, or something similar, explain how *nonphysical thoughts produce physical actions?* There is no question that animals, including humans, *move about,* and it certainly seems like they *govern their own movement.* They go where they want to go and do what that want to do. And it looks and feels like the actions of humans are based on their thoughts. That is what we, as observers, *see happening. Why dismiss empiricism at this juncture?* In *essay eight,* I discussed the possibility that *sunlight itself—photons—*is somehow involved in consciousness. Science may arrive at a better understanding about how consciousness works, and until it does, we should be slow to conclude that the *thoughts* of living organisms do not *control actions.* The *pseudo-scientific superstition* that thoughts do not control actions, and that there is no freewill, if widely accepted, will undermine the entire operation of *faith* that produces the *social systems* as we have described in earlier essays. It will eliminate all justification for law and morality. *Freewill* and *freedom of choice* are basic to all principles of *moral and legal accountability.*

During the twentieth century, B. F. Skinner, with his psychological theory of *behaviorism,* made a strong contention for *determinism* in psychology. His theory was that *external causes* dictate the actions that individuals take, including the decisions that they make. Another variation of the theory of determinism is that internal events—physical and chemical reactions within the individual—determine the actions of individuals, including the decisions that they make. As a lawyer and retired judge, it certainly appears to me that Skinner's theory, as well as all other theories of determinism, if true, undermine the *wisdom of the ages* and the entire theory of *accountability* on which *law and morality* are based.

Skinner still has followers, despite the widely held belief that linguist Noam Chomsky thoroughly discredited his theory. Evidence based on Skinner's theories was presented as expert testimony a few times in my court while I served as judge. I had not fully developed the theories presented here at that time, but think that I successfully intuited that humans do not *participate in consciousness* the same way that rats do. Evidence was offered that given a choice of food or cocaine, the rat would choose the cocaine and starve. In reaching my decision, I found as a fact that the behavior of a rat, with a brain the size of a match-head, compared to a human being with a brain of fifteen hundred cubic centimeters, did not prove determinism in human mental operations. If Skinner had been right, the entire legal system would be meaningless. Of course, the court proceedings themselves would be meaningless, predetermined actions if he were completely right. But the theory of *consciousness* as the *operating system for the biosphere* that is described in these pages provides a meaningful basis for *freewill* and supports the wisdom of the great thinkers who brought the legal system into being and brought civilization as we know it to fruition.

BERGSON AND EVOLUTION

The debate about *freewill and determinism* usually centers on the contrast between *cause-and-effect*, on the one hand, and *end causes or purpose* on the other. But there is at least one other possibility. Earlier in this essay, I suggested that *purpose and end causes* may not be the only alternatives to *cause-and-effect*, with regard to causation. Earlier, I suggested that *evolution* that produces things that are completely new shows that the *system of consciousness* that *operates the biosphere* make choices on the grand scale. So, let's look at that other possibility concerning causation. Henri Bergson wrote about evolution. You will recall our earlier references to his theory of *elan vital, vital force* that was involved in evolution, pushing life to higher forms. He argued that everything that *evolves* is *something completely new*. It didn't exist before. Nothing required it to evolve. How would *cause-and-effect* in a purely *mechanical world,* bring about something completely new? The *future of evolution,* and the *next breakthrough invention* are not predictable. Even though evolution recycles the same *physical matter,* it clothes it with *essences* that are totally new and different. I won't quite join Bergson in arguing that before something evolves, it doesn't even exist as a possibility. Instead, I would say that the possibilities are unlimited. The thoughts in this paragraph apply to *cultural evolution,* group *participation in consciousness*, and nonphysical essences as well as *biological evolution.* The theoretical thinking, the *nonphysical essences,* that are involved in the production of computers have been available since the beginning of time. I suspect that there are many other *nonphysical essences* where those used in computers came from! The supply of *nonphysical essences* for new *inventions, institutionalization of needed social structures,* and *evolution* are probably inexhaustible!

Against the background of infinite possibilities in a biosphere that supports evolution, *cause-and-effect* and *end cause or purpose* do not provide complete explanations for causation. Ongoing *creation* is occurring. Conscious choices make a difference. The simple truth is that we can't predict the weather very well for very far into the future and certainly cannot predict the what is going to happen in *human affairs* that involve humans with freedom of choice. We don't know what is going to be invented next or what is going to happen next, and if *cause-and-effect* were the basis for all that happens, we could make those predictions. But we live life *consciously* at the *cutting edge*, in the *eternal now*, and anything can happen. And humans can help make things happen. Of course, after something happens in the *physical world* structured by *time*, *space*, *matter*, *energy*, and *motion*, *physicalists* can always "explain" why it happened, based on theories of *cause-and-effect*. And the explanations always look good. But that is hindsight. Friedrich Schleiermacher said that everything that happens is, in a sense, a miracle!

Our experience with *cause-and-effect* is strictly based on impressions drawn from the past. We *conceptualize* impressions. Those impressions form the basis for the laws of science. We think we can see *cause-and-effect* in history, and in the stories of things that have happened. But we can't predict the future with any degree of certainty, just on the basis of *cause-and-effect*. That is because many forces are at work. *Consciousness* is at work. *Choices are real*, and they make a difference. That *conclusion* is what *direct perception* reveals. It is supported by all *empirical evidence*. There is no good reason to suspect *semblance*. Any other conclusion makes *nonsense* of *all existence*. *Choices* and *consciousness* play major roles in evolution in the biosphere. Henri Bergson's life force—*elan vital*—makes a difference. Please distinguish the theory I have just described, inspired by Henri Bergson, from any theory of *end causes*. It is not a theory that action is determined on a macroscale by some predetermined goal or purpose toward which we are working. It is a theory that we are all working together in the *eternal now*, in which *anything is possible*, and the future that we build depends on us. And we can't exclude the role of a Supreme Being. And the creator God, acting in the *eternal now* does not have to violate his own laws in the world limited by time, space, matter and energy to bring about what we might regard as miracles! He acts in the *eternal now* of consciousness, and does not violate the laws he created.

11) ULTIMATE MYSTERIES

I DO NOT CLAIM TO have solved the mysteries of the *existence* of *life* and *consciousness* in this series of essays. Cloudy, unfathomable mystery *preceded* the many magnificent accomplishments known to our *consensus reality*. Human faith has produced tremendous accomplishments that were made possible by human *participation in consciousness*. Dwelling among the accomplishments, we seldom think about the deep mysteries. But, despite all the accomplishments made possible by human *participation in consciousness*, and despite the new perspective that I have provided in the preceding essays concerning the nature and role of consciousness in the biosphere, unfathomable, cloudy mysteries remain.

The *biggest mysteries* have not been eliminated by the knowledge that humans have accumulated in the noosphere. When God said, "Let there be light,"[76] he did not remove all the "*darkness*" that was "upon the face of the deep."[77] Clouds of mystery still cloak the entire perimeter of our *consensus reality*. Humans *participate in consciousness*, but evolution of the ability to *participate in consciousness* served the *functional* purpose of survival in the biosphere, not the *philosophical* purpose of unraveling the mysteries that enshroud *existence, consciousness,* and *life* itself. The greatest mystery of all is the very existence of *consciousness.* Humanity's *participation in consciousness* cannot *lift itself by its bootstraps* and explain the consciousness in which it is a mere participant.

Humanity used the cultural tools of language, writing, and reading to construct the magnificent edifice of knowledge that I have identified as *consensus reality.* Participation in society's *consensus reality* greatly increased the ability of *individuals* to *think conceptually,* which steadily increased the *capacity* of *individual consciousness* from the time that *linguistic participation in consciousness* first appeared. The accomplishments of the *noosphere*—the thinking layer of earth's crust—are truly magnificent. *Faith—consensus reality—language*—made those accomplishments possible.

But none of what humans have learned provides a really rational, understandable reason for the *beginning* or the *existence of the physical universe,* or the *consciousness* that is aware of it. I have suggested that the physical universe exists in *consciousness.* But no one can explain the existence of *consciousness,* itself. It just *is.* Once we experience and take to heart the deep *mystery of consciousness,* other unsolved mysteries immediately appear because all that we can possibly know is embedded in *consciousness,* and we do not understand consciousness. So, we don't have answers to some very important questions: (1) What caused the *physical world* to exist? (2) What is *life,* and what caused *it to exist?* (3) What enables individuals to be aware of their surroundings? (4) How does the physical human body acquire or produce thoughts and knowledge? Of course, *individual consciousness* does it, but that begs the question. (5) What is *knowledge?* How does knowledge move from one human mind to another? How do the *individual consciousnesses* of individual minds collect transfer, collect, and preserve knowledge? Of course, humans use speech and writing, but what empowers those capabilities? (6) Is there a *superior creative being* or *intelligence* with whom or to which human consciousness is connected?

The inevitable challenge confronting *faith* is to understand all that we can understand about *ultimate mysteries*, and fully them, even if we are unable to solve them. The human quest for meaning will see to it that we do that. But although faith continually builds and adds to *consensus reality*, it inevitably falls far short of a complete understanding of *ultimate reality*. Wise humans know that the knowledge stored in *consensus reality* is imperfect and incomplete. Ultimately, humanity must cling to *faith*, without a complete understanding of the *ultimate mysteries*.

But the human *quest for meaning* pushes humanity to penetrate as far as possible into the darkness of the mysteries that surround us. When we drive at night, we turn on headlights. Dealing with the mysteries that I am describing is like driving at night. Although we cannot completely penetrate the darkness, *faith* is our *headlights*. Faith empowers us to deal with things that appear within our subjective, existential situation that we cannot engage otherwise. Even though our understanding is imperfect, and faith dependent, it is helpful to understand the critical role that *faith* plays in creating our limited *understanding of reality.*

ABOUT THE AUTHOR

DALE SEGREST WAS BORN IN rural Macon County, Alabama, in 1942. He attended a small, rural public school at Shorter, Alabama. After completing high school at Shorter in 1960, he attended Huntingdon College, a Methodist Church–related liberal arts college, in Montgomery, Alabama, where he majored in chemistry and minored in mathematics. The core curriculum included basic courses in religion and philosophy that instilled a lifelong love of philosophy in him. He served as president of the student government association while a student at Huntingdon.

After completing his work at Huntingdon in 1964, Dale began studying law at The University of Alabama that fall. When he finished his degree, he was in the top five percent of his 1967 law class, and took a job with Hill, Hill, Stovall and Carter, one of the leading law firms back in Montgomery. Although Dale continued to practice in Montgomery, after three years, he, his wife, Betty, and their sons moved back to their home county of Macon.

Dale was elected as a circuit judge in Alabama's Fifth Judicial Circuit in 1982, a four-county rural circuit that includes Macon County, and assumed office in January 1983. He continued in that office until January 2001. During his tenure as a circuit judge, Dale was deeply involved in judicial education, both as a student and a teacher. He received more than 500 hours of training in judicial education. He served on the Alabama Circuit Judge Continuing Education Committee for seventeen of his eighteen years on the bench, planning, participating in, and presenting judicial education. During the late 1980's and early 1990's, Dale participated in several law and literature courses. In 1995 and1996, Dale spearheaded and prepared curricula for two continuing educational events called Foundation in Pluralism, sponsored by Tuskegee University and the Alabama Judicial College. The first of these three-day events focused on the writings of Booker T. Washington and W.E.B. Dubois; the second on writings of Dr. King and Malcolm X. The second of these two educational events received honorable mention as the *best continuing education program in American colleges and universities*. Dale described those events in *Court Reporter*, a magazine for judges. The National Association of Judicial Educators included that article, word for word, in its newsletter, and gave it widespread attention in judicial education circles. Dale earned a master's degree in judicial studies from the University of Nevada, Reno, in 1999. Upon leaving the bench in 2001, Dale established the Segrest Law Firm, reentered the law practice and continues *Of Counsel* with the firm.

Dale's first book, *Conscience and Command*, which dealt with legal philosophy, was published in 1994 by Scholars Press.[78] While writing that book, Dale realized that law is a faith-based *social system*, in that it depends on the faith of the culture for its effective force. So, after its publication, Dale began a study of faith and its functions. He has continually worked on the study that resulted in the present volume since the publication of that first book.

On his return to Montgomery, after completing law school, Dale became very active in Alumni work at Huntingdon College. He served as president of its National Alumni Board, and received its Achievement and Loyalty awards. He became a member of the Board of Trustees at Huntingdon in 1982, and continued on that board until 2004. From 1995 until 1999, he served as chair of the board. Huntingdon awarded Dale an honorary doctorate degree in 1989.

In 1985, Dale was elected as conference lay leader of the Alabama West Florida Conference of the United Methodist Church, and he served in that office until 1990. He was elected to General and Jurisdictional Conference of the United Methodist Church in 1988, 1992, 1996, and 2000. He was a lay speaker in the United Methodist Church for over forty years, and spoke in dozens of churches, well over one hundred. From 1996 until 2000, he served on a denomination-wide task force called the Connectional Process Team that studied the structure and ministry of the entire United Methodist denomination and made recommendations to the General Conference of the Church in 2000.

CLOSING NOTE ABOUT CREDENTIALS

Some scholars may question why a lawyer and retired circuit judge felt qualified to write these essays. I think that a short note about my purposes in writing and a brief description of my credentials may be useful. A major part of the motivation for this book has been concern for faith-based social systems that rely on nonphysical essences for their values and principles. I am referring to law, morality, and religion. It appears to me that the values and principles on which these systems rely, and indeed the viability of the social systems themselves may be at risk in a worldview that is dominated by physicalism. I actually saw that threat in my work as judge, and see it in the affairs of society.

In these essays, I have attempted to define the line between science, that can only deal with the physical, and can only test falsifiable hypotheses, and the values and principles of law, morality and religion. My college major was in chemistry, and it will be a serious error for anyone to see what I have written in these essays as a polemic against science. What I have attempted to do in these essays is to assert the reality of the nonphysical essences that provide the basis for law, morality and religion based on their own merits, while recognizing the value of science. I have tried to assert my position concerning the values that support these faith-based systems positively, rather than fighting the battle for their existence on the turf of science. My credentials are in law, but if morality and religion reap a benefit from my efforts, so much the better.

But I am trying to deal with these issues "on my own turf." My highest academic credentials are in law and judicial studies. I earned a J.D. degree from the University of Alabama, and a Master of Judicial Studies degree from the University of Nevada at Reno. The Degree included course work at the National Judicial College, that is on the UNR Campus. There is no law school at UNR, but several of my professors in that graduate work were visiting professors from the U. C. Berkeley Law School. I dug deeply into legal philosophy, law and literature, law and economics, and law and social sciences. On my own, to bolster my personal knowledge and skills as a judge, I dug deeply into legal philosophy, psychology, and sociology.

In my undergraduate work, I had courses in religion and philosophy at Huntingdon College, but have had no advanced work in those areas. However, as a lay person, I participated in the United Methodist Church at its highest levels, and read extensively.

Credentialism is a strong force in today's academia. Areas of knowledge are narrowly defined, and encroachment into specialty areas is not always welcome. It would have been comforting to have the comradery of colleagues as I worked my way through the interdisciplinary ideas discussed in these essays. But at the same time, that might have limited the thought processes that I applied to reach these conclusions as I explored the issues on my own. Taking into account my purposes in writing and my credentials in law, I am content with the results. In these essays, I feel that I am dealing with issues that I have experienced firsthand, in the world of practical experience. If I had not taken the time and exerted the effort to assemble these thoughts, what better qualified person would have done so?

Dale Segrest

March, 2022

ENDNOTES

---

[1]My own academic credentials are in law, and included judicial studies that dealt with legal philosophy, economics and literature, and I believe that theories described here have important implications for law.

[2]*Stages of Faith,* James Fowler, (1981)

[3]*The Biosphere,* Vladimir Vernadsky, (1926)

[4]*The Phenomenon of Man,* Teilhard de Chardin, (1955)

[5]De Chardin did not call it participation; he did not depart from the traditional view that consciousness evolved in the human brain. But I want to make it clear from the outset that humans participate in consciousness, and it is not something produced by individual brains.

[6]I will develop the definitions of truth as used in this treatise subsequently in this Chapter.

[7]*Creative Evolution,* Henri Bergson, (1907)

[8]See *The Secret of our Success,* Joseph Henrich, (2015)

[9]*The Origin and Goal of History,* Karl Jaspers (1949, translated to English, 1953)

[10]I remember a periodic table of chemical elements from high school that included the elements Alabamine and Virginium. They had been discovered and named by Dr. Fred Allison, who founded the physics department at what is now Auburn University and taught there for thirty-one years. After retiring at Auburn, he taught at Huntingdon College, and I enrolled in physics courses that he taught. Those elements no longer appear in the periodic table of elements, because other scientists could not confirm his findings at the time.

[11]The separation and division is readily apparent in the well-recog-

nized Indo-European language family.

[12]*Stages of Faith,* James Fowler, (1981)

[13]*The Moral Judgment of the Child,* Jean Piaget, (1932)

[14]Bruno Bettelheim's book, *The Uses of Enchantment* (1976) did a beautiful job of describing the role of such stories. I read the book and was impressed with it long before Bettelheim, who endured concentration camps during World War II, was discredited for falsifying credentials, accused of plagiarism, and personality problems. The book received significant recognition prior to those developments.

[15]James Fowler's work was excellent scholarship. It provides a good starting point, but it is not the last word, and I am not aware of efforts to expand his work. An ongoing analysis of faith development is needed. Fowler's stages of faith focus on the psychological development of individuals. But psychology and sociology are inseparable. Every individual deals with people who are completely different from the people that other individuals deal with. He or she receives guidance from parents who are unique and different from other parents and establishes relationships with peer groups that may differ greatly from the peer groups that other individuals encounter. Each individual encounters a culture that is totally different from the cultures that individuals encounter in other parts of the world. All of the groups that immediately surround an individual change with the passage of time, even within the same culture. What impact do these facts have on Fowler's description of faith development?

[16]*The Social Construction of Reality,* James Luckman and Peter Berger, (1966)

[17]See *Narrative Naturalism,* Jessica Wahman, (2015)

[18]An important purpose of this treatise is to expose the possible disparity between faith as described here and the religious faith that many people profess.

[19]*Frames of Mind: The Theory of Multiple Intelligences,* Howard Gardner, (1983)

[20]*Emotional Intelligence,* (1995) Daniel Goleman.

[21]Schleiermacher: *On Religion: Speeches to its Cultured Despisers*, Friedrich Schleiermacher, (1811-1831)

[22]*Motivation and Personality*, Abraham Maslow, (First edition: 1954, second edition: 1970, third edition 1987)

[23]*I and Thou*, Martin Buber, (1923, translated to English 1937)

[24]See *The Embodied Self: Friedrich Schleiermacher's Solution to Kant's Problem of the Empirical Self*, Thandeka, (1995)

[25]*Stages of Faith*, James Fowler, (1981)

[26]James 2:18

[27]James 2:26

[28]Matthew 21:18-19; 20-22 and Mark 11:12-14; 20-25.

[29]Matthew 7:16

[30]Matthew 21:18-22

[31]Genesis 1:28

[32]*Man's Search for Meaning*, Victor Frankl, (1946)

[33]Mark 9:35

[34] Kierkegaard's actual words were "leap to faith," not "leap of faith."

[35] Proverbs 23:7

[36]Hebrews 11:1. "[T]he evidence of things unseen," is very Platonic.

[37]*Roots: The Saga of an American Family*, Alex Haley, (1976)

[38]Nicodemus, a pharisee with strong religious training, would have to change his way of thinking to understand the new view of reality that Jesus was talking about!

[39]Galatians 2:20

[40]John 3:3

[41]Émile Durkheim, who was one of the founders of sociology, made this important point in T*he Elementary Forms of the Religious Life*, (1912)

[42]*On Religion: Speeches to its Cultured Despisers*, Friedrich Schleiermacher, (1811-1831)

[43]*The Varieties of Religious Experience: A Study in Human Nature*,

William James, (1902)

[44]: *To Kill a Mockingbird*, Harper Lee, (1960)

[45]*Born to Be Good*, Dacher Keltner, (2009)

[46]Psalm 117:2

[47]This argument was first articulated by John Austin and Jeremy Bentham, although it had been evolving in the work of eighteenth-century philosophers.

[48]Consider the aphorism of the great legal positivist Oliver Wendell Holmes, Jr. in the context of the things I am discussing: "If you want to know the law and nothing else, you must look at it as a bad man, who cares only for the material consequences which such knowledge enables him to predict, not as a good one, who finds his reasons for conduct, whether inside the law or outside of it, in the vaguer sanctions of conscience." Is law really defined by what a bad man can get away with?

[49]*The Elementary Forms of the Religious Life*, Émile Durkheim, (1912)

[50]Psalms 90:12

[51]Deuce passed away several years ago, after I had first written these lines. This work has been in progress for a long time.

[52]Ideas are human thoughts. Before they became ideas in the human mind, they were nonphysical essences.

[53] Interestingly, an exchange with my editor about this paragraph illustrates the point I am making. After reading this paragraph as I had originally written it, my editor commented, "Please revisit. After agreement, how is there a scope for disagreements." That was an excellent comment, and I hope that I have adequately responded to it!

[54]Without endorsing reincarnation, this concept has interesting implications. The facts that (1) all the matter at or near the surface of the earth is, has been, or could become a part of a living organism, and (2) we do not understand the basis for consciousness, but associate it with life in the biosphere, where life recycles endlessly, and the same matter is used in life forms over and over,

seem to resonate with Plato's theory. In this electronic axial age, we should also note that Buddhism and Hinduism embrace reincarnation.

[55]Peter Berger's description of reality as a social construct is quite similar to my concept of consensus reality.

[56]I am not aware of anything that suggests that Jesus himself was influenced by either Plato or Aristotle. Christianity picked up the Platonic worldview as it moved through the area permeated by the philosophy of Plato.

[57]Genesis 1:3

[58]John 1:1

[59]Hebrews 11:1

[60]1 Corinthians 13:12

[61]*Galileo's Error,* Philip Goff, (2019)

[62]After I had written this essay, I became aware of the fact that philosophers Philip Goff and Sam Coleman believe that consciousness exists in the biosphere and that the human brain participates in it.

[63]It is interesting that Aristotle discussed this very point in *De Anima.*

[64]Panpsychism is a tenet of Buddhism and Hinduism.

[65]*Galileo's Error,* Philip Goff, (2019)

[66]*The Life of the Mind,* Hannah Arendt, (1978)

[67]*Actual Consciousness,* Ted Honderich, (2014)

[68]*Seeing Things as They Are,* John R. Searle, (2015)

[69]Philosophers of the mind who follow the physicality debate will readily recognize this allusion, and further discussion here would serve no purpose, but I make this note for the benefit of readers who are not philosophers of the mind!

[70]*The Mysterious Flame,* Colin McGinn, (1999)

[71]*The Mind's I,* Douglas R. Hofstadter and Daniel C. Dennett, (1982)

[72]*Lila, An Inquiry into Morals,* Robert M. Pirsig, (1992)

[73] *Actual Consciousness*, Ted Honderich, (2014)

[74] *A Treatise on Human Nature*, David Hume, (1739)

[75] *The Life of the Mind*, Hannah Arendt, (1978)

[76] Genesis 1:3

[77] Genesis 1:2

[78] This publisher was associated with Emory University and other universities, and has been dissolved. It is not the self-publisher that is currently in business by that name.